KID MERO -AKA- THE HUMAN DURAG FLAP
McDAB -AKA- TRIZZ KHALIFA -AKA- TIGER BACKWO
KIN MAN! -AKA- CHECK THE GUEST LIST AGAIN CUZ
CC DABATHIA -AKA- DAD OF THE YEAR!
KA- DI-YAYO -AKA- -AKA- BA
MARADONA
ICAN DON DADA -AKA- AIN THERE
KA- ROMEO XANTOS -AKA- ICHE -AKA-
-AKA- CURVE GOTTI -AKA- THE KID MERO
DODS -AKA- I NO FOKIN DONOVAN McDAB -AKA- TRIZ
MY NAME DEF ON THAT BABY! FOKIN MAN! -AKA- CH
! -AKA- BEENSMACKED SHIT -AKA- CC DABATHIA -AK
RLOS XANTANA -AKA- BIYOMBO- KA- DI-YAYO -AKA-
ES DEFINITELY MONEY MARADONA
THE DOMINICAN DON DADA -AK
HE PLANTAIN SUPERNOVA! ON IT! -AKA- ROMEO XANTOS
KID MERO -AKA- THE HUMAN DURAG FLAP
McDAB -AKA- TRIZZ KHALIFA -AKA- TIGER BACKWO
KIN MAN! -AKA- CHECK THE GUEST LIST AGAIN CUZ
CC DABATHIA -DAD OF THE YEAR!
KA- DI-YAYO -AK MUTOMBO -AKA- BA
MARADONA
ICAN DON DADA CARD AGAIN THERE
KA- ROME DUTCHE -AKA-
KA- CURVE MERO
DS -AKA- I N -AKA- TRIZZ
Y NAME DEF ON THAT BABY! FOKIN MAN! -AKA- CHEC
AKA- BEENSMACKED SHIT -AKA- CC DABATHIA -AKA
LOS XANTANA -AKA- BIYOMBO- KA- DI-YAYO -AKA- DI
DEFINITELY MONEY MARADONA

GOD-LEVEL KNOWLEDGE DARTS

NAVIGATING NARCOTICS

&

RELATIONSHIPS

& SHIT LIKE THAT

KIDS!

YOURS and "YOURS"

DESUS NICE & THE KID MERO

This is a work of nonfiction. Some names and identifying details have been changed.

Published in the United States by Random House, an imprint and division of Penguin Random House LLC, New York.

RANDOM HOUSE and the HOUSE colophon are registered trademarks of Penguin Random House LLC.

LIBRARY OF CONGRESS CATALOGING-IN-PUBLICATION DATA
Names: Desus Nice, author. | Kid Mero, author.
Title: God-level knowledge darts: life lessons from the Bronx / Desus & Mero.
Description: First edition. | New York: Random House, [2020]
Identifiers: LCCN 2020003899 (print) | LCCN 2020003900 (ebook) | ISBN 9780525512332 (hardback) | ISBN 9780525512349 (ebook)
Subjects: LCSH: Conduct of life—Humor. | Bronx (New York, N.Y.)—Humor.
Classification: LCC PN6231.C6142 D47 2020 (print) | LCC PN6231.C6142 (ebook) | DDC 818/.602—dc23
LC record available at https://lccn.loc.gov/2020003899
LC ebook record available at https://lccn.loc.gov/2020003900

Printed in the United States of America on acid-free paper

randomhousebooks.com

Cover art direction: Doubleday & Cartwright
Cover design & illustration: Gustavo Dao
Book design: Debbie Glasserman

9 8 7 6 5 4 3 2 1

First Edition

To my mommy, Rocco,
and the Bronx.
—Desus

TO PAPI, MAMI, HEATHER, ADRIAN,
AVERY, AMARI, AZALEA, TITO, INGRID,
VICTOR, & THE BRONX. I LOVE YOU.
—MERO

Contents

Preface
Setting Expectations

HELLO ESTEEMED READER. I AM THE KID MERO. CONGRATULATIONS ON SELECTING SUCH AN IMPORTANT AND CULTURALLY RELEVANT BOOK.

TYPICALLY WHEN PEOPLE CALL SHIT "CULTURALLY RELEVANT" AND "IMPORTANT," IT'S BECAUSE IT SUCKS. BUT THERE'S MAD WHITE GUILT ATTACHED TO TEARING DOWN A POC AUTHOR IN 2020, ESPECIALLY ONE LIKE ME THAT CHECKS MULTIPLE BOXES *USES #2 PENCIL TO FILL IN *BLACK* AND *LATINO** SO I CAN FREELY SAY IT ABOUT MY OWN SHIT. THE FUCK YOU GONNA DO ABOUT IT? I AM POC (I PRONOUNCE IT LIKE 2PAC) AND THEREFORE BEYOND REBUKE.

FORTUNATELY FOR YOU, THIS BOOK REALLY *IS* FUCKING PHENOMENAL AND WILL BE ON YOUR KIDS' COLLEGE SYLLABUS FOR THE CLASS "IDENTIFYING WITH OTHERNESS IN CULTURE" IF THEY GO TO A VERY EXPENSIVE PRIVATE INSTITUTION.

PLEASE ENJOY THIS BOOK OVER AND OVER WHILE YOU COMMUTE TO WORK, TAKE A SHIT, TAKE A SHIT WHILE COM-

MUTING TO WORK. BRUH IF YOU SHIT ON NJ TRANSIT YOU ARE A SPECIAL TYPE OF SAVAGE. WHATEVER. I LOVE YOU. SOME OF THIS ADVICE IS GREAT AND SOME OF IT ABSOLUTELY FUCKIN SUCKS, WHICH, IN A WAY, MAKES THIS A CHOOSE-YOUR-OWN-ADVENTURE BOOK. LOOK AT HOW DYNAMIC THE BRAND IS. I'M GONNA LET DESUS SAY SOMETHING HERE BECAUSE I'M GETTING ANXIETY WATCHING THIS BLUNT BURN IN THE ASHTRAY AND NOT INHALING ITS MAGICAL VAPORS. GO GET EM PAL.

As the child of a New York public branch librarian (go get em Mom!), a former employee of the New York Public Library myself (shouts to Nipple! That's an inside joke, forget you read it), and an English major (shouts to my homie Jane Eyre), writing this book has been a lifelong aspiration.

Ideally this book will last forever, and in 2091 some very sad half-robot/half-human kids will read passages from it and say, "Wow, that's what life was like before the ice caps melted and drowned half the population." (This is said in a weird hybrid Chinese/Minecraft accent).

With this book, we want to give you our hard-won wisdom. Think of it as a fat sack of truth nuggets, a journey inside the minds of myself and Mero. While you probably know us from oh, I don't know, creating some of the best television in the history of television (*GAME OF THRONES* WHO?) and perhaps the greatest and most entertaining and most problematic and damn it just the realest and most Bronx podcast ever, *Bodega Boys,* which is our life, blood, and soul, you've never known us like this. And if you don't know us, welcome to the fucking Bronx.

Mero has mad kids so this probably doesn't feel like having a(nother) child to him, but to me, writing this book has been an amazing experience and feels like I just watched a baby come out a vagina (I'm wearing the traditional "I'm from the hood and this is my baby shower, I ain't pull out in time" Burberry shirt as I write this). If nothing else, you should at least come away from this book with an arsenal of knowledge darts, like the price of a brick of coke (41K in NYC unless you got a connect or can speak Spanish).

So please sit back and enjoy. And keep a glass of water near you while you read because you're going to laugh repeatedly and, sadly, many of you are single, so if you're eating a meal while reading this or listening to the audiobook, there's a good chance your food will go down the wrong pipe and you'll start choking. Unfortunately, you curbed a potential boo a few months ago, probably for a silly reason like he/she used the wrong form of "there" in a text message and you were all, "Umm I have a degree, I'm not putting up with this," and now you're choking alone in your apartment. You try to yell, but between the food caught in your windpipe and the loud sound of the British cooking show playing in the background on Netflix, no one can hear your feeble attempts to scream for help. In a panic, you ram your stomach into the corner of a table to try to get your diaphragm to push up the food, but you've never done that before and *oh shit that hurt* and it didn't help and *oh my god,* you're really dying now, and as you see that white light and head to see your maker, your last conscious thought is a wondrous paradox, the realization that you're dying from us, for us. You're "dying for The Hive," which is one of the top three highest honors one can achieve in this life. Much like a Viking funeral where the body is set on fire and pushed into the water to enter Valhalla, this is your greatest moment. So take that final breath, laugh a muffled, choking laugh, and as you pass out, let your final words be "The brand is brolic."

Thank you for rocking with us.

Sincerely, Dark Desus

Introduction

HELLO READER, IT'S MERO AGAIN, AKA THE PLANTAIN SUPERNOVA. AT THIS POINT, OR PROBABLY AFTER THE FIRST SENTENCE, YOU WERE LIKE, "WHY IS THIS IN ALL CAPS?" IT'S BECAUSE I ALMOST ALWAYS WRITE IN ALL CAPS. IF I'M DRIVING DOWN UNIVERSITY AND FIRING OFF A TEXT I MIGHT NOT USE CAPS, BUT EVERYTHING ELSE IS ON LOCK. IT COMES FROM MY GRAFFITI BACKGROUND, GROWING UP SEEING "BESTER" IN ALL CAPS AND THE SHIT LOOKED SUPER CLEAN AND STYLISH ALL UP AND DOWN TREMONT AVENUE IN THE BRONX. IT WAS SO GOOD AND SO UBIQUITOUS, I THOUGHT "BESTER" AND ITS VARIANTS ("BESTER TFT" & "BESTER OTB") WERE PRODUCTS MADE BY A COMPANY CALLED BESTER. THAT'S WHAT DREW ME INTO GRAFFITI AND MADE ME WRITE IN A "DIFFERENT" WAY EVERY TIME I WROTE *ANYTHING.* THERE ARE ONLY SO MANY WAYS TO DO THAT WITHIN THE RIGID STRUCTURE OF COMPUTERS (ANNNAAARRCCHHHYY!!!) AND ALL CAPS IS ONE OF THEM.

ALSO IF YOU GIVE A SHIT ABOUT CAPS, I'M SORRY, BUT

YOU'RE A HERB, MY GUY. DON'T GIVE ME THE "IT HURTS MY EYES" SHIT EITHER, ARE YOU A FUCKING TODDLER? SOWWY WIDDO BABY EYEBAWS. OH YOU CONSIDER CAPS "YELLING"? YOU'RE KIDDING, RIGHT? HOW BORING ARE YOU? HAVE YOU EVER GOTTEN A BLOWJOB WITH THE LIGHTS ON BEFORE? HAVE YOU EVER BEEN FINGERED IN AN ELEVATOR, NOT KNOWING IF SOMEONE ELSE WAS GONNA GET ON, AND NOT GIVING A SHIT? ARE YOU SOME KIND OF FUCKIN DWEEB WHO'S NEVER GOTTEN YOUR ASS EATEN? IF YOU CARE ABOUT READING IN ALL CAPS AND CHOOSE TO BLOCK YOUR BLESSINGS, YOU ARE A COLOSSAL FUCKING NERD WHO FOLLOWS "INTERNET ETIQUETTE" AND—HOLY SHIT I CAN'T BELIEVE THAT'S EVEN A THING. FUCKIN "INTERNET ETIQUETTE." THE INTERNET IS SUPPOSED TO BE THE WILD WEST, BRUH. I KNOW THIS IS A BOOK AND NOT THE INTERNET BUT FUCK OFF, IT'S ALL THE SAME NOW, IT'S 2020, DAWG. NOT READING MY SHIT BECAUSE IT'S IN ALL CAPS IS LIKE NOT HAVING AMAZING SPONTANEOUS SEX BECAUSE YOU'RE IN A DRESSING ROOM AT NEIMAN'S AND "THaT's NoT ALLoWeD."

Can I interject and thank all the "herbs" and "dweebs" who purchased and are reading this book? I feel like it might not be "best business practices" to insult you out the gate. I would lowkey like to apologize for the number you're about to do to both your brain and your eyeballs. After all of Mero's capital letters, your perfect 20/20 vision will probably drop to something more like 900/300. But I've survived reading Mero this long, so I fully believe you can too, if you put your mind to it. It's actually an important part of you figuring out how to read and imagine Mero talking to you. What he said is true, he's not *yelling* . . . more like speaking at full volume while you're riding in the quiet car with him.

BACK TO ME. I MAY HAVE BEEN HARSH WITH MY ORIGINAL ASSESSMENT BUT I STAND BY IT. YOU KNEW WHAT IT WAS WHEN YOU SIGNED UP! I NEED TO SEE ACTUAL SCIENTIFIC PROOF OF YOU "DOING A NUMBER ON YOUR EYES" BY READING CAPS, I GOOGLED IT AND CAME UP EMPTY. I AM AN UPTOWN/DYCKMAN/BRONX-BORN-AND-BRED/MARRIED FATHER OF FOUR WILD BUT EXCEPTIONAL KIDS. MY LOVELY WIFE IS HEATHER, WHOM I LOVE BECAUSE SHE IS SO FULL OF ENERGY, DYNAMIC, A REAL LEADER, HAS EXCELLENT FIELD VISION, STANDS AN ELEGANT 5'7", GIVING HER THE ABILITY TO WEAR HEELS AND STILL BE SHORTER THAN ME, READS DEFENSES AND MAKES MULTIPLE QUICK DECISIONS UNDER PRESSURE. IF THE STAR RECEIVER IS DOUBLE COVERED, SHE CAN MAKE MULTIPLE READS ON THE FLY AND HAS THE MOBILITY TO PICK UP A FIRST DOWN & MORE. JUST AN INCREDIBLE LIFE PARTNER. ALL THIS PRAISE I'M HEAPING ON MY LIFE PARTNER EXTRAORDINAIRE MIGHT MAKE YOU THINK WE HAVE A PERFECT MARRIAGE BUT THERE IS NO SUCH THING AS A "PERFECT MARRIAGE." DOES ANY GROWN PERSON ACTUALLY BELIEVE THAT'S A REAL THING? MORE ON THAT LATER.

GROWING UP, I WAS HANGING OUT WITH MY PEERS BUT ALSO THE ELDER STATESMEN OF THE HOOD FROM A VERY YOUNG AGE (IT HELPS TO HAVE A GOATEE AT 14), AND IN MY TRAVELS, I CROSSED PATHS WITH DESUS IN SUMMER SCHOOL. I FAILED GYM AT MY ALMA MATER, DEWITT CLINTON H.S. (SHOUT-OUT TO TRACEY TOWERS!! ALSO PLEASE LOOK AT ALL THE DISTINGUISHED ALUMNI!!). I WAS A HIGHLY TOUTED SCUMBAG PROSPECT OUT OF HIGH SCHOOL, SO I WAS ONE AND DONE IN COLLEGE. THEN I JUMPED STRAIGHT INTO THE LEAGUE, AND BY LEAGUE I MEAN ACQUIRING DRUGS ON CONSIGNMENT AND HOPING TO FLIP THEM IN TIME TO GET MONEY TO GO SPEND AT MONTEZUMA'S ON KINGSBRIDGE.

ANYWAY I FLUNKED GYM BECAUSE I WANTED BASKETBALL GYM AND THEY GAVE ME, I'M NOT KIDDING, SQUARE DANCING. SO INSTEAD OF ATTENDING A HOEDOWN, I EITHER CRASHED BASKETBALL GYM OR HUNG OUT AT TAZE'S CRIB AND SMOKED WEED OUT OF A CHALICE PIPE AND TAGGED THE LOCAL STREETS UNTIL IT WAS TIME TO GO BACK TO SCHOOL. THIS RESULTED IN A SMOOTH "F" AND I WAS ASSIGNED TO MY "ZONE SCHOOL," HERBERT H. LEHMAN H.S., FOR THE SUMMER, WHERE DESUS WAS A STUDENT. WE RAN IN DIFFERENT CIRCLES, HE WAS AN UPPERCLASSMAN WITH A SOLID PLAN TO GO TO COLLEGE AND I WAS A SOPHOMORE, NOT GIVING ANY SHITS ABOUT SCHOOL, MORE CONCERNED WITH GETTING MONEY, BOOSTING, GRAFFITI, GETTING STONED & LAID IN THAT ORDER, AND CHARMING GIRLS INTO BRAIDING MY HAIR FOR FREE OR FOR A HIT OFF A BLUNT. I HAD SOME UNSAVORY GUYS AROUND ME ALL THE TIME. TOO MANY "I WILL PUNCH YOU IN THE FACE FOR NO REASON" OR "LOOK I JUST GOT A GUN I'M GONNA COME OUTSIDE AT 3PM IN JULY AND BUST A COUPLE SHOTS IN THE AIR" TYPE GUYS. IT ONLY TOOK ME UNTIL I WAS IN MY MID-20S TO DISCOVER TWITTER, RIGHT THE SHIP, AND USE IT TO PROMOTE THE WRITING I WAS DOING.

I DJ'D AT "BABY'S ALL RIGHT" IN WILLIAMSBURG, WROTE 69 (HEH HEH) ILLUSTRIOUS MUSIC REVIEWS FOR *VICE* WHEN IT WAS A SUSTAINABLE CORPORATION. I WAS OUT HEREEEE. I GOT ON THE FRONT PAGE OF THE *NEW YORK TIMES* ARTS & LEISURE SECTION IN 2013 (SHOUT-OUT TO JON CARAMANICA THE PMF). I WAS BEGINNING UNDER OUR NOW-MANAGER VICTOR'S JEDI-LIKE GUIDANCE TO PICK SPOTS AND GET GIGS IN FRONT OF THE CAMERA. I ALSO PLAYED A LOT OF WHAT I CALL "JOKE TENNIS" ON TWITTER WITH DESUS WHERE A JOKE WOULD START WITH ONE OF US AND THEN THE OTHER WOULD BUILD OFF IT. THEN WE DID A PODCAST WHICH PIVOTED TO VIDEO

WHICH PIVOTED TO CABLE TV WHICH PIVOTED TO BUYING A HOUSE IN BERGEN COUNTY THAT FAT JOE APPROVES OF. (THANKS FOR THE ADVICE, CRILLZMANIA!!)

SINCE I WILL BE EXACTLY 36 (837 IN BRONX YEARS) WHEN YOU READ THIS, I FEEL LIKE I'VE LIVED ENOUGH TO GIVE SOUND ADVICE, AS HAS DESUS. IF THE ADVICE SUCKS, DON'T BLAME ME. I WAS STONED OUTTA MY FUCKING MIND THE ENTIRE TIME WRITING THIS, I'M NOT KIDDING. YOU KNOW HOW MANY TIMES OUR EDITOR BEN HAD TO PUT "ADD: '.'" IN THE GOOGLE DOC?! LOLOLOL NO BUT FOR REAL SOME OF THIS IS GREAT ADVICE SO TAKE A HANDFUL FOR LATER LIKE YOU DO WITH THE NAPKINS AT LITERALLY EVERY RESTAURANT. I JUST BLEW MY NOSE ON A PANDA EXPRESS NAPKIN MY GUY AND YO, HOW DO PEOPLE FILL AN ENTIRE GLOVEBOX WITH TAKEOUT NAPKINS? YOU EVER SEEN THAT SHIT? HOW YOU DRIVING AROUND WITH A FELONY AMOUNT OF BURGER KING NAPKINS IN YOUR CENTER CONSOLE BRUH? LET'S DO BETTER FOR 20WHENEVER-THE-FUCK THIS-COMES-OUT.

HERE WE GO.

GOD-LEVEL KNOWLEDGE DARTS

CHAPTER 1

MAN I AM HIGH AS SHIT LOL AND WRITING ABOUT DRUGS. IS THAT IRONY? I HONESTLY AM ASKING.

Anything can be a drug. Or at least I've been told that. I have a homegirl who said a fresh glass of orange juice gives her the same feeling as smoking weed, and while I'd love to believe her, I also know that's a fucking lie because no one ever comes to work at 8am reeking of orange juice because they needed it to get their day started. Drugs are whatever get you thru life. It could be shopping, it could be playing with your kids (I mean, it isn't, but theoretically it could be).

KIDDING. Drugs are drugs, you know what I'm talking about here. We're talking the rough stuff, the stuff that you can lose custody of your kids over, that stuff that will freeze your jaw and make you spontaneously do the Michael Jackson *Thriller* dance.

DRUGS ARE WILD. I'VE DONE A LOT OF DIFFERENT DRUGS AND BEING HIGH IS DOPE UNDER THE RIGHT CIRCUMSTANCES BUT BEING ADDICTED TO DRUGS FUCKIN SUCKS. I'M NOT HERE TO PREACH, JUST SAYING IT SUUUUCKS. WITHDRAWAL AND ALL THAT SHIT IS THE WORST. THAT BEING SAID, IF YOU ARE READING THIS AND ARE IN YOUR 20S AND/OR HAVE NO REAL RESPONSIBILITIES, FUCKIN GET RIPPED. DO WHATEVER YOU WANT. IF YOU DIE IT'LL BE DOPE CUZ YOU WENT OUT HIGH AS SHIT, UNLESS IT'S ONE OF THOSE GROSS OD'S WHERE YOU CHOKE ON YOUR OWN PUKE OR HAVE A SEIZURE. THAT'S NOT LIT AT ALL.

IF YOU WANNA GET HIGH, GET HIGH. IF YOU DON'T, DON'T. IF YOU'RE AMBIVALENT, I ALWAYS SAY TRY IT . . . BUT DON'T TAKE MY ADVICE, I JUST BURNED A HOLE IN MY CARPET CUZ I DROPPED MY BLUNT THAT I ONLY DROPPED BECAUSE I WAS TRYING TO PICK UP A XANAX I DROPPED BEFORE THAT. HERE'S MY MAIN THING: JUST PUH-LEEEEASEEEE DON'T BE A "HOLIER THAN THOU" JERKOFF ABOUT DRUGS. IF SOMEONE PASSES YOU SOME SHIT YOU AREN'T INTO, A SIMPLE "I'M GOOD, THANKS" WILL SUFFICE. IF YOU LAUNCH INTO A SERMON, I DON'T CARE IF I'M ACROSS THE PARTY, I WILL NARUTO RUN OVER JUST TO DUMP THAT LITTLE TEA LIGHT CANDLE ON YOUR HEAD. THE MOST IMPORTANT THING TO REMEMBER IS THAT DRUGS AFFECT EVERYONE DIFFERENTLY AND NOT ALL DRUGS ARE THE SAME, AND BY THAT I MEAN THE MOLLY YOU GET FROM JULIO IS PROBABLY SOME TOTALLY DIFFERENT SHIT THAN WHAT YOU GET FROM KYLE.

ALCOHOL IS A DRUG BUT IT'S THE BORING DRUG THAT THE OTHER DRUGS SECRETLY TALK ABOUT, SAYING HOW IT'S NOT A "REAL" DRUG CUZ YOU CAN EASILY GET IT ANYWHERE LEGALLY. I GUESS I'M JUST SAYING THAT ON THE OTHER DRUGS' BEHALF. UNTIL YOU MIX ALCOHOL WITH THE "REAL" DRUGS AND FUCKIN

PERISH, IT'S GONNA BE THAT WAY. I GUESS GETTING DRUNK WOULD BE COOL AND ANTI-ESTABLISHMENT IF THERE WAS STILL PROHIBITION, BUT SINCE IT'S LEGAL, PEOPLE MOSTLY OVERDO IT AND NOW IT JUST LEADS TO SLURRED DIALOGUES OUTSIDE OF BARS. DIALOGUES THAT END UP BEING MONOLOGUES BECAUSE YOU WERE SO DRUNK YOU DIDN'T REALIZE THE OTHER PERSON WALKED BACK INSIDE IN THE MIDDLE OF YOU TELLING THEM A STORY THEY'VE HEARD 50LEVEN TIMES, OR WHEN THEY FINISHED THEIR CIGARETTE. EITHER WAY YOU ARE STANDING OUT THERE KICKING YOUR SOLILOQUY WITH A SLOSHING GUT FULL OF FERMENTED WHATEVER, SMOKING A PARLIAMENT LIGHT (YOU DON'T EVEN SMOKE), NOT EVEN REALIZING HOW MUCH MORE FUN YOU WOULD BE HAVING ON SHROOMS. DON'T DRINK AND DRIVE BLAH BLAH BLAH ALCOHOL IS BORING.

SHROOMS ARE FIRE BUT THEY TASTE GROSS. LIKE I MENTIONED PREVIOUSLY, EVERYBODY'S EXPERIENCE IS DIFFERENT AND NO TWO MUSHROOMS ARE ALIKE. THIS IS MY EXPERIENCE ON SHROOMS. YOURS MIGHT BE DIFFERENT. I'VE DONE SHROOMS ENOUGH TO NOT HAVE A SINGULAR "SHROOM STORY" BUT JUST KNOW ONCE YOU EAT THESE THINGS (I RECOMMEND EATING WITH CHOCOLATE OR PEANUT BUTTER), YOU ARE GOING TO BE TRIPPING BALLS FOR THE FORESEEABLE FUTURE. I HAVE NEVER HEARD OF ANYBODY EATING A DECENT AMOUNT OF SHROOMS AND BEING STONE COLD SOBER AN HOUR LATER. I ONCE ATE SHROOMS AND WALKED FROM WESTCHESTER SQUARE & TREMONT AVENUE ON THE 6 LINE TO 218TH & BROADWAY. GOOGLE MAP THAT SHIT, DOG. I WAS TRIPPING MY FACE OFF AND ALSO WRITING WHAT WAS SOME OF THE MOST FIVE-DIMENSIONAL GRAFFITI EVER. MY 40 TASTED LIKE BEING RICH AND EVERYTHING AROUND ME WAS A LIVING ORGANISM. IT WAS FUCKING WILD. IF YOU'VE NEVER WATCHED A

STREETLAMP REACH UP AND NIBBLE AN IMAGINARY TREE LIKE A GIRAFFE GRAZING, EAT SOME SHROOMS AND GO FOR A WALK. SHROOMS ARE HALLUCINOGENS SO I GUESS I SHOULD TALK ABOUT THE OTHER ONES I'VE DONE WHILE WE'RE HERE.

ACID WILL ALSO HAVE YOU TRIPPING FOR HOURS ON END SO MAKE SURE YOU DO THAT SHIT AT THE RIGHT TIME. DON'T DROP ACID AT 3:30AM AND THINK YOUR WORKDAY THE FOLLOWING MORNING IS GONNA BE ANYWHERE NEAR NORMAL. YOU ARE GONNA THINK YOU ARE KEEPING IT TOGETHER WHILE YOUR BOSS'S FACE CYCLES THROUGH EVERY INSTAGRAM FILTER, IN REAL LIFE. YOU ARE NOT KEEPING IT TOGETHER, MY PAL. I TOOK ACID A BUNCH BUT ONE TIME I ENDED UP JUMPING OUT OF A MOVING CAR BECAUSE YOU COULDN'T HAVE TOLD ME THERE WEREN'T SEVERAL SNAKES ON THE FLOOR OF THE CAR. IT WAS IN A PARKING LOT AND I WAS FINE AND WHEN I GOT BACK IN THE CAR THE SNAKES WERE GONE BUT THE LASER SHOW HAD JUST STARTED. EVERYTHING MOVING WAS ACCOMPANIED BY A TRAILING LASER, WHICH MADE ME REQUEST THAT MY FRIENDS DO CIRCLES IN THE AIR WITH THEIR CIGARETTES.

I SMOKED DMT A HANDFUL OF TIMES AND HOE-LEE-FUCKINSHIT. FIRST OF ALL I'M SO GLAD EVERY TIME I SMOKED THE SHIT I WAS INDOORS BECAUSE I LITERALLY HAD TO SIT DOWN AND WATCH AND LISTEN AS OLMEC FROM *LEGENDS OF THE HIDDEN TEMPLE* AND HIS VIBRATING CHECKERBOARD PINK AURA TOLD ME WHAT I HAD TO DO WITH MY LIFE. THEN MY GRANDMA (RIP) WALKED OUT OF OLMEC'S MOUTH ONTO A GLIDING CARPET AND TOLD ME SHE'S PROUD OF ME AND TO NEVER CHANGE. WOW WOWOWOWOW FUCK. THAT SHIT IS MIND-BENDING. I CAN'T EVEN IMAGINE DOING THAT SHIT IN PUBLIC, WHICH MEANS I'LL BE DOING IT WITHIN THE NEXT MONTH OR SO. UNLIKE SHROOMS OR ACID, DMT LITERALLY

LASTED 10 MINUTES THAT, TO BE FAIR, FELT LIKE AN HOUR, AND THE AFTEREFFECTS KINDA SUCK (I FELT NAUSEOUS FOR A COUPLE HOURS), BUT YOU WANNA TALK ABOUT TRIPPING YOUR FACE OFF? FUCKIN DMT IS FOR FEARLESS BRAIN SPELUNKERS BRUH.

Molly is a weird drug because it makes your whole body tingle like you have static cling. And you want to rub up on everyone and hug people and you start to see smells and taste colors. It's not a hard drug that makes you have thoughts like "OMG I'm gonna cut my face off so I can see what I really look like because you can't trust mirrors because the government controls them," but rather a soft mellow one that will make you appreciate the small things in life, like the horns on the song "Safe and Sound" by Capital Cities. Especially at the 2:48 mark of the song. And now you're in the club crying because you just realized that Capital Cities wants to keep you both "safe" and "sound" and that's so beautiful because that's all you ever wanted in life for everyone and then your friend checks to see why you're crying and you respond "your skin is so clear" and y'all make out. Hypothetically.

YEAH MOLLY IS COOL BUT IT'S ONE OF THOSE "OH THIS NIGGA IS DEFINITELY ON FUCKIN MOLLY LOL" DRUGS. THERE'S NO HIDING THE FACT YOU ARE ROLLING LIKE A BOWLING BALL DOWN A WHEELCHAIR RAMP. MOLLY IS WILD BECAUSE EVERYTHING FEELS AMAZING. EATING ICE CREAM FEELS LIKE 3 ANGELS ARE MASSAGING YOUR NUDE BODY ON A DUVET MADE OF CLOUDS, ALL THAT SENSORY BLISS FROM THE SIMPLEST SHIT. GETTING A BLOWJOB FEELS LIKE ASCENDING INTO A UFO MADE OUT OF MILK CHOCOLATE ON ONE OF THOSE TRACTOR BEAM THINGS AND IT'S SOMEHOW MASSAGING YOUR BALLS AND SCALP SI-

MULTANEOUSLY THE WHOLE WAY UP. THEN AFTER A COUPLE HOURS YOUR JAW LOOSENS UP AND EVERYTHING IS BACK TO STANDARD DEFINITION. THIS IS THE PROBLEM WITH ALL DRUGS—SOMETIMES BEING HIGH ON THEM FEELS TOO GOOD. TOO MUCH BETTER THAN REALITY. I SAID I WASN'T GONNA PREACH BUT I DON'T WANNA SEE YOU BLOWING PEOPLE FOR COKE UNLESS THAT'S WHAT *YOU* WANNA DO, IN YOUR HEART OF HEARTS.

Cocaine is more than a drug. It's a literal litmus test for culture. First off, almost everyone does coke. Some of you reading this are immediately like "Desus my guy, that's a pile of horseturds," but I'm right and you're wrong. The reason you don't know anyone who does coke is because you radiate Big Cop Energy and they would never do it / mention it / show it around you. But if you present yourself as a pretty chill person, eventually someone will offer you a little "nose candy." Especially Australians. MY GOD shout-out the AUSTRALIANS.

Professional cokeheads, excuse me coke *users*, are the coolest because they don't judge you as long as you don't judge them. My good friends [REDACTED] and [REDACTED] "tooted some rails" at a Sunday afternoon NY Rangers hockey game. And while that sounds like the absolute worst idea, a good time was had by all and no one got hit with a puck. And trust and believe they weren't the only people skiing at that hockey game.

Also there's like a million slang terms for coke/using coke:

➔ Riding the Metro-North (super regional)

➔ Getting right (pretty general)

➔ Skiing/slopes (classic)

- Bobby Brown jaw (hip-hop related but even Bobby Brown would admit he was wildin in the '90s)

- Chatting with Drew Barrymore and a giraffe at Studio 54 while Chic plays (this one isn't as popular as it was in the early '80s but it's due for a comeback)

- Airdropping (not popular yet but will probably be commonplace when humans and robots start having children together)

One problem with coke is that it operates under the same economics as potato chips, i.e., "once you pop you can't stop." As someone who was once allegedly involved in, um, the, um, logistical distribution of, perhaps, a controlled substance, I've HEARD that coke users will call your phone 26 times in a row at 4am to ask, "You around bro?" and then cop like 300 dollars' worth of whatever you have because "we gotta keep the party going."

Weirdly enough I was terrified of coke growing up because in 2nd grade, my school showed us an antidrug promo where a little black kid (I'm like, oh wow, that's me) and his friend do coke at the friend's house after school. Now, this was total bullshit because the kids were five years old and wearing sweaters in a house in like Maine and . . . what? What five-year-old is doing coke? At five I could barely color within the lines, how am I supposed to chop this diva fuel into equal lines? Anyway, the black kid does coke and feels weird so he runs home and dies in his mother's arms at the door, and then a doctor was like, "He had a heart murmur and the coke stopped his heart." Now, that shit almost literally stopped my heart, because I had a heart murmur (a little bitch-ass one, nothing major, but stay with me). So at that moment I was all, "OMG I'm never touching that stuff" because why would they lie to a child? Fast-forward to me in some unisex club bathroom years later doing bumps with a drag queen and waiting for my heart to explode and it doesn't and I'm immediately shaking my fist at God, because my life was lies, and because the coke had kicked in and now I was God.

COCAINE MAYNE **TERRENCE HOWARD VOICE AND EMOTION.** COKE SUCKS IN THE SAME WAY THAT ALCOHOL SUCKS. IT'S JUST CONFIDENCE POWDER WITH SUPER-CAFFEINE OR SOME SHIT. RIGHT NOW I'M TRYING TO DECIDE IF PRE-VOM ALCOHOL BURPS OR COKEDRIP NOSE SNORTS ARE WORSE. COKE IS ALSO A "OH THIS NIGGA IS SKI'D THE FUCK UP LOL" DRUG, LIKE MOLLY. PEOPLE WILL NOTICE THE TELLTALE SIGNS OF THE DRUG. YOUR UNCONTROLLABLE BOBBY BROWN JAW, YOUR NEED TO USE EVERY WORD IN THE ENGLISH LANGUAGE TO EXPLAIN HOW YOU WENT TO THE SUPERMARKET AND THOUGHT OF WAYS TO MAKE IT MORE EFFICIENT SO HERE'S A PITCH FOR AN APP. STOP. STOP. JUST BE HIGH BRO. COKE MAKES YOUR MIND INTO A LASER BEAM SO USE IT FOR GOOD, NOT EVIL, AND BY GOOD I MEAN MAKING A GREAT ALBUM OR PAINTING. ACTUALLY WRITE THE PILOT YOU WERE TALKING ABOUT AT 4AM WHILE THE DJ PLAYED HIS OWN TERRIBLE REMIXES BECAUSE FUCK YOU, THIS IS THE AFTER-HOURS SPOT AND YOU ARE ALL COCAINE VAMPIRES. BY EVIL I MEAN TELLING ME BETWEEN COKE SNORTS AND WITH PAINSTAKING DETAIL ABOUT HOW YOU ARE GONNA REVOLUTIONIZE HOUNDSTOOTH IN STREETWEAR. I DON'T WANNA HEAR ALL THAT, DOG. IT'S 5AM, MY JAW JUST RELAXED AND I'M SMOKING A BLUNT BECAUSE I'M ABOUT TO EAT SOMETHING OUTRAGEOUS, FUCK, AND SLEEP TILL 3PM.

I NEVER SMOKED CRACK BUT I HAVE PUT TOO MUCH CO-

CAINE IN BLUNTS ON OCCASION SO I GUESS THAT'S TECHNICALLY FREEBASING? IT'S NOT A TERRIBLE HIGH. IT'S LIKE BEING ON COKE JUST SLIGHTLY LESS VERBOSE AND WITH THE ABILITY TO ACHIEVE AN ERECTION EASIER RELATIVE TO BLOWING STRAIGHT YAY AND DRINKING STELLAS. SHOUT-OUT TO DATA, I THINK LIKE 68% OF THE WOOLIES I SMOKED HAD SOMETHING TO DO WITH HIM.

I'VE NEVER DONE ACTUAL HEROIN, BUT I HAVE EATEN MAD OXYS. THE FIRST TIME I ATE ONE I DIDNT KNOW THE SEVERITY OF WHAT THE FUCK I WAS TAKING, SO I ENLISTED MY FRIEND RUSS TO HELP. I CHANGED HIS NAME BECAUSE HE'S MARRIED AND HAS KIDS BUT HE'S GONNA READ THIS AND CHUCKLE AND SHUDDER AT THE SAME DAMN TIME. RUSS PICKED ME UP IN HIS BUICK AND WE HAD ENOUGH MONEY BETWEEN US FOR A DIME OF WEED. I ALLEGEDLY HAD A POUCH FULL OF OXYS BUT I WAS LIKE, "I'M NOT EATING THIS SHIT. I'M NOT SURE EXACTLY WHAT THIS IS BUT I'VE *HEARD* THIS IS BASICALLY HEROIN YOU CAN TAKE WITH A GLASS OF LEMONADE." SO AFTER WE EXPEDITIOUSLY SMOKED OUR SKIMPY DIME, MONEY WAS TIGHT AND HIGHS NEEDED TO BE REACHED, SO WE EACH ATE ONE.

I HAD NO IDEA A 10MG OXY COULD MAKE YOU FORGET YOU HAD A KNIFE STUCK IN YOUR THIGH AND ENTER A SALSA CONTEST. BUT THESE WERE 30MG, MY PALS. RUSS'S BODY SAID "NAH BRUH" BECAUSE HE CALMLY BUT WITHOUT WARNING PULLED OVER AFTER ABOUT 20 MINUTES OF DRIVING AROUND SMOKING NEWPORTS AND LISTENING TO AZ AND BEGAN PUKING HIS EYEBALLS OUT HIS MOUTH. HE THEN RINSED HIS MOUTH OUT WITH WHAT I BELIEVE WAS A BLUE GATORADE, LIT A CIGARETTE, AND PUT THE CAR IN DRIVE LIKE HE DIDN'T JUST EXPEL HIS ENTIRE DIGESTIVE TRACT. BY THEN, THOUGH, IT WAS TOO LATE. DESPITE MOST OF THE OXYCODONE GETTING KICKED OUT OF CLUB GUTS, THERE WAS STILL ENOUGH IN HIS

SYSTEM TO HAVE HIM NODDING OUT AT THE BAR AN HOUR LATER. ON THE OTHER HAND, I THINK MY EXPERIENCE WITH OXYCODONE GOING BACK TO GETTING CRAMBONED BY A CAR AND EATING PERCOCET LIKE M&M'S MADE MY BODY MORE RESISTANT. HATS AND DURAGS WERE ALLOWED IN MY STOMACH LOUNGE. MAN WAS I FUCKIN SLUMPED, THOUGH. I COULD BARELY LIFT A CIGARETTE TO MY LIPS. I WAS SITTING AT A NOTORIOUSLY SEEDY BAR ON TREMONT FREESTYLING OVER R&B SONGS UNTIL MY EYES DECIDED THEY HAD ENOUGH AND CALLED IT A NIGHT MID-FREESTYLE. THE REASON I'LL NEVER DO OXY AND ITS COUSINS RECREATIONALLY AGAIN IS BECAUSE ALTHOUGH THE HIGH WAS FUCKIN BONKERS AND ALMOST TOO GOOD, I KNEW I LOOKED AS HIGH AS I FELT AND THAT WAS OD EMBARRASSING. PEOPLE SAY NARCISSISM IS BAD BUT IT *SERIOUS *60 MINUTES* VOICE* SAVED ME FROM THE RAVAGES OF OPIOID ADDICTION.

WHINY VOICE MERO, YOU ARE PRETTY CAVALIER ABOUT HOW YOU DISCUSS DRUG USE WAH WAH DON'T YOU HAVE KIDS? WHAT IF THEY READ THIS AND THEN DO DRUGS? WAH WAH.

I'M GLAD YOU ASKED, YOU FUCKIN PENIS WRINKLE. DESUS TAKE THE WHEEL, I'M TOO RIPPED TO WRITE ANY MORE AND I JUST REMEMBERED I HAVE THREE EMPANADAS IN THE MICROWAVE.

Why would you throw it to someone with no kids to write about this when you have four kids? But okay. Every parent eventually has to have the drugs conversation with their child. Even more so due to Lil Pump and opioid rappers and things of that nature. Again, as someone who does not have kids ~~(in this country)~~, I have no experience with this and have never even thought about this moment one single time until right now, but also as someone with no children, I'm actually an expert on this if you think about it. I am unclouded by emotion.

Drugs are weird because they're everywhere but you don't see them unless you know what you're looking for. For example: You might think the security guard that always smells like a pack of loud is the big drug head at your job. Meanwhile, there's probably an assistant shooting dope in between their toes on their lunch break. Also, one's knowledge of drugs is usually limited to how much experience you've had with it. So there's people out there who smoked a j once in 1967 and then there are people like me who know how to use cold water extraction to remove opioids from acetaminophen IN THEORY.

OKAY, HE IS CLEARLY JUST STALLING, I'LL DO IT. AS A PARENT THERE ARE MAD OD TIMES WHEN YOU ARE LIKE *DAMN B WOULD IT BE POSSIBLE FOR ME TO OUTSOURCE THIS DRUG TALK WITH MY CHILD? CUZ THIS IS GONNA SUCK*. I FEEL YOU MY GUY, I'M A FATHER OF FOUR. SOMETIMES YOU HAVE TO DO SHIT YOU DON'T WANT TO FOR THE GOOD OF OTHERS. "BUT MERO IF I DON'T CARE FOR MYSELF, HOW CAN I CARE FOR OTHERS?" YOU SERIOUSLY GONNA AVOID THE DRUG TALK WITH YOUR KIDS IN THE NAME OF SELF-CARE? WHAT ARE YOU, SOME KINDA JERK? WHAT DOES THAT EVEN MEAN? IS THAT ONE OF THOSE QUOTES THAT HAS BEEN INCORRECTLY ATTRIBUTED TO MARILYN MONROE? FAM, EVERY BOTTLE WAITRESS GOT MONROE QUOTES ON DECKY, SHE WAS A TIMELESS THOT. ALSO I KNOW THIS WILL SOUND EXTREMELY SCUMBAGGY, BUT WHAT WAS SCUMBAGGY AND SELFISH IN 2005 IS NOW "SELF-CARE" SO . . . IF YOU REALLY NEED SELF-CARE, GO PUT YOUR KID IN FRONT OF AN IPAD AND THROW ON A WOMBAT PLACENTA PORE-CLEANSING MASK. GIVE YOURSELF A MINI SPA DAY WHILE YOUR KID DISCOVERS P-NO ALL IN THE NAME OF MODERN SELF-PRESERVATION.

NOW YOU ALL GOOD? NOW YOU'RE READY FOR THE DRUG TALK, BECAUSE HONESTLY, THE ONE THING YOU ARE GONNA BE FORCED TO DO AT SOME POINT IS TALK TO YOUR KIDS ABOUT SEX, DRUGS (NOT ROCK & ROLL CUZ THAT SHIT IS CORNY, LOL @ "ROCK & ROLL" . . . REALLY? THAT'S THE NAME OF YOUR GENRE? IT SOUNDS LIKE THE NAME OF A FUCKIN BOWLING ALLEY FROM THE FLINTSTONES. FUCK OUTTA HERE "ROCK & ROLL.") I STARTED WITH DRUGS BECAUSE "DADDY'S OFFICE" ALWAYS SMELLS LIKE "HOT CHRISTMAS TREES." NEXT IS SEX BUT I GOT A LITTLE WAYS TO GO SEEING AS HOW MERO JR IS 8. REGARDLESS OF THIS FACT, I HAVE MY BATTLE PLAN READY. OH SHIT I AM STALLING TOO, I JUST REALIZED *THOUGHT LIGHT BULB.*

The sex conversation is a wild one because you used to be able to wait till your kid was 18, then just send them to a brothel (I saw this on *Leave It to Beaver*, I think). Now your innocent lil pookie could just be chilling watching YouTube and they're maybe one click away from HARDCORE P-NO (again I don't have kids so I'm going by what they say on *60 Minutes* every Sunday night). It's not like how it was back in the day. Growing up my mother told me my dick was named "Mr. PeePee" and my sisters had a "pumpum." This was all well and great until we were all in the car and heard a Jamaican song about "ram up ya pumpum" and my poor mother attempted to turn the channel but the damage was done. Nothing was the same after that shit.

YEAH, SEX IS EASY TO TALK ABOUT CUZ YOU CAN JUST SIT DOWN WITH YOUR KID LIKE, YO FAM, BUST IT, GENDER IS A SPECTRUM NOT A BINARY, AIGHT? . . . UHHH NO MEANS NO, SEX IS ONLY CONSENSUAL WHEN BOTH PARTIES ENTHUSIASTI-CALLY AND EXPLICITLY VERBALLY AGREE TO PARTAKE AND

THERE IS NO BACARDI LIMON BEING CONSUMED BY EITHER PARTY CLOUDING JUDGMENT. . . . ALSO CONDOMS SUCK AND FUCKING WHILST ROCKING A LATEX COCK SHEATH IS LIKE WATCHING TV WITH SUNGLASSES ON. IT'S HAPPENING AND YOU CAN TELL IT'S HAPPENING BUT IF YOU WENT RAW DIZZLE YOU WOULD REALLY BE IN BUSINESS. . . . DON'T DO THAT THO BECAUSE [INSERT REASON THAT SOUNDS VALID, I CAN'T REALLY THINK OF ONE]. NICE & TIDY TALKY TALK AND YOU ARE DONE.

OKAY, ENOUGH STALLING. THE DRUG CONVERSATION IS WAY MORE NUANCED. SEX IS ALMOST A GIVEN. LIKE EVENTUALLY YOU WILL BE DOING SEX WITH YOUR GENITALS MY PAL, THAT'S ALMOST CERTAIN. IF THAT'S NEVER HAPPENED FOR YOU, WHY ARE YOU READING THIS BOOK, BRUH? GET OUT THERE AND CHARM THE LITERAL PANTS OFF SOMEONE, FAM. YOU NEED TO HAVE SEX ASAP. IT'S REALLY GOOD, TRUST ME.

BUT DOING DRUGS IS DIFFERENT. IT'S POSSIBLE TO GO YOUR WHOLE LIFE SOBER. YOU HAVE TO TEACH YOUR KIDS THAT IN GENERAL DRUGS ARE "BAD" BUT ALSO HINT AT THE FACT THAT WEED IS SUPER FUCKING LIT SO THEY CAN START SMOKING GANJ IN THEIR TEENS AND YOU CAN HAVE THE ILL WILD CYPH AND FREESTYLE. GETTING SMACKED AND FREESTYLING WITH MY KIDS IS SOMETHING I'M SUPER LOOKING FORWARD TO, NOT REALLY BECAUSE OF THE BONDING OR ANYTHING BUT JUST TO BE LIKE "NIGGA YOU CAME OUT MY DICK LITERALLY" OVER A BEAT. HOW DO YOU COME BACK FROM "YOU EMERGED FROM MY URETHRA" PHRASED AS A DISS? IT'S OVER. I COULD BE LIKE A RAP DAD LAVAR BALL / LUCIOUS LYON FROM *EMPIRE* HYBRID PUSHING MY KIDS TO THE BRINK OF EXHAUSTION IN THE STUDIO SPITTING HOT FIRE. LET ME STOP I'M TINGLING. NEVA LOST!

First I'd basically do the opposite of the speech my father gave me and my sisters about drugs. I was in third grade and it was after school. We were latchkey kids, so we'd come home, make snacks, and wait for my mother to come home and switch off warden duty to my father, who worked at night. I think we were doing homework and watching cartoons and suddenly *BOOM*—my father kinda kicks in the door to the room holding something very small in his hand. It was a plastic container of some sort. I thought my little sister left one of her Barbie toys in the living room, which is apparently the worst thing a West Indian child can do.

My father yells at all of us, "THIS IS CRACK! If I catch any of you using this, I'll break your ass!" We're low-key terrified and he looks at us all in the eyes and turns around and exits. That's it. That was our drug conversation. To this day I have no idea where my father got crack from. Did he find it or did he purchase it for this random-ass display that created more questions than answers? For quite some time after that I thought crack was the colorful top of the vial, not the actual contents. Also what happened to that vial after that fake-ass Nancy Reagan display? My sisters and I figure our father, being the frugal legend that he is, definitely sold it to someone, just to get a return on the investment. So I guess I would want to do a better job than that.

IF THIS WAS AN ACTUAL VIAL THAT WAS ACTUALLY FILLED WITH ACTUAL CRACK THEN YES, I HAVE FURTHER QUESTIONS. PURCHASING CRACK ISN'T LIKE PICKING UP THROW PILLOWS AT TARGET. IF IT WAS AN EMPTY VIAL HE FOUND AND JUST WANTED TO DEMONSTRATE WHAT PACKAGED CRACK LOOKS LIKE, THEN THIS IS PRETTY SOLID DADDEGY (DAD STRATEGY, *FUUUCK* I AM INCREDIBLE AT THIS!) . . . I MEAN, HE DISPLAYED THE CRACK

VESSEL AND THAT IS REALLY ALL YOU NEED TO SEE TO RECOGNIZE CRILLZ FOREVER. EITHER WAY, WHETHER HE COPPED IT FOR REAL JUST TO PROVE A POINT OR WENT SCOURING THE GUTTERS LOOKING FOR EMPTY VIALS, EXCELLENT JOB, DESUS'S DAD. YOU COVERED EVERY BASE OF BEING A WEST INDIAN PARENT. ALSO MY FATHER THREATENING TO "BREAK MY ASS" WOULD HAVE GOTTEN 8-YEAR-OLD MERO TO STRAIGHTEN UP REAL FUCKIN FAST.

It's a razor's edge talking about drugs. You don't want to make drugs seem too cool or appealing and at the same time you don't want to make them so scary that your kids are drawn to them. We've all been teens and nothing is cooler than something your parents told you not to do.

I think the most important part of whatever drug discussion you have is being honest. Growing up I remember a DARE video that said if you smoked crack once, you'd be addicted for life. Who lies to kids? Once I found out you could casually smoke the krills (crack), I was upset. Nancy Reagan had lied to me. Mr. T lied to me. Why would I continue to "Just Say No"?

To have any sort of real drug conversation, you first have to sit down and watch *Intervention*. I mean the real episodes where the girl has sex in the street for like $5 worth of meth, not that stupid-ass "I'm addicted to video games" bullshit. Sometimes you have to let your kids see the dark uncool side of drugs.

IF YOU REALLY WANNA GET INTO IT, I FEEL LIKE THE DRUG TALK IS ACTUALLY A COUPLE OF SEPARATE TALKS. YOUR TALKS HAVE TO BE AGE-APPROPRIATE. YOU AREN'T GOING TO TALK TO YOUR TODDLER ABOUT HPV OR WHATEVER, AND YOU AREN'T GONNA TALK TO YOUR 5-YEAR-OLD ABOUT BLOWING COKE IN BATHROOMS. MY STRATEGY IS THIS: HAVE AN EARLY TALK WHERE

YOU TELL YOUR KIDS WHAT A CRACKHEAD LOOKS LIKE AND TO BE CAREFUL AND NOT TAKE THEIR TIMBS OFF AT ORCHARD BEACH CUZ THEY MIGHT PUNCTURE THEIR FOOT WITH A SYRINGE FULL OF STRAIGHT COOKIE DOUGH HEROIN.

THEN A COUPLE YEARS LATER THE ACTUAL "YOU MIGHT FUCK AROUND WITH DRUGS" TALK. NOW I DON'T KNOW ABOUT YOU BUT I WOULD LET MY KID SMOKE WEED IN THE YARD WITH HIS FRIENDS OR SOME SHIT. WAIT, SHOULD I NOT HAVE SAID THAT? THIS IS A WORK OF FICTION *SWEATING.*

I shared a room with my sister until she hit puberty and then I had to move to the basement because as my West Indian father said, "Your sister, she have breasts now," and then opened the door to the basement like, *get in*. The basement was terrifying because our neighborhood had mad burglaries from fiends and every other house put iron bars on their basement windows except mine because, um, do you have security money? Anyway, I used to keep a mini-machete under my pillow with tape on the handle in case someone broke in. And anytime there was any noise I'd think "Okay, it's go time" but it would always be a cat or something.

I tell that story as a cautionary tale of the wild tales I'm going to tell my kids to keep them off drugs. I'll also tell them that recreational Adderall will make your heart explode. I know that doesn't square with the "who lies to kids" thing I said above, but that's the secret beauty of advice . . . you don't have to take it, not even your own.

As for weed, I honestly think my parents have never smoked. They grew up wild Christian in Jamaica so it's very on brand for them. I actually didn't smoke till I was 30 (had caught a case and was stressed). Had I started smoking earlier, who knows if my life would be what it is now. I guess that's a choice your child has to make and all you can do is give them the tools to make the right decision.

WEED IS HARMLESS AND MY PARENTS KINDA DID ME A DISSERVICE BY ACTING LIKE WEED WAS UNCUT COCAINE DUG OUT FROM UNDER PABLO ESCOBAR'S FORESKIN. I WAS FORCED TO SMOKE WEED IN THE STREET OR IN HALLWAYS AND RISK ARREST BY STATEN ISLAND COPS WHO ARE PISSED OFF THEY HAVE TO WORK IN THE BRONX, INSTEAD OF JUST SMOKING IN MY CRIB DRINKING APPLE JUICE OUT OF THE BOTTLE AND PLAYING VIDEO GAMES. I'M GOING TO INFORM MY KIDS THAT WEED IS HARMLESS BUT YOU HAVE TO DO IT IN MODERATION (LOL) OR YOU WILL BECOME SUPER LAZY AND FAT OR SOMETHING (CHILL, THAT'S FAT SHAMING. I APOLOGIZE TO ALL MY FELLOW FAT PEOPLE). YOU CAN'T JUST TELL YOUR KIDS THERE'S NO CONS TO A DRUG CUZ THEN THEY'LL GO OVERBOARD. ALTHOUGH NOW WEED TECHNOLOGY IS SO FUCKIN ADVANCED THAT BY THE TIME MERO JR IS IN JUNIOR HIGH THERE'LL BE SHIT LIKE WEED THAT MAKES YOU DO YOUR HOMEWORK BETTER. THAT FUCKIN SPECIFIC. LOOK AT HOW SPECIFIC THE SHIT IS NOW! YOU CAN COP AN OUNCE OF SOME SHIT WITH A GOOFY NAME THAT WILL CURE NAUSEA AND ANXIETY IN LIKE 4 PUFFS. SO WE'RE GONNA WAIT AND SEE WHAT THE MARKET LOOKS LIKE IN 2030. THE OTHER STUFF I'LL BE LIKE: CHILL, MY GUY. RECREATIONAL XANAX ARE LIT BUT THEY ARE POINTLESS CUZ YOU CAN'T REMEMBER THE FUN YOU HAD ON THEM. THE REST OF THE SHIT YOU CAN ACTUALLY OD ON AND THINK ABOUT HOW MUCH THAT WOULD FUCKIN SUCK.

I don't think I'll ever smoke with my kids but who knows? Maybe if it's legal. All I know is I'm not paying for my own smoke, dear Lil Desus or Desusia or other. I brought you into this world, the least you can do is hook your old man up. Also please don't have baby lungs and bring disrespect to our family name.

WHEN WILL I STOP SMOKING WEED, YOU ASK? PLEASE TELL ME SOMEONE ASKED THAT AND IT WASN'T A TINY VOICE IN MY SUBCONSCIOUS BEGGING ME TO STOP. CMON, MY GUY, YOU KNOW MY ANSWER IS NEVUARY 200NEVER. WEED IS GREAT. NAME ONE EVERYDAY REGULAR LIFE THING THAT IS NOT ENHANCED BY WEED. DO YOU KNOW HOW MUCH FUN I HAVE AT THE MALL HIGHER THAN A BRONTOSAURUS FINGERING ITS BUTT ON MARS? IF I HAVE SUNGLASSES ON, I'M EXTRA GOOD. I'LL GO TO THE DENTIST SMACKED AND TALK ABOUT THE GIANTS' CHANCES THIS YEAR BUT LIKE REALLY BE INTO IT, NOT JUST SMALL TALK. I'M TALKING OFFENSIVE FORMATIONS WITH FUCKIN DR. GOLDBERG WHILE THE SPIT SUCKY THING IS IN MY MOUTH AND MY LIPS ARE SO DRY IF I SAY "COWBOYS" THEY'LL CRACK. WHO ARE THE OLDEST PEOPLE YOU KNOW THAT SMOKE WEED REGULARLY? CHEECH AND CHONG GOTTA BE AT LEAST 60 AND THEY STILL OUT HERE CHILLIN SMOKIN GAS. WILLIE NELSON OLD AS SHIT. THAT NIGGA PROLLY PURCHASED WEED FROM NATIVE AMERICANS. HE'S CHILLIN. I'M PRETTY SURE HE'S RICH WITHOUT HAVIN TO GOOGLE *GOOGLES ANYWAY* GODDAMN THAT OLD SUMMABITCH IS WORTH 25 MIL!! HOLY SHIT. WOW.

I HAVE 0 MOTIVATION TO STOP SMOKING WEED. I HAVE A WHOLE AREA OF MY CRIB DEDICATED TO SMOKING WEED B. I DIDN'T CREATE THIS AESTHETIC FOR NOTHING. DON'T WORRY THERE ARE NO LAVA LAMPS OR ANYTHING. IT'S VERY UNDERSTATED. BUT NOT SO UNDERSTATED THAT IT LOOKS LIKE THE HOTEL FROM *THE SHINING*... WHICH KANYE'S CRIB KINDA

LOOKS LIKE. ITS OD REPETITIVE, IDK MAYBE I'M JUST SMACKED. ALSO I HAVEN'T SEEN *THE SHINING* IN DUUUUMB LONG. JACK NICHOLSON IS REALLY THE SPIKE LEE OF THE LAKERS LOL. COULD YOU PICK ANYBODY BETTER? JACK NICHOLSON IS LIKE IF DOWNTOWN LA SMOKED MENTHOLS AND WAS A PERSON.

Being old and still smoking is such a flex. You're past the age where you give a shit and you're just still living so you're like fuck it, let me enjoy the time I have left. RIP my uncle Shem who was the coolest person I've ever known. He was always my favorite uncle to have around. He was funny as shit and was constantly cracking extremely inappropriate/nasty Jamaican jokes that made my mother blush. I mention him because he had a photo of Bob Marley and Willie Nelson in the bar he built in his basement (!) and he said they were "his idols." As a child that didn't mean much, but looking back with adult eyes, my uncle was the ultimate stoner. In every photo of him holding me, his eyes are super low and red and he has that smile like "damn man I'm smacked." I remember his house always having a familiar scent to it and now I know what that smell was. My uncle was a true Jamaican with five jobs, so I know the weed didn't stop him, and I'll definitely be smoking until I'm ninety. My nephew will write this same paragraph about me one day. Please nephew, know that I was smoking on that good good.

YOU KNOW HOW ILL WEED IS? YOU CAN'T OD ON WEED. I MEAN YOU COULD BUT YOU WOULD HAVE TO MAINLINE A CRAZY AMOUNT OR SOME SHIT. IDK EVERYBODY IS DIFFERENT BUT I HAVE A SMACKED CEILING WHEN IT COMES TO WEED. WE SHOT A SHOW IN VENICE AND GOT WEED LIBRARY CARDS AND I WAS DEAD-ASS LIKE, *I'M GOING TO GO HAMMER AT THE DISPENSARY*, AND THAT I DID. I GOT WAX, I GOT EDIBLES, I GOT PRE-

ROLLED BACKWOODS DIPPED IN WAX AND KEEF, SHIT YOU ONLY SEE IN FUCKIN MEMES THAT ARE LIKE "WHAT ARE YOU DOIN AFTER SMOKIN THIS." I ATE LIKE 4 BROWNIES THAT HAD FUCKIN SKULL AND CROSSBONES AND ALL IT DID WAS MAKE ME GO 1-15 FROM 3POINT RANGE AND FALL ASLEEP ON A (ACCORDING TO DESUS AND OUR MANAGER, VICTOR) TERRIFYING HELICOPTER FLIGHT TO COACHELLA. ALSO I HAD TWO WEED LEMONADES WHICH, YES, THAT IS A REAL THING.

That trip to Venice proved Mero and I are animals because we took enough edibles to put down a rhinoceros and we kept it moving and filming. Also we need at least 250mgs for a baseline minimum bc New York City reggie will keep your lungs humble. Anyway we got to go to the dispensary and cop whatever we wanted. Usually you go to a weed store and they have all these bogus products like THC Balm for your dick or weed candy you put in your butt. But the place we went to had OFFICIAL product (went out of business shortly afterward) and we got a little bit of everything. There was a muffin that said "not for one person, consume over the course of a week." MERO DA GAWD eats this muffin in about 20 minutes and washes it down with 16 oz. of THC LEMONADE. And with all due respect, Mero is good money! He's still talking, spray-painting, putting up respectable free throw numbers for a Knicks fan. Now he's not exactly speaking words at this point but words were created by the white man, so we don't always need them. Fast-forward to our helicopter ride to Coachella and at a certain point another helicopter is coming directly at us, causing our pilot to swerve and come dangerously low to a mountain. Realizing this would be my last moment in life but also not wanting to be the first to scream (due to toxic masculinity), I turned and looked to see what Mero was doing. I assumed he was probably calling his wife, telling her he loved her and that she was a good wife and he'll be waiting for her at the pearly gates. Or maybe recording a final voice note for his kids to have so they'll always remember their father who would no longer be there.

NOPE.

Mero was knocked TF out. Like 10 sheets to the wind with a little drool coming out the corner of his mouth like a cartoon character. He didn't even feel a thing. When we finally landed I told him we almost died. He looked at me, kinda muttered "word," then shoplifted a Snapple. (THIS IS A LITERAL SNAPPLE FACT.)

TIGER WOODS SLOW FIST PUMP

WEED IS ALSO LIT BECAUSE YOU CAN USE IT MEDICINALLY AS WELL AS FOR CONVINCING YOURSELF YOU NEED A STRAWBERRY HULLER FOR THE CRIB FROM SUR LA TABLE. IF YOU ARE BODEGAHIVE YOU KNOW THE STORY OF A YOUNG CORNROWED MERO FRESH INTO HIS 20S WHO GOT HIT BY A FORD BRONCO WHILE CROSSING THE STREET. IF YOU AREN'T FAMILIAR, WHAT HAD HAPPENED WAS *BOOM,* I'M WALKING TO THE MANHATTAN EXPRESS BUS STOP, RIGHT? CUZ MY GIRL WORKS DOWNTOWN AND SOHO WAS RIFE WITH STORES TO STEAL SHIT FROM, SO I'M HEADED DOWN TO MEET HER AFTER WORK. NOW MIND YOU THESE BUSSES STOP HERE TWICE AN HOUR IF YOU'RE LUCKY. I SEE THE BUS COMING AND PICK UP THE PACE TO BEAT IT TO THE STOP CUZ THESE MUTHAFUCKAS WILL NOT STOP AT ALL IF THERE ISN'T A HUMAN FLAGGING THEM DOWN. I GO FROM JOG TO FULL SPRINT, GLANCE UP AT THE TRAFFIC LIGHT FOR THE STREET I'M ABOUT TO DART ACROSS. THERE'S A FORD BRONCO THAT WAS, IN MY ESTIMATION, AT LEAST HALF A

BLOCK AWAY. *HE'S GONNA SLOW DOWN AND I'M RUNNING LIKE A FUCKIN GAZELLE,* I THOUGHT TO MYSELF.

THREE STEPS INTO THE STREET I REALIZE OJ WASN'T SLOWING DOWN HE WAS TRYING TO BEAT THE LIGHT. *CLUNFF!! SCRRRRAPE!!* I GET CREAMED BY OJ WHO ISN'T ACTUALLY OJ BUT A MIDDLE-AGE PUERTO RICAN MAN. I HAVE NO IDEA HOW I A) DIDN'T DIE AND B) IMMEDIATELY POPPED ONTO MY FEET AND POINTED IN THE DIRECTION OF MY MOM'S APARTMENT. SHE COMES OUT AND IS HYSTERICAL. AMBULANCE IS CALLED, I END UP IN THE ER AT JACOBI, BOOKENDED BY TWO DUDES WHO WERE BLEEDING PROFUSELY. I WENT HOME WITH A SCRIPT AND NEVER ATTENDED TO MY HEALTH AGAIN.

WEED WAS A GREAT PAIN RELIEVER AND EVEN THOUGH THE PERCS WERE LIT, TOO, THE FEELING OF GETTING YOUR KIDNEYS EATEN BY STARVING DEMON HYENAS WHEN YOU OFF THEM SHITS IS DECIDEDLY *NOT* LIT IN THE SLIGHTEST. YEARS LATER, ME AND WEED ARE STILL WILD COOL. WE LINK UP EVERY DAY AND LAUGH ABOUT SHIT ON THE INTERNET, EAT THE FUCK OUTTA CHICK-FIL-A, AND SPEND 27 MINUTES READING THE BACK OF A $9 COPY OF *TEKKEN* AT GAMESTOP, WHILE MY KIDS PICK UP ALL MANNER OF COLLECTORS' TOYS TO SMASH INTO EACH OTHER WHILE PLAYING IMAGINARY *INFINITY WAR* WITH $100 FIGURINES THAT I THEN HAVE TO PURCHASE ALREADY BROKEN. I KNOW EXACTLY WHAT NBA 2K IS BUT I'M STILL READING THE BACK OF THAT SHIT BECAUSE WEED IS FUCKIN LIT. SOME PEOPLE TELL ME WEED GIVES THEM ANXIETY, AND AS SOMEONE WHO SUFFERS FROM ANXIETY I CAN COSIGN THERE'S SOME WEED THAT MAKES ME THINK THE FBI IS GONNA BUST THRU MY DOOR AND ARREST ME FOR MY ROLLING TRAY, THEN WATERBOARD ME AND INEXPLICABLY ASK ME MAD QUESTIONS TRYING TO CONNECT PIO AND RUSSIA.

Weed paranoia is kinda like that color guide that Homeland Security made after 9/11 to scare the hell out of us, because it (the paranoia) comes in different levels. Sometimes your weed paranoia is simple jumpiness, like someone taps your shoulder and you scream because you didn't see them there (narrator's voice: *they were there the whole time*). Sometimes your weed paranoia is just a little bit more intense and you sit there thinking, "What if one of my great-grandkids is a villain and destroys the earth using self-replicating robots who create gray goo (machines who consume all the biomass on earth, triggering an extinction-level event) and the only solution is to send back a killer to stop the bloodline and you hear a knock on the door and yell out, "OMG A TIME TRAVELER IS TRYING TO KILL ME," but of course it's actually the Seamless guy.

I DEFINITELY FEEL LIKE I WOULD RATHER BE DEAD SOBER THAN SMOKE PARANOIA WEED. THE GOOD THING IS NOW YOU KNOW WHAT PARANOIA WEED IS BECAUSE THERE ARE ACTUALLY NAMES FOR THE SHIT. IN THE OLDEN DAYS (2010), YOU GOT WHAT YOU GOT AND IF YOU CAUGHT SOME PDUB (MY ILL NEW WAY TO SAY PARANOIA WEED CUZ TYPING IT OUT MAD TIMES IS TEDIOUS), YOUR PARANOIA WOULD LEAD YOU TO BELIEVE THE WEED WAS LACED (IT WAS), BUT ASIDE FROM THE OTHER ADDITIONAL BLUNTGREDIENTS, THE WEED WAS STILL PARANOIA WEED. SO DUST OR NOT, YOU WERE GONNA THINK THOSE CLOUDS WERE REALLY GOVERNMENT SURVEILLANCE.

SPEAKIN OF GOVERNMENT SURVEILLANCE, CAN I SIDEBAR REAL QUICK? Y'ALL NIGGAS BE BELIEVING MADDDD SHIT. MINNESOTA HAD A DUDE WHO BECAME GOVERNOR WHOSE FORMER JOB WAS GETTING DDT'D ONTO A STEEL CHAIR. THEN HE SAYS SOME WILD SHIT AND MAD NIGGAS BELIEVE IT. I'M NOT

SAYING THE SHIT IS IMPOSSIBLE, I'M SAYING WITH MINIMAL PROOF TO THE POINT YOU CAN CONVINCE A LOT OF AMERICA THE EARTH IS FLAT, HILLARY CLINTON WAS HAVING CHILD ORGY PIZZA PARTIES *SHUDDERS,* AND OBAMA IS ACTUALLY A RANDOM AFRICAN DUDE WHO DECIDED TO RUN FOR PRESIDENT AND WON TWICE . . . BECAUSE OF MUSLIMS(?). *WEEKLY WORLD NEWS* "BATBOY GETS ENGAGED TO TAYLOR SWIFT! SHE'S PREGNANT!"-LEVEL SHIT. AND ALL YOU NEED IS A MICROSOFT OFFICE SLIDESHOW, A NARRATOR WITH GRAVITAS, AND YOUTUBE.COM.

Speaking of wild conspiracy theories, did you know that all animals in zoos belong there because they're political prisoners and we humans worked out a treaty to keep them in exchange the other wild animals don't take over? Heard this in my barbershop so I know it's true.

SPONGEBOB MEME VOICE "BUT MERO WEED MAKES YOU MAD, LAZY, AND UNPRODUCTIVE. ALSO YOU LOSE THE ABILITY TO DRIVE AND RUN OVER A CHILD ON A BIKE." MUTHAFUCKAS REALLY RAN A COMMERCIAL WHERE SOME NIGGAS IN A CAR WERE AT A DRIVE-THRU, GOT THEIR FOOD, AND HOMIE DRIVING WAS SMACKED AND DIDN'T REALIZE THERE WAS A 10-YEAR-OLD ON A NEON BIKE RIDING BY SLOWER THAN A BAD NOVEL. I'VE DONE SOME OF MY BEST DRIVING SMACKED. I'M NOT ADVOCATING FOR THE REST OF Y'ALL TO DO THAT, THOUGH, CUZ

A) EVERYBODY TOLERANCE FOR SHIT VARIES.
B) THAT SHIT IS WILD ILLEGAL.

ALSO YOU MIGHT SAY YOU DID IT CUZ I TOLD YOU OR SOME SHIT. I LOVE YOU AND WANT YOU TO LIVE YOUR BEST LIFE SO

I'M NOT GONNA TELL YOU TO DRIVE THAT RENTAL LAMBORGHINI WITH THE TOP DOWN SMOKIN A BLUNT LISTENING TO DEMBOW, BUT I'M ALSO NOT GONNA TELL YOU NOT TO. ALLEGEDLY. I SEEN MY MAN MIKE DRIVE A STICK SHIFT NISSAN MAXIMA TO CROSSTOWN DINER FLAWLESSLY, BASICALLY WITH HIS EYES CLOSED. I WAS IN AWE.

Weed in and of itself doesn't make you lazy and unproductive. It's more like a stoner voice in your head that suggests things like "hey man, go back to bed, that laundry can wait" or "listen fam, you can nap in the wheelchair stall at work. Stay up till 3am playing *Call of Duty.*" Now, if you listen to that voice, it's on you. But that voice is loud as shit (oh shit, that's why they call weed LOUD).

THERE'S A FALSE CLAIM THAT WEED IS A "GATEWAY DRUG" AND IF YOU SMOKE WEED YOU EVENTUALLY END UP LIKE DUDE ON THE HBO SPECIAL WITH VERY FEW TEETH GETTIN PAID TO GET TOPPY FROM SOMEONE'S GRANDPA. I KNOW THAT TO NOT BE TRUE BECAUSE STUDIES SHOW THAT . . . UHHHHH YOU NIGGAS THOUGHT I ACTUALLY RESEARCHED THE SHIT AND DIDN'T JUST SMASH MY KEYBOARD SMACKED IN MY WEED CHAMBER. LOL. BUT YEAH NAH THERE'S DEAD-ASS BEEN MAD FACTS THAT HAVE DISPROVEN THIS GATEWAY DRUG THEORY SO YOU NEVER HAVE TO STOP SMOKIN WEED UNLESS IT'S FOR A JOB OR SOME SHIT. BONG . . . OH SHIT I WONDER IF BEN THE EDITOR WILL PUT A CHART HERE OF THE PEOPLE WHO GO FROM WEED TO HARD DRUGS WITHIN A YEAR. G'HEAD MY PAL, MAKE THAT HAPPEN. I DON'T EVEN KNOW IF YOU HAVE ANYTHING TO DO WITH THE PROCESS. I APOLOGIZE FOR PUTTIN YOU ON THE SPOT.

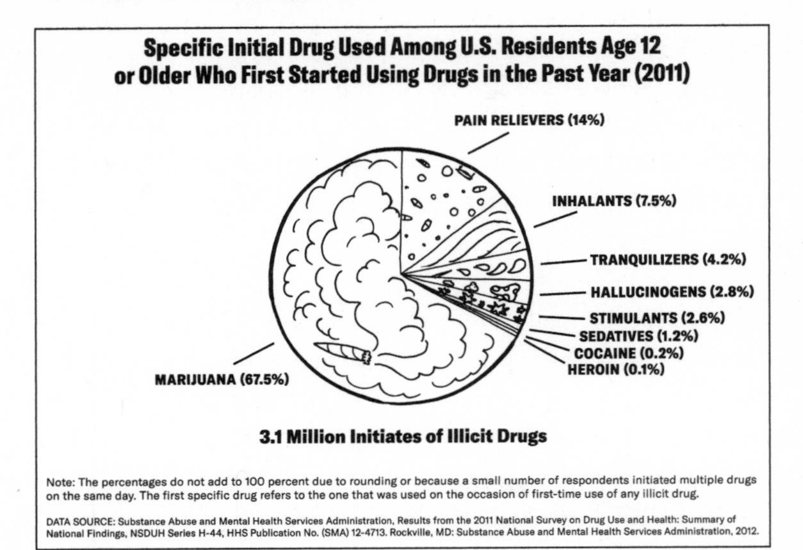

MOTHERFUCKIN BEN DAAWWWGGGG!!! COMING THROUGH LIKE PRE-MAGA MARIANO IN THE CLUTCH!

I've never met a person who made the jump from weed to wild OD hard drugs and I feel like if that's what happens to you, you were probably on that road already if we're keeping it funky. Weed is mad chill, you can pull out a blunt at a concert and people might give you some dirty looks but 9 out of 10 times someone's gonna ask you if they can smoke or maybe "get a puff." Try that with some heroin. If I'm at a Future concert and I see you tying off your arm, I'm calling security. *There are children here!*

LASTLY AND MOST IMPORTANTLY, YOU GOTTA RESPECT THE DEAD'S WISHES. A MUSICAL ICON AND GENERATIONAL TALENT, NATE DOGG, OUR BELOVED HOOK MASTER WITH A VOICE

SMOOTHER THAN ANGEL CHOCH COGNAC WHO WE LOST SEVERAL YEARS AGO, SAID UNTO THEE:

HEY EYYYY EYY EYY-Y.. . . . . SMOKE WEED EVERYDAY!!

SO I'MA DO JUST THAT. REST IN PEACE, NATE. I HONOR YOUR MEMORY WITH THIS 5G BACKWOOD *PRAYER HANDS EMOJI.*

CHAPTER 2

Relationships & Shit Like That

I'll be honest, I have no idea what I'm doing when it comes to relationships so I'm saying right now: Don't follow my advice. Most of what I know about relationships comes from watching *King of Queens* and reading my sisters' *Glamour* magazines growing up. Oh yeah, and watching *Sex and the City,* which in retrospect was a hot mess and championed toxic relationships. Soooo that's me in a nutshell.

I've been a very shallow person in my past 2,000 lives. Shallow being kind, if we're keeping it a buck. I have been a terrible person (GOD'S WORKING ON ALL OF US) and terrible people do and say terrible things. At one point in my life, I would've said the most important quality to look for in a woman is how her mother looks. Like I was really operating at that level of shallow scumbagness.

Once, in the way yonder times before Ubers (back when we rode dinosaurs and everybody carried flattened cardboard in case you had a spontaneous breakdance battle), I was on a date with a young lady I fancied. We took the subway, as most New Yorkers do, and I was climbing the steps behind her. I noticed she had cankles. My mind fast-forwarded to how'd she look in ten years.

Key to this story, I was broke at the time and had nothing going on but a thin mustache and one earring (yikes), so basically, how dare I. But I use that as an example of how I have no idea what I'm doing.

And for you people who need closure to stories: Me and ole cankles dated for a while and then she moved on to marry a great guy (number of earrings unknown).

I THINK PEOPLE HEAR THE WORD "ROMANCE" AND PICTURE RYAN GOSLING KISSING ANTONIO BANDERAS IN THE RAIN. NAH ROMANCE IS KNOWING EACH OTHER AND KNOWING HOW TO MAKE SACRIFICES TO SUPPORT EACH OTHER WHEN NECESSARY. *FLEX BOMB* WHAAAAT NIGGA I JUST **KILLED** THAT!! HAHA WOW. SPIN-OFF MERO & HEATHER (THAT'S MY AMAZING WIFE'S NAME, MY PALS. JUST REMINDING YOU FOR WHEN I EP THE SPIN-OFF.) *PEAKS & VALLEYS* RELATIONSHIP BOOK COMING SOON JUUUHUUURDDD.

DISRESPECTFULLY SLAM DUNKS ON BOOK INDUSTRY

NAH BUT SERIOUSLY MAKING THE "LEAP" FROM DATING TO ROMANCE CAN BE MEASURED IN HOW MUCH "HOUSE OF BALLOONS" YOU LISTEN TO WITH YOUR BLINDS DRAWN SOBBING IF YOU BREAK UP.

FOR REAL, THOUGH: IT HAS EVERYTHING TO DO WITH HOW YOU GUYS "GET" EACH OTHER. AFTER A WHILE YOU BECOME USED TO PEOPLE'S SHIT AND SHIT THAT WAS CUTE AIN'T CUTE ANYMORE. WHAT SEPARATES DATING FROM A RELATIONSHIP—IMA SAY RELATIONSHIP NOW CUZ THE WORD "ROMANCE" MAKES ME THINK OF PEARLS COMING OUT A FRENCH LADY'S

BUTT. SOFT FOCUS, OF COURSE. DON'T ASK ME WHY. I'M SMACKED. I KNOW IT SHOULD BE MOONLIT PICNICS OR SOME SHIT BUT RIGHT NOW IT'S PARISIAN ANAL BEADS. LEAVE ME ALONE. ANYWAY, WHAT WAS I SAYING?

Dating doesn't even feel like a thing anymore. You start hanging out with someone and they're cool and eventually you get their Wi-Fi code and have a pair of slippers in their apartment and then you look at the calendar and it's been two years. Damn, that sounds bleak as hell. But really, dating can be super cool if you find a person who's into the same stuff you are. Unless you're a sicko who enjoys arguing and then you just have a weird relationship where you spend hours on the street arguing on the phone only to go home and make sweet sweet love complete with spitting in each other's mouths. (Or so I've heard.)

Now that I'm older, one thing I look for the most in a possible partner is a desire to have a nice quiet West Indian future together. A simple life with a 3-family house where we live on the bottom floor and rent the rest of the house out to pay for the mortgage. She has a good city union job and I'm on her insurance because I'm too stubborn to have a boss. I spend my nights watering the front lawn and complaining about people parking directly in front of our house (totally legal but so what) and the cost of heating oil. She spends her nights reading her bible and gossiping with her family about her family and about me being shiftless but a good provider.

(My aunt wrote that description, thanks Patrice.)

Something I know is overrated is looking for a partner who makes you laugh. That's all well and good when things are um, well and good, but you can't pay the light bill with laughter. You can only laugh a few times if you live in a car before it's like,

"Okay chuckles, we broke. Save the yakkity yakkity until we have a roof over our heads."

Rather than tell you what you should look for in a partner, here's a quick list of who you shouldn't look for:

1. Geminis—duh
2. People who don't pet dogs when presented with the opportunity
3. Anyone who doesn't enjoy a Filet-O-Fish
4. Red Sox/Patriots fans who don't do that fake "I'm sorry I'm a terrible person" apology after they inform you that they root for evil

Don't get a partner just because you think you'll make cute babies, because the devil will hear you and curse you with a little ugmug that you will find attractive but about whom other people will say things like "When they grow into that head, we'll see" after seeing the photos on your desk.

Another thing to keep in mind when looking for a partner is to find one that has the same gastrointestinal issues as you. You often don't find out these kinds of intimate details until it's too late. Now you're in a committed relationship and you have to refrain from eating Taco Bell because sour cream makes your boo violently fart in her sleep (true story). In fact, after I finish this book I might create a new dating site called Gas.er where you can find the love of your life by filtering them according to what foods they can and can't consume. Maybe a checkbox for fish, beans, kale, etc. For 10 dollars extra a month I'll let you know if they're anemic (anemic people love ice chips so if your boo got the weak bloods, go home and re-create the Spike Lee & Rosie Perez scene from *Do the Right Thing*.)

I've given up on the whole perfect relationship thing so right now I'm just looking for someone to let me inside the house when I leave my keys at home and I can call and ask how many beers are in the fridge while I'm at the store so I don't have to make two trips. The bar is the floor.

Also, be able to save my life if I'm choking because 90% of single people choke to death alone in their apartments but the government covers up these numbers due to kickbacks from Big Heimlich (stay woke).

SURE MY WIFE GETS TIGHT AT ME SOMETIMES. THAT'S PART OF BEING IN A RELATIONSHIP. LEMME TELL YOU SOMETHING, DOG: NO MATTER HOW GOOD YOUR MAMÁ'S LOCRIO DE LONGANIZA IS, IF YOU HAD TO EAT THAT SHIT EVERY DAY FOREVER, ONE RANDOM TUESDAY YOU ARE GONNA SMACK THAT MUTHA-FUCKIN PLATE ACROSS THE TABLE LIKE THE DENZEL GIF. I'M NOT SAYING YOU WANNA SMACK YOUR PARTNER (THAT'S ABUSE) BUT, MAN, IF YOU DON'T WANNA TELL THEM A THING OR TWO . . . BUT STILL, CHILL, THAT'S VERBAL ABUSE. SO JUST HOP ON XBOX LIVE AND LET TYLER IN MINNESOTA FUCKIN HAVE IT FOR CALLIN YOU A "FUCKIN NI99ER NOOB!" AND GET YOUR AGGRESSION OUT THAT WAY. YOU WILL BE VERY MAD AT YOUR SPOUSE AT SOME POINT AND WHEN IT HAPPENS YOU GOTTA GIVE YOURSELF THE DE NIRO IN *HEAT* SPEECH, OR WORK IT OUT.

OH SHIT I REMEMBERED MY POINT ABOUT DATING VS RELATIONSHIPS. IF YOU WANT TO TRANSITION FROM CASUAL DATING TO A ROMANTIC RELATIONSHIP, THERE'S GOTTA BE MUTUAL SACRIFICE. NOW YOU ARE BEHOLDEN TO SOMEONE, THEY AFFECT YOUR EMOTIONS. SOME PEOPLE CAN'T HANDLE THAT AND TO THEM I SAY: IT AIN'T FOR EVERYBODY. SAME WAY I PROBABLY WOULDN'T SKYDIVE BECAUSE IT SEEMS TO ME LIKE

A RIDICULOUS YAKUBIAN DEATH ACTIVITY. SOME NIGGAS AIN'T TRYNA HAVE TO TEXT NOBODY WHERE THEY'RE GONNA BE OR HAVE TO PLAN AROUND FAMILY OBLIGATIONS TO PRIORITIZE WORK OR FUN. THE CHALLENGE IS FINDING THE BALANCE, OR YOU'RE GONNA BE A MISERABLE PRICK DOOMED TO WALK THE EARTH ETERNALLY SAYING WILD SHIT LIKE "*CURB YOUR ENTHUSIASM* WASN'T THAT FUNNY." ALSO DON'T CONFLATE ROMANCE AND HAPPINESS. YOU GOTTA BE HAPPY WITH YOURSELF BEFORE YOU CAN BE HAPPY WITH SOMEONE ELSE. ARE YOU PICKIN UP ALL THIS STARTENDER WISDOM? AHHHH WHAT ELSE? PART OF ROMANCE IS ARGUING AND HAVING CONFLICT. IF YOU HAVE A 100% CONFLICT-FREE RELATIONSHIP, THEN YOU WERE EITHER:

A) MENTALLY BROKEN AT A CIA BLACK SITE OR
B) IT AIN'T THAT DEEP. YOU AIN'T ENGAGED ENOUGH TO REALLY GIVE A SHIT.

What's the best way to find a partner? Again, I'm probably the wrong guy for this because I usually go solo—to ball games, movies, bars, etc. Partners = people who slow me down. (Not you, secret boo.)

There are way more options to find a partner than ever before, even just a few years ago. Twitter, Tumblr, Slack channels, hell even WhatsApp if you want a severely questionable long-distance relationship. But all of these options have one thing in common:

They suck.

Why do they suck? I feel like social media has taken away some of the mystery of dating. Before, you used to have a crush and wonder, "What's this person doing?" or "What kind of stuff do they like?" and you'd have to interact with them in real life to find out. Now in two tweets you can find out someone "is having really bad gas from Otto's Tacos" and "really needs someone to put a thumb in their butt" (okay, those are from my own drafts, but the point stands).

Tinder isn't really for dating dating. It's more like, *Hey I was out, I got wild turned on and I don't have someone to WYD? at 3am so here's an app to help me with that.* Shouts to people using Tinder with my picture tho. I'm not sure how that works when you meet in real life but I'm sure you have that figured out already, hopefully?

The tried-and-traditional method of getting hooked up by a friend still seems to be an option but you have to trust your friends, otherwise you'll end up in a very sad situation. Shoutout to my homegirl who called me 10 minutes before I hooked up with her friend to warn me that that friend had an STD but told me, "I didn't think you'd take it this far." Smh.

Your friends know exactly why the friend they're attempting to hook you up with is single. It's not because "she can't find anyone on her level." It's because she's creating fake Twitter accounts mocking her ex's new girl's dead cats and when you told her to stop she said, "What's it to you, bitch??"

Paying for a dating service sounds like a good idea (umm how is Match.com any different than Backpages? I digress), but anytime money is exchanged it ups the stakes for dating. So in theory you could be on a site looking for a good time, but you just linked with someone who already has a color scheme, location, and date selected for a wedding (Orange and Blue, Foley's Pub on 33rd Street, January 24 in honor of Melo setting the MSG scoring title).

"Back in my day [imagine the blue NYPD cars from the first season of *Law & Order*], a guy used to be able to grab a broad's hand or slap her butt and she'd giggle and next thing you know you got three freaking kids and a house on Rhinelander Avenue in the Bronx." —Anonymous Bronx resident

Attempting to meet people in public is a dangerous game. Number one, most people going from Point A to Point B want to be left alone. Number two, see number one. If you think you have a connection with someone on the subway, I promise you, you don't. And surely you're like, "Desus, what if I see the woman of my dreams?" to which I say this: Leave her alone. If she's fine, you have to imagine about sixty guys already tried to holla at her. So while it's new to you, she's fed up with it. Source: I know women.

Aside: LinkedIn is NOT for dating. Stop being wild thirsty. There's like a billion other people in the world you can rub your genitals on, don't use a professional job connection network for that. Even though no one in history has used LinkedIn to get a job and it's mostly to keep you busy while recruiters don't reply to your résumé . . . actually, you know what? Fuck it. Shoot your shot.

Or perhaps my Auntie had it right when she sent me a WhatsApp message outta the blue, wanting to hook me with some random girl that's probably the head of the party committee at her church. Even though my Auntie knew nothing about said woman's regular life, her hair was always done and she had all her original teeth and she loves Christ, so I'd be lucky to get her.

"Oh and another thing, what kinda man has a dog and a cat? Especially a cat. Nothing of it, it just seems, I don't know, funny to me. A little soft. But if you like it, I love it. Anyway Trevor died, tell your mom. Yours in Christ: Aunt Patrice."

1) MODERN DATING FUCKING SUCKS, B. YOU HAVE ZERO IDEA WHAT'S GONNA HAPPEN, YOU COULD MEET YOUR SOUL MATE

OR YOU COULD MEET SOMEONE WHO'S ALREADY ORDERED AND CONSUMED 2 ENTREES, SAYS THEY ARE GOING TO THE BATHROOM AND SKEDADDLES TF OUTTA THERE.

2) THINK ABOUT RELATIONSHIPS LIKE YOU WOULD LIFE. LIFE IS MOSTLY CHILL UNLESS YOUR LIFE SUCKS BUT BEING ALIVE IS WAY MORE POPPIN THAN BEING DEAD. DID YOU KNOW ONCE YOU DIE YOU CAN'T SMASH CHEEKS ANYMORE? *SHUDDERS* THE DAMP *THWOP THWOP* OF A ROUND BUTT EATING YOUR PP WILL BE A SOUND YOU NEVER HEAR AGAIN, MY GUY. IS THAT WHAT YOU WANT?! NO. SO REGARDLESS OF YOUR SEXUALITY AND ASSUMING YOU AND YOUR PARTNER RESPECT EACH OTHER'S AGENCY (MERO PULLS UP FROM 50' WITH A 3PT WOKE SHOT! SWISH!) YOU ARE GIVING UP SECURE CONSENSUAL SEXUAL ENGAGEMENT AND STABILITY FOR THE POSSIBILITY OF A DOWNGRADE OR SOMEONE YOU THINK IS GONNA BE BETTER. I'VE HAD MARITAL ISSUES AND WORKED THROUGH THEM BECAUSE AT THE END OF THE DAY, MY WIFE AND I LOVE EACH OTHER AND HAVE BEEN WORKING TOWARD A GOAL FOR MORE THAN A DECADE, AND THAT GOAL IS EVER CLOSER. ONCE YOU LOSE SIGHT OF THAT GOAL, WHATEVER IT IS FOR YOU AND YOUR PARTNER, THEN YOU MIGHT AS WELL JUST SAY FUCK IT AND SEE WHAT ALTERNATIVES THERE ARE TO BACKPAGE SINCE IT GOT SHUT DOWN *TEARS UP.*

"BUT MERO, WHAT IF MY PARTNER AND I REACH OUR 'GOAL'?"

CONGRATULATIONS, HYPOTHETICAL PERSON! THAT ISN'T POSSIBLE. ONCE YOU REACH A GOAL, SET A HIGHER ONE. REACH NIRVANA, MY GUY. I ALSO SUGGEST IF YOU COMMIT TO EACH OTHER ON SOME LEGAL SHIT LIKE YOU GET PAPERED UP WHERE YOU HAVE TO CALL CELLINO & BARNES IF YOU WANNA BREAK UP, RUN AROUND A BIT TOGETHER BEFORE YOU HAVE KIDS. DON'T INTERPRET THAT AS ME SAYING KIDS ARE A NUI-

SANCE, BUT THEY ARE A RESPONSIBILITY. IT'S LIKE THOSE WEIRD PEOPLE THAT BRING THEIR DOG WITH THEM EVERYWHERE. YEAH, YOU'RE ON THE BEACH IN PUNTA CANA DRUNK AS SHIT HAVING A BLAST UNTIL ROVER GETS STUNG BY A MANTA RAY AND NOW YOU'RE DOING YOUR BEST DRUNK DAVID HASSELHOFF (REDUNDANT) IMPRESSION RUNNING INTO THE WATER TO SAVE YOUR CHOCOLATE LAB.

I OWN A SHIH TZU. I VACATION WITHOUT THAT LIL BITCH (THAT'S THE PROPER TERM, I'M NOT BEING PROBLEMATIC) BECAUSE SHE'S ANOTHER THING I HAVE TO KEEP AN EYE ON. SAME THING WITH KIDS EXCEPT IF ROVER DROWNS ONLY WHITE PEOPLE WILL FEEL SORRY FOR YOU, JIMMY KIMMEL MIGHT EVEN START A GOFUNDME AND CRY LIVE ON AIR. BUT GOD FORBID SOMETHING HAPPENS TO YOUR KID, THEN NOT ONLY DO YOU HAVE TO LIVE WITH THAT FOREVER BUT YOU'RE ON EVERY NEWS SHOW FOR A WHOLE 24-HOUR CYCLE AT LEAST.

A GORRILLER?!!? *BOWS* GOOD NIGHT.

Alexa, play "I Hate This Part" by Pussycat Dolls.

Okay, we all want that dream relationship like the old people in the beginning of *Up* had, but life is short and full of twists and turns and everything is finite, like Spike Jonze said.

The million-dollar question is: "When is it time to leave a relationship?" Now, of course the answer is "Immediately," as soon as we see the signs, but that's not how life works at all. There are all types of reasons to stay in a relationship—you have kids together, the other person lives halfway between your job and your apartment or above your favorite ramen place, etc. Sometimes you'll stay too long in a relationship because you love the other person, sometimes you'll stay too long because the other person has central A/C and you have a fuckin box fan.

So in the real world, when is it time to leave a relationship?

When has it reached the point where you have to leave because if you hear this motherfucker blink one more time you're going to catch a murder charge (have you never heard someone blink? Get mad at your boo and watch how loud those lashes become).

My relationship test is a simple one: How do you feel when the other person texts you? Do you get excited and nervous like *OMG it's them*? Or do you sigh and roll your eyes to prepare for whatever bullshit they're sending you? And when you're over your boo, anything they send you is bullshit. They could ask you to pick up milk while you're out and in your head you're yelling "Jesus Christ how much milk are you going to run thru, you dairy wasting bitch!!!!!" but you just respond "Okay."

Now ask yourself this: Are *you* going through something? Are you hungry? Did your team just lose? Did you lose your AirPods (hope those are still a thing)? Are you just taking this anger/stress out on your relationship? Did they recently shave their head and you're just noticing they have the wild big Charlie Brown domington and you can't live like this? Because a text shouldn't send you from zero to ten, my dude.

Honestly I think one of the worst situations one can be in is knowing you should leave a relationship but feeling like you can't. Like if you can now properly spell Munchausen syndrome because you googled it after your boo served you clam chowder that tasted like antifreeze, but other than that the soup was banging, one could get confused. Or your bae is the wild bird but when you watch her get dressed in the morning you're still stuck on stupid like "Damn Ma them titties perky as shit, boy" or you're a chick and your man has waves or is a great scammer or got you dickmitized. These are very hard situations to leave.

If your friends are telling you to leave your current boo, theoretically you should because they are probably right . . . BUT . . . don't do it. You don't want them to be right, and anyway, you know they secretly enjoy the constant drama you provide the group text.

Your mind will tell you when it's time to leave a relationship. For example, that moment when during sex maybe they ask you to choke them harder and for a split second you think, "Okay, you want to leave hair in the fuckin drain?" and start seeing red and almost go too far? Yeah man, time to bounce.

When you get to the point where little things make you sick (the loud blinking as mentioned before), you have to get out of there for your own safety. Like this is the person you chose to be with, there's no reason for them to be the cause of your distress.

Sometimes you just have to count your losses. And while you're tempted to stay because you know their family, you've already linked your Netflix accounts, y'all got a cat . . . just know it's probably for the best. And you can replace all that.

January is tricky because you just got out of the Christmas/Hanukkah/Kwanza/three kings period so emotions are still high and family members saw y'all together so if you just break up now it's hella messy. And Valentine's Day is coming up and if you break up with someone just before Valentine's Day, that is also hella messy. Once Valentine's Day passes, the next major holiday is St. Patrick's Day (if you're white) or Easter (everyone else), so try to thread the needle. If you miss, the next major date to avoid is Memorial Day where you're basically telling the world this is who you're spending your summer with (also always break up before summertime because um fun). If you make it to Labor Day just stay together because being single in the winter sucks even if the relationship is wack, let's be real.

Some more specific instructions: Sundays are a terrible breakup day because you have work the next day and you don't want to ruin their week. Friday is worse because now you've ruined their weekend before it's even started. My suggestion is to break up with someone on a Tuesday; that way they have Wednesday through Friday to come to terms with it and hopefully will drink/smoke/cry through it on Saturday and Sunday.

You're welcome.

YOU'RE IN A BORING RELATIONSHIP, MY PAL? WHY? NOT WHY IS IT BORING, WHY ARE YOU IN IT IF IT'S BORING? IS YOUR NAME ON THE LEASE? ARE YOU MARRIED AND LAWYERS ARE OD EXPENSIVE (THEY BILL BY THE HOUR, DIQUE, BUT I SWEAR THEY JUST BE MAKING UP NUMBERS WHEN IT'S TIME TO MAIL YOU THAT INVOICE). ANYWAY, IF YOUR RELATIONSHIP IS BORING YOU CAN DO SOME THINGS . . .

A) WHAT I SAID EARLIER, TAKE STOCK OF YOUR LIFE AND GOALS AND GET THE FUCK UP OUTTA THERE OR

B) TRY TO MAKE THE SHIT NOT BORING, DUH NIGGA LOL YOU THOUGHT THERE WERE MORE THAN TWO OPTIONS? I'LL ADD ANOTHER ONE TO FILL MY WORD COUNT.

C) WATCH MAD DIANE KEATON FILMS TOGETHER.

I'M KIDDING, BUT THERE IS ONE ROM-COM WITH HER AND STEVE MARTIN THAT ISN'T BAD BUT STEVE WASN'T LAYIN THE PIPE CORRECT, HE'S TOO GOOFY. LIKE I CAN BE GOOFY BUT I CAN ALSO HIT IT FROGGY STYLE, YOU FEEL ME? FOUR KIDS LATER, FROGGY STYLE HAS NOT FAILED ME, IT'S LIKE THE D TRAIN EXPRESS TO OVARY JUNCTION. SO FOR FEAR OF MORE KIDS, I'VE RETIRED FROGGY STYLE FOREVER. *MERO, I JUST READ THE WORDS "FROGGY STYLE" LIKE 5 TIMES AND I DON'T WANNA GO TO URBAN DICTIONARY. I PAID FOR THE HARDCOVER OF THIS, CAN YOU JUST TELL ME WHAT IT IS?* OKAY FINE, MATTHEW. FROGGY STYLE IS WHEN YOU GOT THE OD AKUMA RAGING DEMON BONER AND IT'S KINDA LIKE DOGGY STYLE BUT YOU'RE HIGHER UP SO YOU POINT THE SHIT DOWNWARD INTO YOUR PARTNER'S AWAITING ORIFICE (LOL I JUST READ THAT OUT

LOUD AND IT SOUNDED WILD GROSS IMA GIVE U A SECOND TO TAKE A BREATHER. . . .)

As someone not trying to make mad kids, I suggest one be careful before attempting Froggy Style. That's a high-level sex move and if you're not ready for it you could hurt your back or destroy the other person's bed . . . or inadvertently create a life. Also, it's problematic because it's appropriating the style of sex frogs have, and that's like interspecies cultural theft or something.

ENOUGH ABOUT MY KID-MAKING PROCESS. WHAT WAS I SAYING? YOUR RELATIONSHIP IS BORING? THAT'S VERY VAGUE, MY PAL. LIKE WHAT IS BORING ABOUT IT? YOU'RE IN A RUT? THE YEEKS ARE TRASH? YOU DON'T TALK? LISTEN, I'VE BEEN MARRIED FOR LIKE 937 YEARS AND MARRIAGE IS UPS AND DOWNS. FAM, YOU ARE PROBABLY FATIGUED FROM SEEING EACH OTHER EVERY FUCKIN DAY AND EVERY DAY IT'S THE SAME SHIT.

THEREIN LIES THE KEY, MY ESTEEMED BALLBAG. SWITCH IT UP. GO DO SOMETHING DIFFERENT. GO FOR A WALK, I FUCKIN DARE YOU, EVEN IF YOU LIVE IN THE WILD HOOD. IF YOU DON'T SAY A SINGLE WORD TO EACH OTHER, WHO CARES, JUST ENJOY EACH OTHER'S PRESENCE. IF YOU CAN'T STAND THEIR PRESENCE, THAT'S A FUCKIN HUGE RED FLAG, B. AND IF Y'ALL START TALKING BUT ARE MILDLY BEEFING, AT LEAST YOU'RE STILL COMMUNICATING, WHICH IS GOOD. IT'S ALWAYS GOOD TO TALK EARNESTLY. AND FUCK IT, TAKE NOTES IN YOUR PHONE. LATER WHEN YOU HAVE TO RECALL THE SHIT IN AN ARGUMENT YOU CAN BE LIKE "NNNNNNAHHHH FAM *POINTS TO HELVETICA FONT ALL CAPS NOTE* IT'S IN MY NOTES APP. JULY 7TH, YOU SAID YOU "DON'T GIVE A SHIT IF I SEPARATE MY DARKS AND LIGHTS," NOW YOU READY TO CRUCIFY A NIGGA? HOW YOU FEEL NOW? BONG!!" I CALL IT A "BONG!" WHEN YOUR PARTNER

SWEEAAARSSS UP AND DOWN THEY ARE RIGHT ABOUT SOMETHING AND YOU ARE SEVERELY WRONG, THEN YOU FIND OUT YOU WERE RIGHT ALL ALONG. IT'S THE MARITAL VERSION OF DUNKING ON YOUR SPOUSE, IT FEELS SO FUCKIN GOOD. YOU EXPLAIN HOW YOU WERE RIGHT THE WHOLE TIME THEN END IT WITH AN EXTRA LOUD "BONG!" I DO FINGER GUNS BUT GUN CONTROL IS A HOT-BUTTON ISSUE SO NOW I JUST KEEP MY HANDS IN MY POCKETS AND YELL "BONG!" IT'S NOT AS DRAMATIC BUT IT'S OD MORE WOKE.

BUT YEAH, DO DIFFERENT SHIT OUTSIDE YOUR COMFORT ZONE. YOU'LL NEVER KNOW YOU REALLY FUCK WITH SOMETHING TOGETHER UNLESS YOU TRY IT. HOW DO YOU THINK I GOT INTO FROGGY STYLE, MY PAL? DAWG, DO FUN SHIT—WHAT THE FUCK ARE YOU DOING? PUT SOME MOLLY IN YOUR BUTT, FUCK IT B. GO TO THE BALLET WITH MOLLY IN YOUR BUTTS. YOU'LL NEVER APPRECIATE THE BALLET LIKE THAT AGAIN. DOES THAT SOUND BORING? PURE FUCKIN MDMA BEING ABSORBED BY YOUR ANAL WALLS WHILE YOU WATCH A GLOWING SET CHANGE AND PEOPLE DANCING WITH A FUCKIN ORCHESTRA PLAYING! SHIT'S CRAZY B. DEFINITELY CALL AN UBER HOME THO FOR REAL.

OH SHIT, THE ANAL MOLLY BALLET REMINDS ME: YOU GOTTA BE ABLE TO LAUGH AT EACH OTHER. I DON'T MEAN MERCILESSLY ROAST EACH OTHER TO DEATH, BUT SHIT, THAT MIGHT EVEN WORK AND BRING YOU CLOSER TOGETHER. BY LAUGH AT EACH OTHER, I MEAN FIND HUMOR IN EVERYDAY SHIT AND LAUGH TOGETHER. THAT SHIT IS IMPORTANT. WHEN I MAKE MY WIFE TEAR UP LAUGHING, IT FEELS LIKE SPLASHING A 3 WITH 2 SECONDS LEFT IN THE GAME.

Communication is key to a good relationship. But more important is memes. If you have a person you can share memes with, and they send you memes, you're creating a strong bond never seen since back in the "everyone had Afros" days. Also, if you have that moment where you send each other the same meme/tweet at the same time, that's a great sign that you are with "the one."

The problem with my meme relationship law is that it implies that sharing memes with a third party is essentially cheating. Sorry. Dem's the Twitter rules.

BUT MERO, WHAT IF THE SHIT IS JUST DONE? HOW DO I GET OUT? IF IT'S NOT TECHNICALLY A "RELATIONSHIP" YET, YOU CAN BE THE WILD DICKHEAD AND GHOST A PERSON COMPLETELY. THE LONGER THE RELATIONSHIP, THE BIGGER JERK YOU ARE IF YOU GHOST ON YOUR S/O . . . WOW I REALLY JUST ABBREVIATED "SIGNIFICANT OTHER." WHO THE FUCK DO I THINK I AM, DAN SAVAGE? YOU COULD ALSO JUST BE LIKE: "YEAH THIS AIN'T IT, MY PAL" AND THEY SHOULD UNDERSTAND.

SO TO SUMMARIZE: EITHER MAKE IT FUN, CANDIDLY AND EARNESTLY GET THE FUCK OUT OF THERE, OR GHOST. HONESTLY UNLESS THE SHIT IS LIKE 6+ MONTHS LONG OR YOU'RE TRYING TO DATE THEIR COUSIN, YOU SHOULD ABSOLUTELY JUST GHOST. THAT'S WHY BEING MARRIED IS SUCH A BIG DEAL. IF MY WIFE & I DECIDE TO "THROW IN THE DAMN TOWEL!!" THE SHIT HAS TO BE LITIGATED. WE CANNOT JUST GHOST. IF YOU SINGLE AND WANNA HAVE A KID YOU REALLY ROLLIN THE DICE, THAT WAS MY LITERAL NIGHTMARE IN MY LATE TEENS AND EARLY 20S, HAVING A BABYMOMS THAT YOU CAN'T STAND BUT HAVE AN ETERNAL BOND WITH. WHEN I WAS 22 I DUMPED THE GIRL I HAD BEEN DATING SINCE I WAS 19 BECAUSE I FELT LIKE WE WERE HEADED IN THAT DIRECTION AND I WAS LIKE: "CHILL, I CAN'T HAVE A BABY WITH THIS GIRL. SHE CUT ALL MY JACKETS IN HALF WITH A BOX CUTTER BECAUSE ANOTHER WOMAN

HUGGED ME. I GOTTA BE SINGLE FOREVER." THAT WAS FUN UNTIL I THOUGHT ABOUT BEING LIKE 70, SINGLE AND CHILDLESS, AND I GOT DEPRESSED.

Okay, this book is messy and many of these concerns, such as the "childless and 70," are starting to feel like personal attacks, but like Mario says in the go-kart racing game that bears his name: "Let's-a-go!"

How to know when to settle down with someone is a question older than time itself, one of those terrible queries that you ask older people and they respond with the nonsense statement "When you know, you know."

"When you know, you know."

WHAT THE HELL DOES THAT MEAN?

If a definite sign is what it takes for a commitment, then I'm doomed. I'm Ray Charles when it comes to signs from the universe. The universe could literally send an asteroid crashing 5 feet in front of me with the name of my future life partner etched all over it and my response would be: "Whoa, that was close, better buy a lottery ticket because today is my lucky day!" I don't know what "knowing" means because every time I've felt it, within a few hours I've caught that person either chewing their toenails (disgusting but flexible) or tweeting about how lotion causes homosexuality (maybe?).

There's no standard time or age for everyone to settle down because as a wise man (me) once said: "We're all riding our own horses." Maybe you want more than your current life and you can't achieve that with your current partner. Maybe you need your current partner to help you achieve what it is you want in life. There are so many variables that you gotta test for yourself.

Also never never **never** let an ultimatum cause you to settle down. Getting into a relationship is a big deal; this isn't Spotify where you just click and hope for the best. And if after 3 years you're still not sure, maybe it's time to break up? But to guilt the other person into something just because of time passed is a terrible idea. It's also embarrassing to both parties and if you invite me to the wedding I'll be gossiping wild brazy at the table like: "Yeah, they didn't want to do this but she was all *we not getting younger* and he was like *damn, fuck, fine, I guess.*" And what's more romantic than that?

However, one clear sign that you should *definitely* say fuck it and settle down is your washed level. We will get into washedness and its forms in a later chapter, but it must be addressed here, too, as it pertains to relationships. Are you still hitting the club but have no idea what songs they're playing? You're washed. Did you attempt to do one of the new popular dances all the kids are doing but when you tried it at home in front of the mirror you think you pulled something? Washed. Turned to MSNBC from an NBA game because Rachel Maddow had breaking news? WWWWWWWASHED.

If you're washed, like the legendary character Guile from *Street Fighter II* said: "Go home and be a family man." Even Kobe knew when to retire. Don't fight it. Embrace the wash. Retire the Jordans and get yourself a nice comfortable pair of Skechers. Maybe even treat yourself to a Dr. Scholl's gel pad. Let the world know you won't be following fads anymore. Get a good sturdy pair of Wrangler jeans and a braided man-belt. Baptize yourself in the washedness.

Jay-Z has an old verse on the "Can't Knock the Hustle" remix where he says: "The only thing worse than getting old is not getting old." Let me put on my Ari Melber hat and break this down for you. Eventually it all gets old—popping bottles, seeing the same people at the same club every night. As a club employee, I saw this firsthand. I watched people age through the club circuit. Suddenly the hottest chick a year ago isn't getting as much attention as the new hot club girl. Maybe that baller-ass dude isn't as big a draw as he was a few years ago. Now what? Are you going to keep doing this? Till when?

When you start getting those feelings, when you get tired of sliding in DMs and chasing people, you're washed, so settle down. Sadly this sounds very dramatic and like you have to let life break you. But maybe that's the truth. Maybe the key word in the phrase "settle down" is "settle."

HOLY SHIT IS THIS NIHILISTIC. LET LIFE BREAK YOU? KEY WORD IN SETTLE DOWN IS "SETTLE"? JESUS CHRIST I JUST TOOK 10 ZOLOFT WITH A SHOT OF PLASTIC BOTTLE VODKA. THEY DON'T CALL HIM DARK DESUS FOR NOTHING, FOLKS. YOU NEVER KNOW WHEN A FUCKING WINDOW AC UNIT IS GONNA COME TUMBLING DOWN 10 STORIES ONTO YOUR CRANIAL, SO I LIKE TO BE A LIL MORE GLASS HALF FULL WHILE I'M HERE. YES, A LOT OF THINGS SUCK. COUNTERPOINT: MAD THINGS ALSO DECIDEDLY DO NOT SUCK.

Listen, don't let my black-hearted words in this book ruin love for you, or make you think that meeting someone, getting into a long-term relationship, and being corny together until you both die is a bad thing. I'm just giving both sides, and one side happens to be pessimistic as fuck. So I guess my feeling is you settle down once you find either the person you want to be with for the foreseeable future or the whole life thing beats you down to the point where you can no longer recognize your own face in the mirror and you feel eerily aware of the cold, clammy hand of death hovering nearby.

DAMN DUDE. CAN WE LIGHTEN THIS SHIT UP A LITTLE, TALK ABOUT A PERFECT DATE OR SOMETHING? WHEN YOU'RE LIKE ME (MARRIED WITH FOUR KIDS, WASHED) YOUR "PERFECT DATE" IS WIIIILD DIFFERENT THAN WHEN YOU WERE 22 AND HAD NO RESPONSIBILITIES EXCEPT NOT GOING TO JAIL OR SPREADING HERPES, OR BOTH (AIM HIGH, KIDS, SKY'S THE LIMIT). A PERFECT DATE CAN BE ALL KINDS OF STUPID SHIT. IF YOU'RE SINGLE AND POPPED LIKE I WAS BACK IN THE DAY, THEN A PERFECT DATE IS ONE THAT YOU DON'T PAY FOR AND THAT EVENTUALLY ENDS UP WITH YOU RECLINED RECEIVING TOP-PINGTON. IF YOU ARE BOTH ON SOME ADRENALINE JUNKIE SHIT YOU COULD SMASH OUTDOORS IN THE SERENGETI OR . . . I DONT KNOW, FUCKIN 69 WHILE HANG-GLIDING? GO KAYAKING STANDING UP? FLY KITES ON ACID. I'M JUST SPITBALLING HERE. I CAN NO LONGER FATHOM A DATE THAT ISN'T ABOUT ACHIEV-ING OD RELAXATION. IF MY WIFE AND I CAN GET OUT TO DIN-NER SOMEWHERE LOW-KEY, CHILL AND HOUSE A BOTTLE OF MALBEC? THAT'S PERFECT. SOME MAY CALL THAT CORNY BUT THOSE PEOPLE ARE PROBABLY STILL HAVING THE $200 DATE CONVERSATION ON TWITTER OR ARE OLD. NOT WASHED, JUST OLD, WHICH IS AWFUL. SOME MUTHAFUCKAS HOLD ON TO THEIR GLORY DAYS UNTIL THE SECONDHAND EMBARRASS-MENT IS PALPABLE.

TO ME, RIGHT NOW AS I WRITE THIS, A PERFECT DATE IS ME AND HEATHER ON A BEACH WITH A 4 GRAM BACKWOOD AND SOME ALCOHOLIC DRINK THAT DON'T TASTE LIKE AN ALCO-HOLIC DRINK UNTIL I GET IN THE WATER AND AM SO SMACKED I START FLOPPIN AROUND LIKE A MANU GINÓBILI-FISH ON THE DECK OF THE SS *CHANCLETA*. THEN I GET MY BEARINGS AND START FLOATING AND LAUGHING UNCONTROLLABLY BECAUSE IT'S A BEAUTIFUL SUNNY DAY AND I HAVE MONEY AND I BOUGHT

HEATHER TITTIES AND THEN SHE SWIMS OUT AND WE SHARE A WARM EMBRACE. THIS IS THE PART WHERE YOU THINK IT'S ABOUT TO GET INTO SOME WILD FUCKING & SHIT LIKE THAT.

NO! (JUELZ SANTANA VOICE)

THAT SHIT WAS STARTING TO SOUND LIKE FAN-FIC EROTICA, WHICH I DON'T EVEN WANNA KNOW THE POSSIBLE EXISTENCE OF. ALSO, FUCKING IN THE OCEAN IS WILD RECKLESS AND NOT LUBRICATED. LET ME GET BACK TO THE POINT. YOUR PERFECT DATE IS GOING TO BE JUST THAT, *YOUR* PERFECT DATE. THERE'S SOMEONE OUT THERE WHOSE IDEA OF A HOT DATE IS GETTING KICKED IN THE BALLS REPEATEDLY TO "THIS CHARMING MAN" WHILE WEARING AN ADULT DIAPER WITH A DICKHOLE CUT OUT. BUT HEY, WHO AM I TO JUDGE? I DON'T KINK SHAME OR DATE SHAME. IF YOUR IDEA OF A PERFECT DATE IS SITTING NEXT TO YOUR PARTNER ON A COUCH AND JUST TALKING? THAT'S OKAY! DON'T EVER LET ANYONE DATESHAME YOU B. THAT'S FOUL. NOT ALL OF US HAVE GOAT YOGA POLO LOUNGE MONEY. THAT'S WHY I'M WRITING THIS BOOK. I NEED GOAT-YOGA-WITH-LUNCH-AT-THE-POLO-LOUNGE-RIGHT-AFTER TYPE MONEY, AND I'M NOT THERE YET. I MEAN I GUESS I KINDA AM BUT IT WOULD BE WASTEFUL OF ME TO SPEND THAT MONEY THERE AND NOT ON A DESPERATELY NEEDED DYSON SO I CAN SUCK ALL THE CHEERIOS AND GOLDFISH, WHICH APPARENTLY APPEAR OUT OF THIN AIR IN THE FUCKIN LIVING ROOM WHEN I *CLEARLY* SAID NO EATING WITHIN 20 FEET OF THE GOD DAMN TELEVISION, SHOUT-OUT TO DYSON, THOUGH.

House dates are cool but you have to have the right setup to pull it off. Like if you're trying to illegally watch Netflix on a MacBook while drinking White Claws, that's cool if you're 19. But people want effort. You gotta at least get a Chromecast and watch that on the big screen. Little details like that make or break the date.

Also, and this is key: Either make food or get food delivered. If you have old Chinese food from the night before, don't offer it to your guest. That's really quite rude, which should go without saying but doesn't.

IF YOU HAVE ABSOLUTELY NO IDEA WHAT TO DO FOR YOUR OWN DATE, I MEAN . . . WHY YOU EVEN DOIN THIS? YOU GOT SERIOUS PROBLEMS B. BUT OKAY IF YOU REALLY WANT MY ADVICE ON WHAT YOUR PERFECT DATE SHOULD INCLUDE, IT SHOULD AT LEAST INCLUDE THESE 2 THINGS:

1) ROOM TO TALK: YOU NEED TO KNOW WHAT THIS PERSON IS ABOUT AND IF YOU GO PAINTBALLING AND YOU CLAPTIZE HER IN THE GRILLATIN WHEN SHE HAS HER MASK OFF, THERE AIN'T MUCH TO TALK ABOUT FAM. IF YOU GO TO A RESTAURANT LIKE STK, THE SHIT IS MAD LOUD AND YOU CAN SPEND $50 ON MAC & CHEESE AND NOT HEAR WHAT THE FUCK YOUR DATE IS TALKING ABOUT.

2) A VERY OD CLOSE UBER PICKUP POINT.

OH ALSO DON'T ASK "WHAT DO YOU DO FOR WORK?" THAT SHIT IS BORING. INSTEAD, ASK: WHEN'S THE LAST TIME HE/SHE JAYWALKED, LIKE "FUCK YOU TOYOTA CAMRY I DARE YOU." THAT SHIT IS A CURVEBALL AND IT'S NOT CREEPY EITHER. VERY INNOCUOUS QUESTION, YOU FEEL ME? IF THEY LIKE "WOW YOU'RE LAME!" THEN FIRST MAKE THEM FEEL OD UNWOKE BY TELLING THEM "LAME" IS AN ABLEIST TERM, THEN GET OUTTA THERE BECAUSE I'MA BE REAL, IF YOU CAN'T LAUGH WITH EACH OTHER AND AT EACH OTHER THIS WILL BE YOUR FIRST AND LAST DATE.

I WOULD GO OUT TONIGHT BUT I HAVEN'T GOT A STITCH TO WEEEEAAAHUHHHH. LMAO I JUST SPELLED THAT PHONETI-

CALLY THEN HIT THE WILD DABINGTON. YO I'M SMACKED YOU HEAR ME? YO IS MORRISSEY CANCELED? IS HE PROBLEMATIC? I DON'T KEEP UP WITH THE YAKUBIAN TIMES. LIFE IS WILD. YO I USED TO PAINT THE CORNERS OF OUR CRIB WITH THAT ROACH-KILLING CHALK THAT HAD A DEAD ROACH AND WHAT I ASSUMED TO BE CHINESE WRITING ON THE PACKAGE. THAT SHIT WAS DECIDEDLY NOT FDA APPROVED. DO Y'ALL REMEMBER THAT SHIT? IT WAS A LITERAL CHALK AND YOU WOULD DRAW A LINE WHERE THE WALL & FLOOR MEET AND I SHIT YOU NOT IT WAS LIKE *WALKING DEAD* BUT STARRING ROACHES. THEY WOULD COME OUT IN DROVES, EAT THE CHALK, AND INSTANTLY SEIZURE AND PERISH. SHIT WAS LIKE THE HOTTEST HOT BAG OF ALL TIME. FUCKIN HUNDREDS OF ROACHES WOULD PULL UP TO GET SMIZZY AND STRAIGHT OD, NO NARCAN IN SIGHT. *TOMA!* FUCKIN *CUCARACHA*. AS A NIGGA GROWING UP IN THE HOOD, NOTHING WAS MORE SATISFYING THAN STOMPING OUT A ROACH OR SPRAYING THAT LIL MOTHERFUCKER TILL IT PERISHES, OR CATCHING THAT FUCKIN MOUSE THAT FUCKED UP YOUR OFF-BRAND DORITOS ON A GLUE TRAP. LISTEN. JUST *HAVE FUN* ON A DATE B. GO BOWLING. BOWLING IS TYPE LIT.

Wow, that was a lot. Anyway, I think perpetually single can be seen as either waiting for the right one or just being too damn picky. And it all depends on what you bring to the table. If you have a good job and your stuff together, then waiting for the right person makes sense. However, if you ain't bringing the heat lifewise, maybe it's time to take your standards down a bit, Prince Charles.

I know a few people here in New York City who would describe themselves as the ultimate catch, which they define as: good job, no kids, no record, etc. Now, I don't know what the bar is but that seems kinda low (also any guy that describes himself using those terms is more than likely a jerk who wears square-toed shoes to brunch).

So if you're the ultimate catch, then why are you perpetually single? Is it a fear of commitment? Are you terrified of having sex with one person for the rest of your life? Are you a tiny man-child that lacks self-control sexually and anytime you see fat ass it's like someone jingling keys in front of a toddler and you get distracted and forget that you are in a relationship ~~like wtf Desus what's the matter with you?~~

HOT TAKE: I think being perpetually single beats being constantly in and out of relationships just because you're afraid of being alone or you need someone to constantly text memes to. At least the perpetually single person isn't dragging someone else down with them or is honest enough to say "Hey, I'm not a relationship person." Meanwhile, your best friend just "met the love of his life" for the 3rd time this year and it's March.

Dating is weird and operating by other people's timetables is even weirder. Many of my (white) friends in college were married by 22, which was wild to me because at that age I was still perfecting my beer pong game (sidenote: a very disgusting game that probably has killed off more Americans than we know).

BEER PONG IS HOW WHITE PEOPLE SPREAD THE BLACK PLAGUE IN MEDIEVAL TIMES. I'M DEAD-ASS. THEY CALLED IT "ALE TIDDLYWHO" AND THEY USED A MUSKET BULLET. SUPER GROSS. THEY LET RATS PLAY AND THEN HALF OF EUROPE GOT WIPED OUT. IT'S STILL A EUROPEAN TRADITION TO THIS DAY TO HONOR THOSE WHO GAVE THEIR LIVES TO RAT SHIT IN FERMENTED LIQUID.

THE TRUTH IS, I CAN'T EVEN REALLY SPEAK TO DATING ANY-

MORE BECAUSE I GOT MARRIED WHEN IT WAS NOT CONSIDERED GAUCHE TO INTRODUCE YOURSELF TO SOMEONE IN PERSON, WHICH IS HOW I MET MY WIFE. I APPROACHED HER AND SAID, "HELLO, I HEAR YOU ACROSS THE HALL. YOU ARE LOUD AS SHIT!" SHE LAUGHED AND IT WAS ON. NOW WE HAVE A MORTGAGE BUT STILL SMASH IN DRESSING ROOMS CUZ YOU GOTTA KEEP SHIT SPICY. BUT YEAH DATING IN 2020 SOUNDS LIKE A HELLSCAPE.

WHEN I GOT MARRIED I DIDN'T HAVE SHIT SO AT THE VERY LEAST I KNOW SHE AIN'T IN IT FOR THE MONEY. TRUE LOVE IS DATING A BROKE MUTHAFUCKA LIVING IN A DILAPIDATED APARTMENT AND TRYING VALIANTLY TO MAKE IT LIVABLE. I DUNNO MAN, JUST LISTENING TO MY SINGLE FRIENDS' WAR STORIES AND WATCHING THE JUGGLING MAKES MY FUCKIN HEAD HURT. DOES MARRIAGE SUCK SOMETIMES? HELL YEAH, MY GUY, BUT IF THERE'S MORE GOOD THAN BAD I'LL TAKE HEATHER BEING PISSED OFF AT ME FOR A WEEK CUZ I WAS TOO LAZY TO WALK TO THE BATHROOM AND PEED IN A SNAPPLE BOTTLE IN THE WEED CHAMBER OF CHATEAU DU MERO OVER 2 DIFFERENT DATES IN A WEEK WHERE I WEAR UNCOMFORTABLE SHOES AND WE TALK ABOUT WHERE WE WENT TO SCHOOL FOR 3 HOURS. *SHUDDERS*

The new cutoff for settling down and getting married seems to be 30. Why? I don't know, but every show has people panicking about turning 30 and not having their shit together, as if at midnight, you die when you hit the big 3-0. And then apparently life after 30 is terrible, because if you're an unmarried guy in his thirties, people have questions about your life choices and/or just assume you're a fuckboy.

The message also seems to be that if you're a female over the age of 30 you might as well not exist. You're like a bruised can of corn marked half-off in the discount aisle at your local supermarket. If you have kids, FOH, nobody dealing with all that, Ma. If you don't have kids it's either you have wack pussy or you're a crazy cat lady. These are the options out there. Don't quote me.

And if I can throw on my Social Justice Warrior hat: Calling someone perpetually single is appropriation of Auntie culture. Now for those of you who aren't immigrants, Auntie culture is the world where your Auntie, because she's older than you, is allowed to say the rudest stuff right to your face for no other reason than you're blood relatives (and sometimes you're not even that). In Auntie culture, a proper greeting is "Wow, you got fat" or "Still not seeing anyone? Better hurry up. Your eggs are drying up," and you can't respond with anything other than a smile because even as an adult you could still get popped in the mouth.

I think perpetual singleness can be a good thing. Imagine you've spent your whole life meeting people and you've just never connected with someone. Maybe it's for the best because you realize what you *don't* want and sometimes that's more tangible than knowing what you *do* want.

On the other hand, maybe it's you. It could be time to take a good, close, realistic look at yourself. Are you attempting to date outside of your dating pool? Are you a weirdo dating younger people because you can control them? I do think that attaching an age range to this issue is weird because my grandfather (RIP) had two girls when he was ninety-six. Bless that man. Still doing numbers right before hitting the triple digits, what a legend. If you still got it, you still got it.

MAKE SURE YOU FUCK YOUR PARTNER REGULARLY AND WITH VIGOR. ALSO, BE NICE TO THEM AND TALK TO THEM AND SHIT

LIKE THAT. YOU GOTTA BE PRESENT WITH YOUR PARTNER, WHICH SEEMS IMPOSSIBLE TO ME IF YOU HAVE MORE THAN ONE PARTNER. MAN, I WAS WATCHING THAT *SISTER WIVES* SHIT THE OTHER DAY AND THAT SHIT LOOKED LOW-KEY STRESSFUL. I KNOW, I KNOW, HAVING SISTER WIVES IS A LOOPHOLE TO GETTING SOME EXTRACURRICULAR COOCH. BUT IT'S ALOTTTTAAAA WORK FOR NOT THAT GREAT A PAYOFF. IT'S LIKE TRAINING AND PLAYING MAD BASEBALL FROM TEEBALL TO LITTLE LEAGUE TO SCHOOL TO TRAVELING TEAMS AND THEN PEAKING AS A MINOR LEAGUE ALL-STAR. ACTUALLY THAT MIGHT BE GREAT IDK LEMME GOOGLE HOW MUCH THESE NIGGAS GET PAID HOLD UP *PLAYS SMIF N' WESSUN—"LET'S GET IT ON" IN THE BACKGROUND WHILE HE GOOGLES* DAMN $1,100 A WEEK?! THAT'S FUCKING CRAZY B. YOU MEAN TO TELL ME I SACRIFICED MY BODY AND WORKED MY ASS OFF PLAYING THIRD BASE FOR THE SCRANTON BILLYBOBS FOR "I'M-THE-ILLEST-SALES-NIGGA-AT-BEST-BUY" MONEY? BUT YEAH, SISTER WIVES IS KINDA WACK. THAT'S TOO MUCH RESPONSIBILITY. SHIT LOOKS LIT ON THE SURFACE BUT WHAT IF THEY ARE BOTH DUBS? DAMN. *STARES INTO SPACE HIGHLY* BUT I GUESS PEOPLE ARE PEOPLE AND IT'S THE SAME FOR SISTER HUSBANDS OR BROTHER WIVES OR NON-BINARY GENDER-FLUID HOMIES.

ANYWAY, YEAH, IF YOU BLOW SOMEONE THAT'S PROBABLY CHEATING UNLESS YOUR PARTNER DON'T GIVE A FUCK, THEN I GUESS IT'S NOT? ALL I KNOW IS IF MY WIFE CATCHES ME SMASHING SOMEONE ELSE I'D HAVE A LOT OF EXPLAINING TO DO, MOST OF WHICH WOULD BE IN A COURTROOM. THEN I'LL BECOME AN IRRESPONSIBLE RECKLESS WEEKEND DAD WHO GIVES ZERO FUCKS AND SMOKES NEWPORTS BACKWARDS WELCOMING DEATH'S EMBRACE. I LOVE MY WIFE AND I LOVE MY KIDS. SO TO ME THE PROSPECT OF MULTIPLE PARTNERS OR CHEATING IS LIKE ASKING ME "HEY, WOULD YOU RATHER BE

RICH AND CONTINUE TO HAVE YOUR SPOUSE'S ENDLESS LOVE AND ORIFICES WHILE YOU PROUDLY WATCH YOUR KIDS DO COOL SHIT? OR WOULD YOU RATHER BE BROKE AS FUCK AND HAVE YOUR KIDS CALLING YOU "JOEL" INSTEAD OF "DAD" ON THEIR MONTHLY SLEEPOVER?

Yup. In other words: Don't let your partner catch you blasting out the wild brazy dick pics.

A DICK PIC IS NEVER OKAY, FAM. I BEEN OUT THE GAME FOR A MINUTE BUT JUST ON GENERAL PRINCIPLE YOU GOTTA BE SUPER THIRSTY TO SEND A PICTURE OF A BONER YOU WORKED UP FOR THE SPECIFIC PURPOSE OF TAKING A SELFIE OF SAID BONER. WHEN YOU STEP BACK AND THINK ABOUT IT . . . IT'S WILD, MY NIGGA. FIRST OF ALL, AN UNSOLICITED DICK PIC IS VIOLENCE, OKAY? I CAN'T EVEN IMAGINE WHAT IT WOULD BE LIKE TO RECEIVE A DICK PIC FROM MY MAN, LET ALONE FROM AN ABSOLUTELY RANDOM DUDE. LIKE, BRUH, IT'S 4PM. THE FUCK ARE YOU DOING? ARE YOU FUCKIN KIDDING ME? AND NOW I HAVE A PHOTO OF YOU AT HALF-MAST FOREVER. NICE ONE, GENIUS. I'M AN INCH AWAY FROM LITERALLY HAVING YOU BY THE BALLS, STUPID. YO I'M SORRY WHETHER YOU LIKE DRAKE OR NOT, *SCORPION* IS FULL OF BANGERS. IF YOU OUT HERE SENDING UNSOLICITED DICK PICS, DON'T EVEN WAIT TO FINISH THIS SENTENCE BEFORE YOU STOP THAT SHIT RIGHT NOW. AS A CISHET MALE I FIND VAGINAS TO BE LIT, THEY LOOK LIKE BLOOMING FLOWERS. DICKS JUST LOOK LIKE SNUFFLE-UPAGUS OFF MAD XANS ON A FLIGHT TO MIAMI. EVEN AT THEIR MAX GIRTH AND LENGTH, DICKS ONLY HAVE A SMALL WINDOW OF SEXINESS IMHO. BUT AGAIN, YOU'RE TALKING TO A GUY WHO DOES NOT FIND DICKS APPEALING. MAYBE A TON OF PEOPLE IN THE WORLD LIKE ANGLED PHOTOS OF FLACCID

COCKS. IF YOU FALL INTO THAT CATEGORY, THEN YOU CAN IGNORE THIS WHOLE SHIT AND GO REREAD THE DRUGS PART. IT'S INFORMATIVE.

SITS BACK IN CHAIR AND PONDERS FEROCIOUSLY

YOU KNOW WHAT? PUTTING MYSELF IN THE SHOES OF SOMEONE WHO LIKES PENIS WHILE NOT ACTUALLY BEING A FAN OF PENIS MYSELF IS POTENTIALLY PROBLEMATIC. SO FORGET EVERYTHING I JUST WROTE. MY NEW ANGLE IS THAT I AM PROUD OF MYSELF AND MY BODY, FLAWS AND ALL, AND MY DICK LOOKS MAJESTIC WHEN IT'S FRESHLY SHORN IN THE SHOWER AND AT MAXIMUM CAPACITY. IT'S LIKE A VEINY BROWN MISSILE WITH A BUILT-IN G-SPOT SEEKER. MY DICK IS LIKE IF WIDENECK GUY AND SKINNYNECK GUY HAD A BABY AND THAT BABY WAS A HUMAN DICK. I'M KIDDING, I DON'T HAVE A FOOT-LONG WIENER. ALL I WILL INTIMATE IS THAT MY PENIS IS WELL ABOVE AVERAGE FOR LENGTH AND VERY GIRTHY. WOW I REALLY JUST SPENT SEVERAL SENTENCES DESCRIBING MY DICK TO Y'ALL, MAN. I MAY HAVE CROSSED A LINE AND I APOLOGIZE. IF YOU ARE SEX-POSI, THOUGH, AND NOT OFFENDED, NOW YOU DON'T HAVE TO GUESS WHEN YOU ARE WRITING YOUR CREEPY FAN-FIC.

Man's really out here describing his penis in vivid detail. It was too much, but at the same time, it was art. Like hearing Michelangelo describe the dick on one of his statues but in a Dominican accent.

BUT FOR REAL, NEVER EVER EVER EVER SEND AN UNSOLICITED DICK PIC. I'M PRETTY SURE IT'S AGAINST THE LAW. I DON'T CARE IF THEY'VE SEEN YOUR PENIS BEFORE OR EVEN TOUCHED IT. THEY DIDN'T ASK FOR THE SHIT SO DON'T SEND IT. LISTEN CLOSELY MY NIGGAS, TRANSNIGGAS, AND GENDERQUEER NIG-

GAS WITH DICKS: **DO NOT SEND UNSOLICITED DICK PICS.** THEY ARE RARELY IF EVER MET WITH APPRECIATION AND MORE SO MET WITH SCORN AND MOCKERY IN THE GROUPCHAT:

YOUR DIC PICK GETS POSTED TO THREAD

"EWWW YO WHY IT MAD ASHY ON TOP"

"EWWW HE NASTY I DEADASS THOUGHT THAT SHIT WAS A HALO FILTER."

"*BARF EMOJI*"

"*MULTIPLE BARF EMOJIS*"

"THIS NIGGA DICK LOOK LIKE A BURNT HOTDOG WHY YOU PUT THIS IN THE CHAT YESENIA YOU OD BLOWIN MINE WITH THIS SHIT"

"NAH HOLDUP I GOT SOME SHIT FOR YOU . . ."

SOMEONE POSTS A DIFFERENT DICK PIC

"YOOOOOOOOO"

"WOW. WOWWW"

"OH LORDT"

NOW YOU GOT SOME OTHER POOR JERK'S DICK THROWN IN THE MIX CUZ YOU VERY LITERALLY COULD NOT KEEP YOUR DICK IN YOUR PANTS. MY SISTER AND I ARE VERY CLOSE AND HER GROUPCHATS ARE OUTRAGEOUS. SHOUT-OUT TO INGRID, I LOVE YOU MAMA. I GUESS THIS SCENARIO IS SOME CHICKEN OR EGG SHIT. BUT YOU GET WHAT I'M SAYIN. DICK PIC VIOLENCE BEGETS DICK PIC VIOLENCE.

MERO, YOU SAID UP THERE NEVER SEND A DICK PIC UNLESS ASKED FOR.

WELL, TO QUOTE NBA MEGASTAR AND GRANDFATHER OF

THE GOAT LEBRON JAMES, GREG ODEN: "I SENT IT CUZ SHE ASKED FOR IT AND SHE HAD ALREADY SENT ME A BUNCH OF STUFF." (I'M PARAPHRASING.) SO HE SENT A DICK PIC BECAUSE HE FELT LIKE HE OWED THE OTHER PERSON. DON'T DO THAT. THAT AIN'T SUPER SOUND LOGIC. ESPECIALLY IF YOU ARE A SINGLE NBA PLAYER SMASHING GROUPIES CROSS-COUNTRY. THAT'S HOW DRAYMOND GREEN'S TWO-TONED COCK ENDED UP ON SNAPCHAT. NIGGAS BE MAD EAGER TO SEND A PIC OF THEY ASHY DICK LIKE IT'S GOING TO TURN YOUR SEX PARTNER ON IMMEDIATELY. IF SHE IS AT WORK AND YOU ARE HOME PLAYING *RED DEAD REDEMPTION 2* AND YOU PULL YOUR PJ PANTS WAISTBAND UNDER YOUR NUTS AND FIRE OFF A GOOD MORNING DICKPIC WITH YOUR COCK ASLEEP, JUST KNOW THAT YOUR SHIT IS HEADED STRAIGHT FOR THE GROUPCHAT. IF YOU KNOW YOUR PARTNER WELL ENOUGH, YOU'LL KNOW WHEN TO SEND A DICK PIC TO SIGNAL THE DEEP ATTACHMENT YOU HAVE TO THEM. BECAUSE NOTHING SAYS COMMITMENT LIKE A DUDE WITH LOW CONFIDENCE IN HIS BRACIOLE SENDING YOU A PICTURE OF IT.

I was once at a BBQ and one of my friends got a dick pic (notice I didn't indicate a gender for my friend because I am an ally, and also my friends just kinda go with whatever energy) and that dick pic got passed around the BBQ like a newborn baby at a family function. And the photo didn't get passed around because it was an amazing photo but rather because it was unsolicited. So, Mero was right about all that. And it's fucking wild to me, too. Y'all out here just cyber sending your meats all around Al Gore's Internets and you have no idea who's looking at them. Probably a person on the Geek Squad right now with your Tootsie Roll saved to their recent photos, smh.

CHAPTER 3

I've heard some people say, "Have kids in your twenties so by the time you're in your forties, they're gone and now you have free time." But by the same logic, I've spent 20 years doing shit y'all couldn't do and my body was better built for it and it was the shiiiiiit. And now that I'm washed I can (theoretically) have a baby in peace.

The whole *at what age should you have a kid* discussion is strange to me because in the Bronx, you don't really plan to have a baby. You usually get the phone call and you're like, "Are you serious?" followed by a "Oh my god baby I'm so happy" or "Nah fuck outta here that shit ain't mine." And this starts when you become sexually active, so that's like, ugh I want to say 11?? (Again, the Bronx, and I actually know kids who started earlier but I don't want to get too dark.)

If you're really planning for a baby, it's less about your age and more about your pay grade. I don't know how much kids cost but every now and then I hear some wild number and I'm like, oh hell no. Daycare is on average 16K a year for an infant in NYC. 16K. Just gone, with nothing to show for it. WILD. Do you know how much Pampers cost? And babies use MORE THAN ONE DIAPER A DAY?? WILD.

RAISING KIDS IS DUMB EASY B, ALL YOU NEED IS A ZILLION DOLLARS AND AN ENTIRE STAFF OF PEOPLE TO DO EVERYTHING FROM CHANGE DIAPERS TO GIVE BATHS SO YOU CAN DO THE COOL SHIT LIKE PLAY CATCH AND DO GRAFFITI ON THE SIDEWALK WITH BABY CHALK. NAW, THAT'S SOME FANTASY WORLD SHIT, AND BY THE TIME I WOULD EVER SEE THAT KINDA MONEY, MY KIDS & I WILL BE IN THE POOL HOUSE CYPHING PLAYING NBA 2K34 ON XBOX1 WHILE THEY ASK WHY WE CAN'T USE THE SONY BRAINSTEM INTERFACE TO PLAY INSTEAD.

My whole thing about having a child was that I wanted to be well off enough to provide a great life. My parents raised four of us and there were times we didn't necessarily have the best stuff, yet we were always provided for. But the wild stress my parents went through always stuck with me. How hard my father had to work and he never saw us. Doesn't that kind of defeat the whole purpose of having a kid?

As for how old is too old to have a child, let's just ask Jeff Goldblum. Jeff Goldblum had his first child at sixty-five. SIXTY-FIVE. People are having babies at later ages now (correction: rich people). So I imagine that's an option for some people (rich people again). And there's always adoption (correction: for some people).

IN ALL HONESTY, RAISING KIDS IS NOT DUMB EASY. IT'S WILD COMPLICATED. A KID IS A HUMAN PERSON WITH THEIR OWN DEMEANOR, THEIR OWN PERSONALITY QUIRKS, THEIR OWN

AMBITIONS AND DREAMS AND NEEDS AND THEN FUCK MAN, HERE COME (FOR ME) 3 MORE. I JOKINGLY TELL PARENTS OF ONE OR TWO KIDS: YOU GOOD FAM, YOU CAN DOUBLE-TEAM THE KID OR PLAY COMBO MAN COVERAGE AND FOCUS ON YOUR STAR TROUBLEMAKER. I'M OUT HERE RUNNING A ZONE WITH NO FREE SAFETY.

MY PERSONAL APPROACH IS TO TAKE STOCK OF WHERE HEATHER AND I ARE AS PEOPLE, FOCUS ON OUR STRONG SUITS, AND LEAVE THE EXTENSION CORD ASS-WHOOPINGS BACK IN THE '80S WITH CRACK AND REAGAN. IF YOU CAN PERFECT THE DOMINICAN DAD "DON'T YOU FUCKIN DARE EMBARRASS ME IN PUBLIC" LASER DEATH STARE, YOU'RE GOOD. IF THAT FAILS, SOME OF Y'ALL GONNA WHOOP A KID'S ASS. THIS IS AN OD CONTROVERSIAL TOPIC: SOME PEOPLE ARE ALL ABOUT TIME-OUTS AND BEHAVIOR MODIFICATION CHARTS AND SOME PEOPLE ARE LIKE "WHOOP THAT LIL NIGGA ASS, HE'LL GET IT TOGETHER!" HERE'S WHAT I DO: IF I'M AT A STORE WITH ALL FOUR KIDS AND SOME OF THEM ARE ACTING WILD, I'LL BREAK OUT THE DDDS (DOMINICAN DAD DEATH STARE). IF THAT DOESN'T WORK, SINCE I'M WAY BIGGER THAN ANY OF THEM, I'LL JUST PICK ONE UP FROM UNDER THEIR LIL BITTY ARMPITS, RAISE THEM UP TO MY EYE LEVEL, AND, USING MY SMOKY BENICIO DEL TORO GROWL, STERNLY SAY: "CHILL . . . CHILL." THAT WORKS 175% OF THE TIME, BUT MY KIDS ARE ALL LITTLE. MERO JR IS 8 RIGHT NOW, SO I CAN'T TELL YOU SHIT ABOUT RAISING TEENS. MY NEIGHBOR SAW ME CHASING MERO IV, WHO IS 3 AND BUCK FUCKIN WILD, DOWN THE BLOCK. WHEN I CAME BACK DOWN THE STREET WITH HIM UNDER MY ARM LIKE DON DRAPER HOLDING THE *NY TIMES*, I WAS LIKE "YOUR KIDS ARE OLDER! MUST BE NICE! *NEIGHBORLY CHUCKLE*" AND SHE WAS LIKE, "NAH CHIEF . . . LITTLE KIDS, LITTLE PROBLEMS. BIG KIDS, BIG PROBLEMS." THEN I REMEMBERED WHAT A HELLA-

CIOUS TEENAGER I WAS AND WONDERED HOW MY PARENTS COULD POSSIBLY STILL LOVE ME.

SO I GUESS RAISING A TEENAGER IS TOUGHER THAN PREVENTING A 3-YEAR-OLD FROM UNSCREWING EVERY KNOB ON YOUR DRESSER (HOW THE FUCK DID YOU DO THAT? AT 3AM?). ALL I KNOW IS WHEN I WAS A LIL BADASS 16-YEAR-OLD DOING GRAFFITI, FIGHTING, AND INGESTING DRUGS, I RESPECTED MY POPS, BUT I WANTED TO BE THE BIG DOG IN THE HOUSE. SO I WAS ALWAYS GOADING HIM INTO A SCRAP, MUCH TO THE CHAGRIN OF MY POPS WHO, LIKE A DJ RECEIVING A DRUNKEN SONG REQUEST FROM A WHITE GIRL, DID NOT PLAY THAT SHIT. MY DAD WAS VERY BIG ON DEFERENCE AND RESPECT. BUT I WAS 16 AND STUPID SO I BROUGHT HOME A PIT BULL THAT WAS GIVEN TO ME, WITHOUT SO MUCH AS MENTIONING IT TO MY POPS FIRST. HE SAW IT, GLARED AT ME, AND SAID, "GET THE FUCK OUTTA HERE WITH THAT SHIT, WE LIVE IN A FUCKING 2-BEDROOM APARTMENT YOU JERK." (I'M PARAPHRASING.) IT WAS AT THAT MOMENT THAT I SHIRTLESSLY UTTERED THE PHRASE "FUCK YOU NIGGA!" AND SQUARED UP. REGARDLESS OF THE FACT THAT I WAS TALLER THAN MY DAD, HE HAD GORILLA HANDS FROM DOING CARPENTRY FROM THE AGE OF FUCKING 7 AND LITERALLY HAD A BLACK BELT IN JUDO. SO WE FISTICUFFED IT OUT, AND I GOT SWIFTLY WASHED OUTSIDE. I THINK THE WORST DECISION I MADE WAS NOT PURPOSELY MISSING MY POORLY THROWN PUNCH INTO MY DAD'S VIBRANIUM NECK. I'M NOT KIDDING, THIS MAN'S NECK IS HARDER THAN TAKING THE LSAT ON ACID. HAD I MISSED, HE MIGHT HAVE BEEN LIKE "AW THAT'S CUTE." BUT I MADE CONTACT AND IT HURT MY HAND. MY MOM AND SISTER WERE OD EMBARRASSED. AT THE TIME, MY LOGIC WAS "IF I BEAT MY DAD UP, I RUN THE HOUSE." LIKE OUR CRIB WAS A FUCKIN RIKERS DORM. AND THAT'S THE ONLY THING I KNOW ABOUT RAISING TEENS . . .

THAT EVENTUALLY MY KIDS AND I WILL FIGHT SHIRTLESS IN FRONT OF THE CRIB AND THOROUGHLY EMBARRASS MY WIFE AND DAUGHTER. SO AT 4AM DAILY, I DO 500 PUSH-UPS (THE ONES WHERE YOU CLAP TWICE) AND PRACTICE MY 52 HAND BLOCK TIGER STYLE IN ANTICIPATION OF THIS INEVITABLE STANDOFF/POWER STRUGGLE.

That fight every guy has with his father is such a game changer. Because you're just chilling in the crib learning about life and you have wild hormones and teen angst going on and then your pops gets in your face over some bullshit and it's suddenly like "Damn, it's not father and son right now, I'm about to fight some regular dude in the street." Except your pops made you and has been waiting to knock you the fuck out to teach you a lesson about respect.

I remember fighting my father and actually saying "oh shit" out loud when I heard his punch whiz past me. I'd either dodged it, or he wasn't really trying to kill me, but I felt the wind behind it. The wind was more terrifying than getting clocked . . . had me like "Oh my god, I'm about to die, this was a huge mistake."

RAISE YOUR KIDS TO QUESTION SHIT. THAT WAY THEY'LL THIRST FOR KNOWLEDGE THE WAY MICHAEL ANTHONY THIRSTS FOR A BUNDLE. THEY WON'T BE FOOLED BY YAKUBIAN TRICKNOLOGY AND COINTELPRO AND DIQUE FREE GAMES WITH IN-APP PURCHASES. MY DAD PUT ME ON TO A LOT OF SHIT RIDING AROUND IN THAT ECONOLINE VAN, SENDING ME OUT TO EVERY BODEGA TO HAND OUT STICKERS FOR HIS 2.5-MAN HVAC OPERATION. SHIT WAS NOT A GAME. I LEARNED THE STREETS AT A VERY YOUNG AGE, NAVIGATING HOOD BASEMENTS WITH MY POPS. DRIVING THROUGH HUNTS POINT WHEN YOU COULD GET 2 PATELITOS AND SOME TOPPY FOR LUNCH WITHOUT BREAKING

A 20. MAYBE DON'T EXPOSE THEM TO THAT SHIT AT 8 YEARS OLD, BUT LET YOUR KIDS ASK QUESTIONS, LET THEM ROAM, MAKE SURE THEY HAVE PHONES AND ALL THAT, AND MAYBE AN RFID CHIP. I GOT ONE IN MY SHIH TZU. IF YOU LIVE IN A CITY, THEY'LL LEARN TO SEE THE MASTURBATING GUY WITH PAPER SHOES A MILE AWAY. THIS IS A LITTLE-KNOWN FACT, BUT CHILDREN BORN IN THE 5 BOROS HAVE A SPECIAL OLFACTORY DUCT THAT HELPS THEM DETECT AND NEUTRALIZE BUM PISS. I TOOK PUBLIC TRANSIT AS A KID WHEN IT WAS EXPONENTIALLY MORE DANGEROUS AND I WAS FINE.

LOOK, JUST DON'T RAISE HERBS. I'M 98% SURE ALL MY KIDS WOULD LITERALLY TELL A CREEPY STRANGER "I DON'T FUCKIN KNOW YOU. DON'T TOUCH ME YOU FUCKIN ASSHOLE." VERBATIM. THEY MIGHT GET PUNCHED IN THE FACE BUT THEN THEY'LL LEARN TO EAT A PUNCH, WHICH IS A CRUCIAL EXPERIENCE. ALSO IF AN ADULT KNOCKS OUT A SMALL KID ON A CITY BUS OR TRAIN, THAT GUY IS GETTING BEAT TO SHREDS BY A RANDOM PERSON OR ARRESTED OR BOTH. YOU GOTTA GIVE YOUR KIDS LICENSE TO CURSE TO WARD OFF DANGER. THERE'S NOTHING WILDER THAN AN 8-YEAR-OLD ON THE A TRAIN THREATENING TO FUCK UP A 40-YEAR-OLD, USING THE PHRASE "I'LL DEADASS FUCK YOU UP." *WHIPS OUT BOX CUTTER* THAT'S WILD, BRUH. YOU WERE WATCHING *PEPPA PIG* 6 MONTHS AGO, NOW YOU'RE GETTIN BROLIC ON NIGGAS ON PUBLIC TRANSIT. *SINGLE TEAR*

I actually agree entirely with everything he just said.

I'M PEAKING, MY DUDE, STAND BACK. YO, AS FAR AS FOOD AND SHIT, GET THEM EATING GREENS EARLY, I GUESS? THAT'S WHAT WE DID AND ALL MY KIDS ARE AT LEAST IN THE 65TH PERCEN-

TILE FOR HEIGHT AND WEIGHT. I MIGHT BE LYING—HEATHER, AM I LYING? FUCK, I'M STARTING TO CRASH.

HEATHER: 55th, not 65th. Adr . . . I mean . . . "Mero Jr," is in the 55th percentile for height and weight.

OKAY. ALSO MERO IV IS A 3-YR-OLD JUNIOR FULLBACK FOR THE U. HAVE YOU EVER SEEN A TODDLER BUILT LIKE MIKE TOLBERT? THAT IS MERO IV. MERO JR AND MERO III ARE AVERAGE SIZE, AND THE BODEGA PRINCESS IS RIGHT THERE, TOO. YOUNG NUDY "THE RACE" REMIX W TAY-K IS SUPER HARD. JUST HAD TO THROW THAT IN THERE CUZ I GOT IT ON LOOP WHILE I WRITE AND THE SHIT SLAPS. BUT YEAH NAH YOU DON'T WANT YOUR KID TO GET SOME WILD CONDITION FROM SUPERMARKET BRAND SODA, HOLD UP LEMME ASK HEATHER, I'M OUTTA MY ZONE, FUCK.

HEATHER: Soda?? Never soda. Water or milk are our kids' options. Juice on special occasions but even that is like the vodka at an all-inclusive resort: half water. Kids can be picky so your best bet is to expose them to all sorts of different foods from all food groups early. It certainly isn't a promise that your dinnertime will go peacefully, with your kids eating what you put on their plates, but hopefully it expands their palates and gives you some options as their parents. Vegetables are a hard sell in our house, even with a vegetarian mom. I convince myself that fruit is an acceptable substitute. Personally, I love the kids' plates with the different sections—it helps me visualize, like "Okay they have protein, grain, dairy, and fruits & veggies." The rest of mealtime depends on the day . . . does the food go into their mouths, or does it get thrown at their brother or sister? Do they use it to decorate my hair? Do they slip it to our dog, Brownie?? Who knows?! But I know I did my best and that's all I can do. Good luck!

MY OPERATING PARENTING PHILOSOPHY IS TO JUST KINDA ROLL WITH THE KIDS LIKE THEY ARE LITTLE ME'S. YO, WE'RE AT THE MALL, YOU WANT CHICK-FIL-A? AIGHT LIT, LET'S GO TO FOOT LOCKER. OH SHIT, THE MICROSOFT STORE GOT *MARVEL VS. CAPCOM 3* ON A GIANT MONITOR! WE HOLDING THIS SHIT DOWN LIKE A JAIL PHONE. LET'S JUMP AROUND IN A ROOM MADE ENTIRELY OF TRAMPOLINES. LET'S GO TO GAMESTOP, GET *MARIO PARTY* BECAUSE IT IS FUCKING LIT, AND THEN I'LL DRIVE HOME AND WE CAN JUMP UP AND DOWN TO LIL PUMP IN THE CAR. MAYBE I'M IMMATURE BUT I WOULD DO ALL THAT SHIT DOLO AND SMACKED. IT'S JUST 20X BETTER WITH YOUR KIDS BECAUSE THEY ARE EXPERIENCING IT FOR THE FIRST TIME, SO NOT ONLY ARE YOU HAVING FUN AND RISKING PERSONAL INJURY, YOU ARE ALSO WITNESSING A MILESTONE. REMEMBER THAT AMAZEMENT AND WONDER AND "OH SHIT THEY REALLY DO HAVE INDOOR SKYDIVING, IT'S NOT A RUMOR" FEELING? WELL NOW YOU ARE WITNESSING THAT WHILE ON A 100MG EDIBLE AND THERE IS ABSOLUTELY NOTHING ON EARTH FUCKING WITH THAT. CHUCK E. CHEESE IS EVEN LIT. HAVE YOU EVER SEEN YOUR KID'S FACE WHEN YOU SINK A JUMPER ON THOSE ARCADE MACHINES FROM WAY BEYOND THE ACTUAL GAME? THE SHIT IS MAD EASY, BUT TO MERO JR I MIGHT AS WELL HAVE CLIMBED ON A DRAGON AND HAD IT EAT THE DUDE IN THE CHUCK E. CHEESE MOUSE SUIT. SHOUT-OUT TO THE CHUCK E. CHEESE ON ROUTE 17 . . . YOU DON'T *REALLY* HAVE TO SWIPE YOUR PLAYCARD TO GET INTO THE LITTLE TUNNEL-MAZE THING. JUST YANK THE DOOR OPEN. TECHNICALLY IT'S STEALING, BUT ALSO TECHNICALLY I DON'T GIVE A FUCK. IN A NUTSHELL, MY

CHILD-RAISING ADVICE IS VERY SIMPLE. YOU ARE RAISING A HUMAN SPONGE, SO BE CAREFUL WHAT YOU LET THEM ABSORB. OTHERWISE YOU'RE GONNA END UP WITH A DOODLEBOB ON YOUR HANDS. BUT AS MUCH AS YOU CAN, BE YOURSELF.

The wackest part of having kids is that having kids isn't fair at all. There are people who are complete pieces of shit who have kids with ease and don't take care of them, abuse them, or worse. Then you have people with so much love in their hearts who can't have kids because of medical conditions or other reasons. There's no rhyme or reason to this, so my apologies to anyone reading who is going through that.

Some people say "Don't have kids too late in life because you won't be able to play sports with them," but the flip side of that statement is, some of y'all are young as fuck and can't hoop and are teaching your kids terrible shooting form and subpar defense. Plus, have you ever played any sport against kids? *Everything* is impressive to them.

FOOTBALL IS WILD DANGEROUS, THE SHIT CAUSES PERMANENT BRAIN DAMAGE. IT'S MAD FUN TO WATCH, BUT WOULD I LET MY KIDS PLAY IT? PROBABLY NOT, WHICH IS SAD BECAUSE MERO IV IS LOOKING LIKE THE SECOND COMING OF TONY GONZALEZ AND HE'S ONLY THREE. THE WACK THING ABOUT PLAYING FOOTBALL AND ASPIRING TO HAVE A CAREER IN IT IS THAT YOU HAVE TO PLAY THAT SHIT FOR-E-VERRRRR TO EVEN BE ON ANYONE'S RADAR. THERE'S ALWAYS "MIRACULOUS UNDERDOG WALK-ONS" THAT MAKE ROSTERS BUT OTHER THAN THAT, IT'S NIGGAS THAT PLAYED HIGH SCHOOL AND COLLEGE BALL FOR YEARS. THIS AIN'T THE NBA WHERE AN 18-YEAR-OLD CAN POP OUT AND MAKE A GAZILLION DOLLARS WITHOUT PUTTING A TREMENDOUS TOLL ON THEIR BODY. IF IT WASN'T FOR THE IN-

FORMATION ABOUT CTE AND A LOT OF NFL PLAYERS DOING WILD SHIT DUE TO IT, I MIGHT HAVE BEEN LIKE "GO FOR IT" TO MY KIDS, BUT WHEN YOU WEIGH THE RISK/REWARD, IT'S NOT WORTH IT. WOULD I LOVE TO BE IN A ROOM FULL OF PARENTS AND HAVE MY KID DRAFTED FIRST BY THE NY GIANTS? OF COURSE I WOULD, WHAT AN INCREDIBLE RETURN ON MY INVESTMENT. THEN NOT ONLY CAN I FLEX MY OWN ACCOMPLISHMENTS BUT ALSO BRAG ABOUT MY KID WHO HAS THE MOST TOTAL YARDS & TDS OF ANY GIANTS ROOKIE TIGHT END EVER. I'D BE WILD ANNOYING LIKE "LOOK AT THIS BLOCK YO!! HE BODIED THIS DUDE!! HE PLAYS BOTH SIDES OF THE BALL!!" I WOULD STAND UP WITH HEATHER AND WE WOULD GROUP HUG AND CRY TEARS OF JOY AS HE ASCENDED TO THE PODIUM AND PUT THE HAT ON.

BUT I CAN'T WITH A CLEAR CONSCIENCE DO THAT SHIT BECAUSE I DON'T WANT MY KID HAVING SUICIDAL THOUGHTS OR DOING COMPLETELY FOUL OUT-OF-POCKET SHIT LIKE BEATING UP HIS GIRLFRIEND OR FIGHTING COPS. (ACTUALLY FIGHTING COPS COULD BE KINDA LIT. I WOULD NEED A LIL MORE CONTEXT.) SO HOPEFULLY WE CAN GET HIS HAND-EYE COORDINATION AND THAT BAT SPEED UP SO HE CAN PLAY 1B FOR THE YANKEES. THERE ARE SO MANY BETTER OPTIONS FOR KIDS. I KNOW HIGH SCHOOL AND COLLEGE FOOTBALL IN THE SOUTH AND SOUTHWEST IS BASICALLY RELIGION. BUT IF YOU'RE A 6'6" RECEIVER WITH SPEED, A VERTICAL, AND GOOD HANDS, WHY NOT PLAY BASKETBALL? DO COLLEGES HAVE SOCCER TEAMS? DO PEOPLE EVEN RECRUIT COLLEGE SOCCER PLAYERS? WHERE DO ALL THESE EURO DUDES COME FROM? LEMME ASK VICTOR, THAT NIGGA KNOWS LITERALLY EVERYTHING ABOUT SOCCER. HE KNOWS THE AMOUNT OF YAY MARADONA DID IN HIS LIFETIME DOWN TO THE MILLIGRAM.

VICTOR APPEARS IN THE FORM OF ZORDON

"They are bred in football academies owned by pro teams, the most famous being La Masia owned by Barcelona. If you think the NCAA is exploitative, peep La Masia."

WOW THAT'S WILD, B. I JUST YOUTUBED THEIR SHIT. THESE LIL MOTHERFUCKERS ARE LIKE 12! YO SOCCER MONEY IS GUARANTEED AND I GOT MONEY NOW. MERO JR IS GOIN TO LA MASIA. FUCK THAT, I DON'T EVEN CARE IF IT'S A SCHOOL, HE'S DORMING. I GUESS I'M LUCKY BECAUSE EVEN THOUGH MY KIDS LIKE TO PLAY FOOTBALL, WHEN I ASK THEM WHAT SPORT THEY WOULD PLAY PROFESSIONALLY, THEY SAY: BASKETBALL, BASKETBALL, AND BASEBALL, IN ORDER FROM OLDEST TO YOUNGEST. DON'T WORRY, I'M NOT SEXIST B . . . I ASKED MY DAUGHTER AND SHE JUST SAID, "GEH. GEH. DADADA!" AND I HAVE NO IDEA WHAT SPORT THAT IS.

Off the rip, every generation of kids is softer than the generation before it. Gotta remember that in the Dark Ages, people were getting married at age 7 and had to farm turnips or dig coal or kill dragons or something along those lines. Fast-forward to the industrial revolution and you had 14-year-old coal miners working a full shift and getting black lung. Yet my generation thinks we're tougher because we rode bikes without helmets. FOH.

But at the same time there are different threats now for kids. Not going to lie, I don't really keep up with, for lack of a better term, "kids' shit in the news," but I don't remember peanut allergies when I was in school. Maybe those allergies existed, and we just rubbed milk on kids going into anaphylactic shock. Also, and completely unrelatedly, whenever we did a lice check in school, the nurse at PS 83 would skip the black kids because "we couldn't get lice," which is a straight-up lie.

I grew up online but it was nothing like the social media of today. At most we had ENet, which was a bunch of nerds trading MP3s and such. Now kids have Instagram and Finstagram and TikTok and probably other platforms I haven't discovered yet. The cyberbullying seems terrible because, unlike real bullying, there's no one to punch in the face, which is one way to end the whole situation.

There's a notion that today's parents are too protective, but maybe that's for the best? There were SEVERAL instances in my childhood that definitely should've killed me, like the time I got a concussion by slamming my bike into a stopped car, and instead of telling anyone, I just went home and slept it off . . . smh. Looking back, I probably would've appreciated some parental supervision there (that head trauma statistically put me at a greater chance of ending up on Death Row, but I've dodged that).

I think kids being soft also depends on their neighborhood. I see kids in the Bronx all the time and they have the hardened faces of adults who've been through too much. There are news reports of kids in the Bronx as young as 12 committing wild crimes, but it's always been like that in the hood.

It's not all on the kids, either. I think parents, given social media and too much free time, are messing kids up. Take, for example, parents who don't vaccinate their kids. I want to say that's crazy, but crazy is an ableist slur now. Why would you let a YouTube video or a Facebook post make you say "Ayy fuck you Dr. Jonas Salk and your so-called polio vaccine. We'll take our chances with this almond milk, thank you very much."

Again, I'm not a parent, but some of this stuff seems like common sense.

Kids don't get beat as much nowadays, I hope. My parents used to beat my ass. I was the last one of four to still get beatings. Sometimes I see my father's thick black leather belt and reminisce about my days getting spanked and letting a single tear roll down my cheek like Denzel in *Glory*.

WHEN I WAS GROWING UP, MY PARENTS WHOOPED MY ASS. I'M NOT SURE IF SOME PEOPLE WOULD CLASSIFY IT AS ABUSE. ESPECIALLY NOW THAT I'M A PARENT, I SEE HOW TAXING KIDS CAN BE AND SOMETIMES YOUR OWN FRUSTRATION COMES OUT ON YOUR KID. IN MY HUMBLE OPINION, THAT'S WHEN YOU'RE ABUSING YOUR KID. I NEVER FELT LIKE MY PARENTS HIT ME BECAUSE THEY HAD A BAD DAY AT WORK OR THEY WERE FIGHTING OR SOMETHING. IF MY DAD WHOOPED MY ASS, I KNEW *I'D* FUCKED UP.

IN RETROSPECT, I'M GLAD I NEVER FELT ABUSED BECAUSE I REALIZE MY DAD WAS JUST RAISING ME THE WAY HE WAS RAISED. LIKE I SAID, THERE'S A MILLION DIFFERENT OPINIONS ON THIS. IF YOU WHACK YOUR KID BECAUSE THEY SMASHED A GLASS SERVING DISH AT TARGET AND THOUGHT IT WAS HILARIOUS, YOU AREN'T ABUSING YOUR KID (*SCREAMS* IN MY OPINION). YOU ARE SAYING: "HEY ASSHOLE. YOU JUST FUCKED UP A BUNCH OF PEOPLE'S DAY FOR A LAUGH. THE GUY THAT HAS TO CUT 20 MINS OFF HIS 45-MIN LUNCH BECAUSE NOW HE HAS TO GO PUT UP A CUTE LIL SIGN AND SWEEP UP THE GLASS? THE PERSON THAT MAY HAVE BEEN ON THEIR WAY TO BUY THAT SHIT AND YOU SMASHED THE LAST ONE? MOST IMPORTANTLY, YOU LITTLE DICK, YOU COULD HAVE HURT YOURSELF. A SHARD OF GLASS COULDA FLOWN IN YOUR EYE. ANYTHING COULDA HAPPENED. THIS WHACK IS TO REMIND YOU VERY QUICKLY THAT THAT WAS RECKLESS AND YOU SHOULD NEVER DO IT AGAIN."

I DON'T CONDONE PUNCHING OR HITTING YOUR KIDS ON SOME GROWN SHIT. THEY'RE KIDS. YOU CAN'T FUCKIN DECK

YOUR KID BECAUSE THEY LET THE TUB OVERFLOW. BUT IIINNN MMMYYYYY OOOPPPPIIIIIIINNNNIIIIIIOOOONNNN A SLAP ON THE GLUTES IS OKAY HERE. CUZ HAVING SOMEONE IN HERE TO FIX THE LEAK IS GONNA COST A COUPLE GRAND AND IT WASN'T AN ACCIDENT. SOME PEOPLE MIGHT SAY "MERO, YOU ABUSE YOUR KIDS." *SHRUGS* ASK THEM? THEY ARE WELL-ADJUSTED, WELL-ROUNDED KIDS, AT HOME. AT SCHOOL MERO JR GIVES ABSOLUTELY NO FUCKS ABOUT ANY KIND OF RULES OR STRUCTURE BUT WE'RE WORKING ON THAT. I MEAN IT SUCKS FOR TEACHERS TODAY, THEY CAN'T DO SHIT TO MAINTAIN ORDER.

I REMEMBER WHEN I WOULD GET IN TROUBLE IN 6TH GRADE THE DEAN WOULD MAKE ME WRITE SOME SENTENCE OF HIS CHOOSING A ZILLION TIMES AS PENANCE FOR KISSING NANCY RODRIGUEZ IN THE STAIRWELL WHEN I WAS "GOING TO THE BATHROOM" DURING 6TH PERIOD. IF YOU DID THAT AS A TEACHER OR DEAN NOW? YOU ARE GETTING FIRED SO FUCKIN FAST YOUR EYEBROWS WILL COME OFF AND THE *NEW YORK POST* WILL PUT YOU ON THE COVER DOING THE PERP WALK WITH SOME DICKISH HEADLINE LIKE "TORTURE TEACHER!"

SO YEAH, THAT SHIT BEGINS AND ENDS IN THE DOMICILE.

Having a terrible family is such trash. Your family is your first gang, crew, support group, and yet sometimes they don't live up to the title. Sometimes your family is the greatest stressor one can have in your life.

What are the signs your family is terrible? In my humble experience, if just the thought of being around your own family makes you sad or tired, they're probably terrible. Are they always hitting you up for money or demanding you take care of them? Do they not respect your boundaries? Do they leave inappropriate comments on your Instagram photo instead of texting you directly? (Okay, the last example might be a reach.)

My advice for dealing with a terrible family would be simply to cut them off. Block them on everything and wash your hands of them.

LOL YEAH RIGHT. If that seems even remotely possible for you, best of luck. The reality is, most of us can't just completely cut our family off for financial or emotional reasons. You're stuck with this family for life.

YOU SEE KIDS THROUGH A DIFFERENT LENS WHEN YOU YOURSELF ARE A PARENT. YOU EITHER WANT KIDS OR YOU'RE LIKE: "KIDS WILL RUIN MY LIFE." THERE'S NOBODY THAT'S JUST ON SOME AMBIVALENT SHIT ABOUT KIDS. THAT SAID, THERE ARE SOME SHITTY KIDS OUT THERE, BUT IT'S NOT THEIR FAULT, THAT'S LIKE BEING MAD AT A SPONGE YOU USE TO WIPE UP PISS FOR SMELLING LIKE PISS. KIDS BY AND LARGE ARE A PRODUCT OF WHO IS RAISING THEM. SO IF YOU THINK YOUR KIDS ARE DICKHEADS, YOU'RE PROBABLY A DICKHEAD, TOO. THE APPLE DON'T FALL FAR FROM THE TREE, MY GUY. I TOTALLY ACKNOWLEDGE WHEN MY KIDS ARE DICKS CUZ I ACKNOWLEDGE WHEN I'M BEING A DICK WITHIN 24 HOURS OR LESS. SOMETIMES I SLEEP FOR 8 HOURS, SOMETIMES I SLEEP LIKE DRAKE TOOK THE WHOLE XAN ON "SICKO MODE." YOU MIGHT HAVE TO WAIT FOR MY ACCOUNTABILITY, BUT THAT SHIT IS COMIN NEXT DAY AIR AT THE LATEST. SO IF YOU AS A PARENT ARE LIKE "MY KIDS ARE SHITTY," OF COURSE YOU'RE A BAD PARENT! LOL, FUCK YOU MEAN, MY PAL?? YOU MADE THIS KID! ITS DNA IS HALF YOURS, HALF YOUR PARTNER'S. MAYBE YOUR PARTNER IS A PIECE OF HUMAN GARBAGE. WHO KNOWS? YEAH FAM, YOU'RE A BAD PARENT. YOU SUPPOSED TO LOVE YOUR

KIDS UNCONDITIONALLY. THAT DOESN'T MEAN YOU GONNA LIKE THEM 24/7/365, IT JUST MEANS YOU LOVE THEM NO MATTER WHAT. I KNOW THAT SOUNDED REDUNDANT, BUT IF YOU GOT KIDS YOU UNDERSTAND WHAT I'M SAYING.

FOR THE UNINITIATED, THIS MEANS THAT IF YOUR KID WAS BUGGIN THE FUCK OUT ALL MORNING, THEN YOU AT THE PLAYGROUND, AND HE FALLS DOWN, YOU TINYSMILE EVILLY BEFORE RUNNING OVER LIKE "OH MY GOD, ARE YOU OKAY?!" OF COURSE HE'S FINE, HE FELL INTO A PILE OF DICED TIRES, BUT HE'S SHOOK AND IT'S WEIRDLY SATISFYING. AT YOUR CORE, THOUGH, YOU ARE LEGITIMATELY CONCERNED, AND IF YOUR CHILD WAS SERIOUSLY INJURED YOU WOULD BE FRANTICALLY TRYING TO HELP THEM. THIS IS TANGENTIAL BUT IF YOU RESENT YOUR KIDS AND YOU DON'T GOT A THERAPIST BUT YOU GOT HEALTH INSURANCE OR ARE RICH, DEFINITELY GET ONE. IT'S GOOD TO SAY SHIT TO A PROFESSIONAL WHOSE STRATEGIES FOR LIVIN YOU CAN IMPLEMENT FOR YOUR BETTERMENT. OH SHIT, THAT RHYMED. LOL WOW I JUST READ THAT BACK AND IT JUST CAME OUT IN A JERU THE DAMAJA VOICE. SO YEAH, IF BY SHITTY YOU MEAN LIKE "UGH GET THESE KIDS OUTTA HERE. I'M ABOUT TO SEND THEM TO LIVE WITH MY MOM / PUT EM ALL IN A CAR AND DRIVE IT INTO A LAKE AND SAY A RANDOM BLACK MAN DID IT," YES, YOU ARE A BAD PARENT.

NOW, ON THE OTHER HAND, IF BY SHITTY YOU MEAN YOUR KIDS ARE SOMETIMES DICKHEADS BUT FOR THE MOST PART ARE WELL-ADJUSTED MEMBERS OF SOCIETY, THEN NO, YOU ARE NOT A BAD PARENT. AS A MATTER OF FACT, YOU'RE AN ABOVE-AVERAGE PARENT FOR RECOGNIZING AND ADMITTING THAT NOBODY IS PERFECT, AND THAT INCLUDES THE SEED Y'ALL PUT IN THE BUSH FOR LIFE. YOU LOVE THEM EVEN WHEN YOU DON'T LIKE THEM AND YOU CAN'T PICTURE NOT BEING WITH THEM. PAT YOURSELF ON THE BACK, BECAUSE YOU ARE

INVESTED IN YOUR KIDS. THAT'S DOPE BECAUSE A LOT OF PEOPLE DON'T GIVE A FUCK ABOUT THEY KIDS.

YET YOU NEVER REALLY HEAR OF ANYBODY BEING MAD AT A PUPPY FOR PEEING ON THE FLOOR. IT'S USUALLY LIKE "AWWWW!! LIL BOPPY POO DID WEEWEES?" MEANWHILE, IF YOUR POTTY-TRAINING HUMAN CHILD PEES ON THE FLOOR, IT'S LIKE "EWWW UGH OH MY GODDDD UGHHHH I CAN'T STAND YOU!!!!"

LISTEN MAN, I'M FIRST GENERATION. WE THINK DIFFERENTLY ABOUT ANIMALS AND I'M NOT ABOUT ANIMAL CRUELTY, BUT I'M ALSO, LIKE, ON THE MIKE FRANCESA SIDE OF THE HARAMBE SITUATION (GOOGLE IT, I'VE SECRETLY REFERENCED IT TWICE ALREADY, FOR CRYING OUT LOUD). NOW DON'T GET ME WRONG, IF YOU'RE A SHITBAG BIG-GAME HUNTER THAT IS GONNA EVISCERATE AN ANIMAL FOR ITS LEFT TESTICLE AND LEAVE IT TO DIE A MISERABLE DEATH, YOU'RE A FUCKING WORM. AND IF YOU GET FATALLY GORED OR MAULED, YOU WERE ASKIN FOR IT. BUT IT AMAZES ME THAT AMERICAN CULTURE VALUES THE LIVES OF ANIMALS OVER HUMANS AND IT'S *NOT EVEN CLOSE.* I'VE POSED THIS SAME THEORY MAD TIMES AND A LOT OF THE RESPONSES I GET ARE "WELL, PEOPLE ARE SHITTY! DOGS ARE NEVER SHITTY!" ARE YOU KIDDING? THAT'S YOUR LOGIC? THAT AN ANIMAL THAT HAS A BRAIN WITH 3 SETTINGS IS COMPARABLE TO A HUMAN BEING WITH A COMPLEX MIND AND THE ABILITY TO REASON? I'M SURE IF YOUR GERMAN SHEPHERD COULD REASON/TALK, IT WOULD CALL THE COPS ON ME FOR WALKING INTO RITA'S ITALIAN ICE AND FROZEN CUSTARD WITH A 36" CHAIN ON LISTENING TO FRENCH MONTANA. IF YOU DID A SOCIAL EXPERIMENT WHERE YOU POSTED A COUPLE FUNDRAISERS, ONE FOR KIDS AND ONE FOR STRAY DOGS, THE ONE FOR STRAY DOGS IS WINNING EVERY TIME, ESPECIALLY IF YOU CAN SEE THE DOG'S RIBS OR IF IT GOT A MISS-

ING LEG. IF YOU WANT TO GET GUNS UNDER CONTROL IN THIS COUNTRY, SHOOT UP A KENNEL. DON'T SHOOT A SINGLE HUMAN. MATTER OF FACT, CLEAR OUT ALL HUMANS AND THEN JUST GO HAMMER AND CLAP EVERY DOG AND CAT IN THERE. 40 SCHOOL SHOOTINGS A MONTH, NO GUN CONTROL. BUT SHOOT UP A BUILDING FULL OF ABANDONED GOLDEN RETRIEVERS AND WATCH HOW FAST THE UNITED STATES OF TRUMPISTAN TURNS INTO WHATEVER COUNTRY IT IS WHERE GUNS ARE COMPLETELY ILLEGAL. DOES MIKE VICK EVEN PLAY FOOTBALL ANYMORE? WHITE WOMEN OVER 40 *STILL* HATE HIM WITH A BURNING PASSION THAT IS UN-FUCKING-MATCHED BECAUSE OF THE DOGFIGHTING SHIT. LITERALLY OVER A DECADE LATER B. THEM DOGS WOULDA BEEN DEAD BY NOW ANYWAY. DOGS GOT LIKE 10-YEAR LIFE SPANS. I LOVE MY DOG, SHE'S COOL, BUT I'M NOT AN IDIOT. I KNOW SHE'S HERE MAD TEMPORARILY, AND IF A CAR WERE HURTLING TOWARD HER AND MERO JR AND I CAN ONLY SAVE ONE, BROWNIE GETTIN BAKED, SORRY MA. I LOVE YOU DEARLY, BUT IN DOG YEARS YOU ARE IN YOUR TWILIGHT AND HAVE LIVED A BEAUTIFUL LONG LIFE FULL OF LEISURELY WALKS AND BARKING AT DOGS 80X YOUR SIZE. ALSO ALL DOGS GO TO HEAVEN.

Damn that was dark af but, again, it's all correct.

I GOT WAY OFF TOPIC BUT I'M STILL SMACKED AND PASSIONATE AND THIS IS WHAT YOU LOVE ABOUT MFS FORMAT (MERO FUCKING SMACKED) . . . I'M VERY TOUCHED BY THE NUMBER OF PEOPLE THAT READ MY OLD "I MAKE NO MONEY, I'M FURIOUS AT THE WORLD, AND I DON'T CARE" STUFF. YOU ARE APPRECIATED. BUT TO GET THIS TRAIN BACK ON TRACK, I'M GONNA WRAP THIS SHIT BY SAYING MAYBE "SHITTY" IS THE WRONG WORD TO DESCRIBE KIDS. BOTTOM LINE: IF YOU RESENT YOUR

KIDS CONSISTENTLY FOR REASONS THAT HAVE NOTHING TO DO WITH THE ACTUAL CHILD BEYOND THEM EXPLORING THE WORLD AND OCCASIONALLY GETTING IN TROUBLE, YOU'RE A BAD PARENT. YES, I AM PASSING JUDGMENT. ASK ME IF I GIVE A FUCK. "MERO, DO YOU GIVE A FUCK?" NO I DO NOT. AND IF THESE LITTLE SNIPPETS OF MY HOME LIFE DON'T WARM YOUR MISERABLE COLD HEART, I DON'T WANT TO BE ANYWHERE NEAR YOU, BECAUSE YOU ARE A BLACK HOLE OF ANGUISH AND I DON'T NEED THAT TYPE OF ENERGY IN MY LIFE! *SAGES ROOM*

CHAPTER 4

This chapter is about sports, and the beauty of having me and Mero discuss sports is that we pretty much suck at all of them. But it's not fair—our lack of athletic ability comes from our Bronx childhoods. For example: Because of budget cuts, some of my schools literally didn't have sports teams. So instead of going to gym, we'd cut class and take the train into the city and hang out in Manhattan because that's what you'd do, too, don't judge. Also, I think tearing your ACL is one of the most avoidable injuries in life, and the surest way to avoid said injury is to *watch* sports, not *play* them. To be fair, I have a really nice TV and speaker system, and an Instant Pot that makes very fire-hot wings, so I'm biased. But yeah, the Bodega Boys are not world-class athletes unless you count porn references and blunt rolling as Olympic events, in which case you're looking at two Usain Bolts.

I do love watching sports, though, which is something you have to develop as a Knicks fan. There's an art and more than a bit of sadism in looking forward to watching a game you have no chance of winning. I'll take it even further. I purchase Knicks tickets all the time just to be in Madison Square Garden. SAD! Naturally, we have to come up with ways to keep sports entertaining, so I live-tweet Knick losses to keep my fellow fans from committing seppuku.

THEN THERE'S BETTING ON SPORTS, WHICH IS LIT AND MAKES EVEN MEANINGLESS GAMES EXCITING. YOU KNOW WHEN COLLEGE BOWL SEASON ROLLS AROUND AND YOU DON'T KNOW SHIT ABOUT THE MISSOURI STATE TECH HAYSTACKS TAKING ON THE NORTH DAKOTA COLLEGE COW TIPPERS BUT THEY ARE GOING HEAD TO FUCKIN HEAD TO SEE WHO WILL WIN THE DUNKIN' DONUTS COFFEE COOLATA BOWL AND YOU KNOW THE SPREAD IS 45.5 PTS FOR SOME REASON AND YOU ARE LIKE FUCK IT THERE'S NO WAY THE FIGHTIN TIPPERS LOSE BY 46 PTS? THESE ARE BOTH TEAMS I'VE NEVER HEARD OF IN MY LIFE THROWING A TOYS R US (RIP MY NIGGA TOYS R US) FOOTBALL, BECAUSE I SWEAR A COLLEGE FOOTBALL LOOKS WAAAAYYYY BIGGER THAN AN NFL FOOTBALL . . .

ANYWAY, YOU LOOK AT THAT SPREAD AND IT'S VERY ENTICING.

I WILL, HOWEVER, PREFACE THE RESTA THIS SHIT BY SAYING: IF YOU HAVE A GAMBLING ADDICTION, IT IS NO LAUGHING MATTER. AND I SAY THAT AS SOMEONE WHO HAS WATCHED *SOPRANOS* MAD TIMES. REMEMBER THE SPORTS STORE DUDE THAT LOST HIS PROVERBIAL SHIRT AND HIS LITERAL STORE PLAYIN CARDS? HE WAS DEFINITELY A DG—A DEGENERATE GAMBLER.

YOU GOT AN UNCLE OR COUSIN OR SOME SHIT WHO SAYS "YO I'LL BET YOU $5 THIS SHIT GOES IN" AND EXPECTS PAYMENT UPON THE HEINEKEN BOTTLE GOING IN THE TRASH FROM 3'

AWAY, AND THEY DO IT LITERALLY ALL THE TIME FOR EVERYTHING? THEY ARE A DG.

IF YOU WALK INTO YOUR LIVING ROOM AND YOUR FRIEND'S HANDS ARE ON HIS SWEATY HEAD WATCHING THE LAST SECONDS OF A DIVISION 3 WOMEN'S VOLLEYBALL PRESEASON SCRIMMAGE STANDING LIKE HE'S ABOUT TO SHIT IN HIS PANTS, HE'S A DG. THAT DESCRIPTION IS VERY VIVID BECAUSE I ONCE HAD A FRIEND CALL HIS BOOKIE AND ASK FOR A LINE ON A RANDOM PENN STATE WOMEN'S VOLLEYBALL GAME. I'M NOT KIDDING AT ALL. ALSO IMA TAKE A LEFT LIKE I'M AMBI DEX, GAMBLING ON SPORTS IS LEGAL IN DOMINICAN REPUBLIC, WHICH IS HILARIOUS BECAUSE THERE'S ALWAYS A DUDE AT EVERY "BANCA" THAT DOESN'T SPEAK A LICK OF ENGLISH BUT CAN TELL YOU HOW MANY POINTS SOME RANDOM SLOVAKIAN DUDE ON THE MINNESOTA WILD HAS FOR THE SEASON WITHOUT GOOGLING IT.

Mero lives in New Jersey now, so anything he says about sports betting does NOT apply to me. I mean, I'd have to gamble illegally, and that would involve Italian guys in Scarsdale, NY, and maybe meeting them in Metro-North parking lots after dark, which is something I'd never get involved in, even if I was scratching my neck because I needed something, *anything,* to gamble on, and the only thing on was the Division 3 women's volleyball team at my beloved college. MOUNT SAINT VINCENT STAND UP!

But if I could, I'd totally bet on my Knicks because the lines for Knicks games have to be something like "Bet $5 dollars and win $5,000."

I GUESS THIS IS WHERE I TELL YOU ABOUT SPORTS BETTING AND YOUR ROAD TO RUIN.

I'VE ENLISTED THE HELP OF MY FRIENDS: MY MAN STACKS AKA SLIME STACKAVELI, AND MY MAN JIMMY AKA RICAN HAVOC, WHO DEFINITELY HAVE ABSOLUTELY NOTHING TO DO WITH GAMBLING WHATSOEVER. AT ALL.

STACKS: I'll never forget the time I received a phone call to be in some focus group shit for $150 while I was in the middle of putting my bets in and told the guy, "Fuck outta here, I'm about to crack my bookie's cookie!!" I felt it. I immediately hung up and got back to business. Sure enough, I cracked it big. When it comes to muthafuckas that get cracked (lose a bet), they pay juice (interest and a payment) each week until they settle their debt. Never had an issue, and if so, "Big Tony" was always a phone call away. There's always a "Big Tony."

RICAN: I took a parlay, which means I bet a bunch of different shit all together. If they all hit, I cracked it. Low stakes, high reward . . . depending on how many underdogs you got in your parlay. Parlays are a double-edged sword: A win will definitely gas you into thinking you found the perfect combination of women's college soccer, NBA basketball, and the Slovakian hockey league. Me? I took a seven-team parlay with FL/MLB/College Football/NHL for $50 that paid out 20 racks. One of my teams was losing by 21 in the 4th quarter so I went to bed like fuck it, I got work tomorrow, only to wake up to my phone exploding with my boy telling me I'm about to win 20 racks. So I get up, check the parlay, and see that the team that was down 21 came back and covered. The only game left was Padres/Dodgers. Ninth inning. TWO OUTS. Padres up by FOUR RUNS. All I needed was for the Padres to win, and I was sure they were gonna. THEN THESE DODGERS MOTHERFUCKERS HIT 4 HOMERS IN A FUCKING ROW TO FORCE EXTRA INNINGS!!! So in the bottom of the 10th, the Padres go up 10-9, sigh of relief. Two outs AGAIN and the pitcher walks the next batter, so now there's a man on first with two outs. THEN NOMAR GARCIAPARRA DECIDED TO SHIT ON MY DREAMS and hit a two-run walk-off. I was so sick to my stomach that I swore I'd never gamble again.

YOU CAN BET MONEYLINE IF THE KNICKS ARE PLAYING THE LAKERS AND YOU THINK LEBRON IS GONNA STEP ON KEVIN KNOX'S STERNUM ON THE WAY TO A DUNK. YOU BET MONEYLINE THERE BECAUSE YOU THINK, "THESE NIGGAS ARE WINNING, NO QUESTION." BUT . . . THIS BET IS BORING. BETTING THE SPREAD IS MORE FUN BECAUSE EVEN IF THE TEAM THAT WAS EXPECTED TO WI—"MERO, WHAT'S BETTING THE SPREAD?" FAM, DON'T YOU HAVE GOOGLE? I'M KIDDING, YOU PAID HARD-EARNED MONEY FOR THIS KNOWLEDGE BIBLE SO I'M GONNA EXPLAIN HOW BETTING THE SPREAD IS MORE EXHILARATING AND DANGEROUS AND SOUL-CRUSHING.

IF YOU ARE LOOKING AT A SPREAD (ASK SIRI. I'M SERIOUS, CHIRP SIRI. THEN BE LIKE, WHAT'S THE SPREAD ON THE YANKEES GAME, SHE'LL TELL YOU) AND YOU'RE LIKE YO, THERE IS *NO WAY* THE WARRIORS ARE GONNA COME INTO THE GARDEN AND BEAT THE KNICKS BY 20.5 POINTS!! NO FUCKIN WAY!! SPLASH BROTHERS MY DICK B!!" AND AS YOU'RE WALKING OUT OF THE ARENA WITH YOUR HAT IN YOUR HAND AFTER A 26-POINT BLOWOUT, YOU THINK ABOUT THE $500 YOU PUT ON THE KNICKS JUST TO COVER! JUST COVER! THAT WHOLE FUCKIN GAME YOU WERE THINKING: *DON'T GET BLOWN OUT AT HOME, YOU'VE BEEN PLAYING GREAT AT HOME, I KNOW IT'S THE WARRIORS, BUT MAKE IT INTERESTING, LOSE BY LIKE 5 OR 2. OR SOMETHING. PLEASE*. NOPE, SMOKED AT HOME, AND NOW YOUR LIGHTS ARE GETTING TURNED OFF BECAUSE YOU THOUGHT THAT SPREAD WAS A LOCK. NOW YOU'RE SOBBING BY CANDLELIGHT. SHIT IS BLEAK.

OR THE OPPOSITE HAPPENS AND JULIUS FUCKIN RANDLE GOES FOR 40 WITH 25 REBOUNDS AND 6 BLOCKS IN A RIDICULOUS CAREER PERFORMANCE. RJ GETS RED HOT, GETS THE GREEN LIGHT FROM FIZ, GOES 10-12 FROM 3, ENDS UP WITH 42 AND 8 ASSISTS. KEVIN KNOX GOES FUCKIN BONKERS AND

DUNKS ON STEPH 8 TIMES. THEY FUCK AROUND AND WIN BY 17 AND YOU IMMEJUTLY BUY A ZIP OF ZKITTLEZ ON CREDIT.

THEREIN LIES THE DICHOTOMY B. WHEN YOU CRACK IT YOU FEEL INVINCIBLE, ESPECIALLY IF YOU HIT A COUPLE OF PARLAYS IN A ROW. YOU LIGHTIN NIGGAS UP, BUYING J'S, ALL THAT. THEN YOU GO ON THE WILD LOSING STREAK AND YOU'RE LOOKING UP THE BLUE BOOK VALUE OF A '99 CAMRY. I'M ALLEGEDLY NOT TELLIN YOU NOT TO ALLEGEDLY GAMBLE. I'M JUST TELLIN YOU THERE ALLEGEDLY ARE HIGHS AND LOWS. ALLEGEDLY.

Sports gambling always ends badly. Always. Are you listening to me? ALWAYS. You were up for a little while, started throwing money everywhere, and then you take an L. So you put some more cash up to make up what you lost . . . and you lose again. Then you're stressed so you think, *I gotta clear my head and relax*. You turn on the TV and what's on? Sports. And there you go, all over again. Why aren't you listening to me? I told you to listen, stupid. The highs and lows of fandom should be enough on their own.

I HAVE TWO FAVORITE SPORTS MOMENTS. THE FIRST WAS A SERIES OF MOMENTS AND THE OTHER IS A SINGULAR MOMENT. BOTH WERE IN THE '90S BECAUSE I JUST MADE THE CUTOFF FOR BEING A . . . MILLENNIAAAAALLLLL.

PLAYS THAT ROBBIE WILLIAMS SONG

THE FIRST WAS THE '96 YANKEES WORLD SERIES, BECAUSE I VIVIDLY REMEMBER THAT TURNING ME FROM A CASUAL YANKEE FAN INTO A "27 RINGS, BRO!!" YANKEES FAN. THEY HADN'T WON SHIT IN YEARS AND GENERALLY WERE NOT GOOD. 1996 WAS DEREK JETER'S ROOKIE YEAR, AND THAT MUTHAFUCKA WAS CAPTIVATING. HE WAS THE COOLEST BASEBALL PLAYER I

HAD SEEN SINCE KEN GRIFFEY JR. BEING COOL IS HARD TO DO AS A YANKEE BECAUSE THEY MAKE YOU SHAVE, YOUR NAME ISN'T ON THE JERSEY, AND TYPICALLY "THE YANKEES" ARE BIGGER THAN "THE PLAYER." BUT JEETS WAS SPECIAL. MY MAN HAD THIS ENIGMATIC SWAG THAT HE STILL CARRIES TO THIS DAY EVEN THOUGH HE NOW LOOKS LIKE A DIABETIC UNCLE. GREATEST YANKEE OF ALL TIME, YEAH I SAID IT, DON'T EVER DISRESPECT THE BEAUTIFUL BIRACIAL ANGEL THAT IS "THE CAPTAIN."

THE YANKEES LOST THE FIRST TWO GAMES AT HOME TO THE BRAVES, AND I STILL REMEMBER TURNING MY TV OFF AFTER THE FINAL OUT OF GAME 2 LIKE, "FUCK. THE BRAVES ARE REALLY GOOD." HINDSIGHT IS 20/20 THOUGH, BECAUSE I WATCH VIDEO OF THOSE FIRST TWO GAMES NOW AND IT'S LIKE THAT WAYANS BROS MOVIE WHERE MARLON DIES AND BECOMES A GHOST WHO HELPS HIS TEAM WIN OR SOME SHIT LIKE THAT. I HAVE NO IDEA HOW YOU TURN THAT PREMISE INTO A 90-MINUTE FEATURE FILM, BUT THEY DID THAT SHIT. ANDY PETTITTE THE YOUNG ACE GETS FUCKIN INEXPLICABLY CREMATED IN THE FIRST GAME, WADE BOGGS'S THIGH GETS IMPALED BY A BROKEN BAT WHILE MAKING A THROW TO FIRST THAT LED TO THE RUNNER BEING SAFE. DARRYL STRAWBERRY HADN'T FOUND GOD YET AND WAS THROWING THE BALL TO HOME PLATE WITH THE ACCURACY OF THE 2008 RAMBO REBOOT FINAL SCENE WHERE HE'S JUST BUCKING WILD SHOTS ALL BRAZY ON THE BACK OF THE PICKUP TRUCK WITH THE .50-CAL. MARIANO DUNCAN, ONE OF MY FAVORITE YANKEES OF ALL TIME, BOOTED A DOUBLE-PLAY BALL AND WAS GENERALLY WACK. I TOTALLY FORGOT TIM RAINES GOT HIT IN THE BALLS BY JAVY LÓPEZ'S CATCHER'S MASK WHEN LÓPEZ WENT TO CATCH A POP FOUL. SO YEAH, THE YANKEES GET SMOKED AT HOME IN GAME 1. IT WASN'T JUST BECAUSE THE BRAVES WERE SUPER

TALENTED OFFENSIVELY, THE YANKEES WERE JUST STINKIN UP THE JOINT OD. GAME 2, SAME SHIT.

THEN THEY GO DOWN TO ATLANTA AND I'M WATCHING LIKE "DAMN. IF THEY LOSE THIS GAME IN ATLANTA, IT'S A FUCKIN WRAP." BUT THEY DIDN'T. DAVID CONE PITCHED A FUCKIN GEM AND BERNIE WILLIAMS WASN'T PLAYING PUERTO RICAN JAZZ GUITAR FULL-TIME YET BUT HE *WAS* HITTING LIKE HE WAS USING ONE AS A BAT. OD CLUTCH. YANKEES CRACKED THE SHIT OPEN IN ATLANTA AND I KNEW AFTER GAME 5 THE YANKEES WERE GONNA WIN THE WORLD SERIES. IT WAS LIKE A FUCKIN OVERSCRIPTED MOVIE, IT WAS SO HAM-FISTED. I REMEMBER SITTING DOWN FOR GAME 6 WITH A BAG OF DORITOS I HAD GOTTEN FROM THE BODEGA AND A TROPICAL FANTASY ORANGE SODA. I'LL NEVER FORGET THE AIR, THE SOUNDS, EVERYTHING FROM THAT NIGHT. IT FEELS WILD CORNY SAYING IT OUT LOUD, BUT MY DAD HAD GONE TO BED EARLY BECAUSE HE HAD TO WORK EARLY. I WAS ALONE IN MY LIVING ROOM WATCHING ON A 27" ZENITH (BELIEVE IT) WHEN CHARLIE HAYES CAUGHT THAT POP-UP, HEARING "THE YANKEES ARE CHAMPIONS OF BASEBALL!" AND WATCHING THE DOGPILE ON THE PITCHER'S MOUND. WADE BOGGS RIDING A FUCKING HORSE AROUND THE STADIUM. THE HORNS HONKING OUTSIDE THE MOMENT CHARLIE SECURED THE BALL, GUNSHOTS, ALL THAT SHIT. IT WAS PURE HAPPINESS FOR A LITTLE KID FROM THE BRONX.

I'm about to tell you the tale of my favorite sports moment and I ask you to bear with me because I'm probably going to tear up while writing it.

Now . . . key to this story is the date: February 2, 2009. I attended a Knicks game with my older sister. It was the Knicks vs. the Lakers and I remember a scalper offering us $200 for each ticket, which we seriously considered as we stood there. However, because we're Knicks fans (till death!), we went into the game.

BUT. That night, one Kobe Bean Bryant (R.I.P.) turned my beloved MSG into a literal hell. The night started with the crowd cheering for the Lakers during the opening players announcement. And there was nothing weird about that because it's the Lakers and they have lots of fans in NYC, and also the Knicks stunk that season (they finished 29-53). But the first warning sign that the night was going to suck was the crowd chanting "MVP" anytime Kobe touched the ball. We real Knicks fans booed, but every time Kobe hit a shot the chants got louder.

Kobe must have heard those chants because he WENT OFF. I sat there in a Latrell Sprewell jersey and watched as Kobe dropped 61 points on my beloved Knickerbockers. 61 POINTS. He hit threes, smashed wild dunks, he even hit a couple of half-court shots because why the fuck not. It was devastating. We watched as he set the Madison Square Garden record for the most points scored. I saw it in person and will always remember that night. It's the most disrespected I've ever felt as a Knicks fan, which is saying a lot. It was also an honor and a blessing to see Kobe do this. RIP to the GOAT.

So fast-forward to the good night of January 24, 2014. Times had changed and, shouts to my homegirl Jean, I had damn near floor seats. Literally sitting close enough to the court where the players could hear everything I yelled. We had pregamed a little so I had a little buzz going as I got to the seats, but I knew the feeling I was feeling wasn't just that buzz . . . this night was going to be special. I was amped because the Knicks where playing the Bobcats and I'd get to see my boy (not really my boy, I hadn't met him yet) Kemba Walker from the BX drop some points at the same arena where he'd once led UConn to victory in the NCAA.

Anyway, they announced Kemba wouldn't be playing that night so I was bummed, but going to Knicks games is one of my life's greatest joys, so I was going to have a great time regardless. No Kobes in sight.

Knicks legend CARMELO ANTHONY DA GAWD must've agreed it was gonna be a good night because he launched his first shot, boom, sinks it. Then his next shot. Then another. I stood up and said, "HE'S GOING FOR THE SCORING RECORD!" I felt it. Tonight was the night.

Melo went off. Hitting threes, set shots, everything. With each shot I stood up and yelled louder and louder. Eventually the usher came over and told me to calm down or I'd be thrown out (shout-out to Keith, he's the usher, and I've been coming to so many games that he knows me by now and he's extremely excited that I'm on TV). I calmed down so as not to be removed from the Mecca.

Melo knew he had to drop at least 61 to tie the record, but Melo said eff that. My man dropped 62 points and the Garden absolutely exploded. And the worst part is they immediately took him out. Melo and I and every other Knicks fan knew that he should've run his points up to like 85 to assure that no non-Knick would ever break it. But that night was amazing. The Knicks felt like winners. We all had that moment. Sadly, that would go down as Melo's greatest Knicks moment. But I was there and that night lives in me forever.

I left the Garden all woozy and went back to my crib and made sweet sweet record-breaking love to my then-girlfriend. And to pay homage to Melo I wore a compression sleeve and hand band while doing so.

Maybe. I can't remember if that last part happened or if it just seems like it should have.

MY OTHER FAVORITE SPORTS MOMENT WAS WILD BECAUSE IT LITERALLY WAS NOT SUPPOSED TO HAPPEN. THE '98-'99 KNICKS WERE AN 8TH SEED GOING INTO THE PLAY-OFFS. THEY KNOCKED OFF #1 SEED MIAMI EN ROUTE TO THE FINALS WHERE THEY GOT FUCKIN ANNIHILATED BY THE SPURS. BUT THE EASTERN CONFERENCE FINALS CONTAINED ONE MOMENT I WILL REMEMBER FOREVER: LARRY JOHNSON'S 4-PT PLAY TO GIVE THE KNICKS A 1-POINT LEAD AGAINST THE HOE-ASS PACERS. I LOVED THAT KNICKS TEAM AND FELT TERRIBLE FOR PAT EWING BECAUSE HE WAS ON THE BENCH IN A VERY '90S SUIT. I HAVE NEVER BEEN SO INTENSELY FOCUSED ON THE LAST MINUTE OF A BASKETBALL GAME IN MY LIFE. I WAS WATCHING THE SHIT OUT OF IT. WHEN LARRY HIT THAT 3 AND I HEARD THE WHISTLE BLOW AND THE ARENA EXPLODE LIKE SPAGHETTI SAUCE IN A MICROWAVE, I LITERALLY LEAPED OFF MY PARENTS' BED (THEY HAD THE CABLE BOX IN THEIR ROOM AT THAT TIME), HIT MY HEAD ON THE CEILING, AND BIT MY TONGUE, BUT ASK ME IF I GAVE A SHIT? I DID NOT. THE KNICKS HAD DONE THE IMPOSSIBLE. I THINK I BOOSTED A LARRY JOHNSON REPLICA JERSEY AT MODELL'S THE NEXT DAY OR SOME SHIT. *THROWS L UP* I'M SERIOUS, LOOK THIS SHIT UP ON YOUTUBE, IT'S ELECTRIC. EVERYBODY REMEMBERS LARRY FROM THE HORNETS BUT LJ IS ONE OF MY FAVORITE KNICKS OF ALL TIME, BECAUSE OF THIS PLAY AND BECAUSE HE HAD A GOLD TOOTH.

The worst sports moment I've ever had is surprising, since I'm a lifelong Knicks fan and so you'd probably think it would be about them. WRONG. The Knicks haven't been able to hurt me since Game 7 of the NBA Finals in 1994 when they broke the heart of Little Desus by losing to the Houston Rockets. I cried that night because, even then, I knew I'd probably never see them in the Finals again in my life. So now some meaningless

Knicks blowouts on a Tuesday night can't hurt. It's like being stabbed in the same place for years. It's all scar tissue now.

That said, what really hurts, and still hurts to this day, is the Yankees epic choke against the hated ~~racist~~ Boston Red Sox. I can't put into words the pain I experienced that week but it's all still very real. Let me attempt to paint a picture.

Desus in 2004 was a super Yankees fan, a super baseball fan. I'd wake up every morning and check out River Ave Blues and Lohud to find out updates about my Yankees and fight with people in the comments. My next stop would be *Boston Dirt Dogs*, a Red Sox blog where I'd read scouting reports and game recaps because I didn't have NESN and couldn't watch their games. I was a baseball nerd and I was obsessed with the rivalry. This was our year and I knew it. I felt it.

Play-off baseball is completely different from regular-season baseball. For a regular-season game, you can pull up to any bar wearing any outfit and just enjoy it. The play-offs require planning; you have to wear your lucky shirt with your lucky hat and get the perfect bullshit juju aligned to help your team win. I had my fresh Aaron Boone T-shirt with the matching brand-new fitted. I was ready.

Now, I wasn't about to watch Game 6 of a critical series against our division rivals at home like some sort of loser (this would change when I became washed recently). So my first mission was to find a venue that would be Yankees-fan friendly. Here's where the story gets sad and washed. I just, right now, googled the name of the bar where I watched this series and there's no trace of it ever existing (it was underneath/next door to a hotel on 3rd Avenue across the street from that terrible bar The Continental).

What adds an extra layer of sadness to this story is that I wandered all day through NYC looking for the perfect viewing bar. This particular bar had windows that opened to the street and Yankees banners flying. I felt the vibe and it was perfect for winning. They even had a chalkboard that read "LET'S GO YANKS." I had found my place and my people.

Mind you, I still lived on East 233rd in the Bronx at the time but was going to be in the city anyway before game time each game, so this was my Yankees bar for that whole series. When the games were over, I'd have an hour or more ride home on the subway, which is not fun if you're sober and even worse if you're shitfaced. But my Yankees had been killing it all season so I wasn't worried about any of that.

I took the series so seriously that I refused to let my girlfriend at the time watch with me because I needed total concentration. My method for watching was one beer per inning with a glass of water in between half innings, while checking my BlackBerry(!!!) for updates. I'd picked a seat with perfect reception and room to pace around when the bases were loaded or any other suspenseful moments in the game. I was ready for anything.

In the beginning, the series was not that big a deal. The Yankees won the first two games, then took Game 3 19–8, and we were in that bar taking shots and talking cash money shit to Boston fans. I mean just absolutely roasting them, probably the happiest moment in my life. Imagine not only smacking the living shit out of your division rivals but you're also about to sweep them. I actually considered buying a broom and bringing it to Game 4 (which is corny, but I was pretty corny back then).

Then the Red Sox won Game 4, but I was okay with it. Yeah, we didn't get the sweep but Game 5 is ours! Can't wait! World Series here we come! And then the Red Sox won Game 5 and the energy shifted in the bar. Red Sox fans who had never had any kind of backbone were suddenly talking shit in their quiet

Red Sox way. Back then, we Yankees fans had the 1918 chant, which was a reference to the last time the Sox had won the World Series. We'd been chanting it for this entire series, but after Game 5, the chants just weren't as boisterous.

It was okay, though. I *knew* my Yankees had this. I still felt it. I had an offer to watch Game 6 somewhere else and immediately rejected the offer. If the Yankees had won games 1–3 because I was at that bar, they'd need me back there for this game. Of course this logic makes absolutely no sense because I was also there for the losing games, but whatever. I got on the train and went to my appointed position at the bar.

Not only did the Yankees lose Game 6, we lost to Curtis Motherfucking Schilling and his bullshit bloody sock (it was a ketchup packet, fight me you coward). I remember ESPN or Fox or whoever saying it was basically impossible for any team to come back from being down 3–0 in the series, and they kept harping on this stat, and even now I feel the fucking bile rising in my throat as I'm typing this.

So there we were. Game 7. No way the Yankees blow this, right? Right? I kept asking myself that question all day long. I don't remember most of the morning. I was floating around in a fog like someone in a tracking shot for a Spike Lee movie. Every conversation sounded like the muted trumpet talking teacher from Charlie Brown.

Finally it was time. I had on a pair of G-Star Japan Savage jeans and a Mariano Rivera shirt. The Yankees had this. I kept repeating this phrase over and over to myself: *They got this.* I slammed down my first Heineken and then another. I was a mess.

The Red Sox scored two runs immediately in the first inning. Then four runs in the second. The bar exploded. It was now full of Red Sox fans. I yelled out *fuuuuuuck* and slammed my fist on the bar. I remember a red-faced Red Sox fan who came over to me, grabbed me by the shoulders, and said, "Cmon man, just let us get this." He was right, but fuck him still to this day.

I left in the 9th inning. Didn't even wait to see the final pitch. I felt like I needed to throw up. It was raining when I came out of the bar, which just added insult to injury. After slamming beers for 9 innings I was a wobbly mess and stumbled to the 2 train . . . from the East Village, sans umbrella. And then it happened. I tripped and fell. So now I was in a puddle, just cursing my life. A searing pain rushed up my leg and I looked down just to see my jeans had been ripped at the kneecap and I had a nasty cut on my knee. The night couldn't get worse.

I finally made it to the train and just sat there zoned out. Each stop passed and it didn't even matter. My Yankees had choked and things would never be the same in the rivalry. I probably was shaking my head in this super-quiet train, which wasn't just Yankee fans but a cross section of all the other heartbroken New Yorkers. And at 96th Street a lady gets on the train and sees my hat and yells, "Did we win??" I don't remember what I said. She was a demon from hell.

I'm now upset all over again, sitting at my computer thinking about all this. To this day, when it rains, my knee hurts from that injury. Just another sad reminder of one of the worst weeks of my life.

Fuck Boston.

A YOUNG MAN ONCE ASKED ME IF YOU CAN EVER SWITCH TEAM ALLEGIANCES, AND THAT PERSON WAS DAN AT ICM, OUR BOOK AGENT. SHOUT-OUT DAN AT ICM. HE SOLD THE SHIT OUT THIS BOOK. ALSO HE GOT THE OFFICIAL WHITE GUY "I'LL MAKE YOUR GIRL LEAVE YOU" HAIRCUT. I KNOW I PROBABLY SHOULDA

WROTE THIS IN THOSE PAGES WHERE YOU ACKNOWLEDGE YOUR PEOPLES BUT NAH, I'M SHOUTING YOU OUT RIGHT HERE, DAN. YOUR TINDER IS GONNA BE FUCKIN BLINGIN NOW. ANYWAY NAH YOU CAN'T SWITCH TEAMS NIGGA, ARE YOU STUPID?

THERE IS ONE EXCEPTION. YOU CAN ONLY CHANGE THE TEAM YOU ROOT FOR IF IT'S TO ROOT FOR YOUR HOME TEAM. FOR EXAMPLE, YOU FROM NEW ORLEANS AND YOUR FAVORITE TEAM IS THE ATLANTA FALCONS (GO FIGURE). ONE DAY YOU'RE LIKE, "FUCK THIS, THE FALCONS ARE ALWAYS REALLY GOOD BUT NEVER WIN A CHAMPIONSHIP. AS A MATTER OF FACT, THEY LOSE IN SPECTACULAR FASHION AND I'M FUCKIN SICK OF IT!" I HEREBY DEEM IT OKAY TO THEN ABANDON THE FALCONS AS YOUR TEAM *BUT ONLY* TO BECOME A SAINTS FAN. DREW BREES OUT HERE PLAYING MADDEN ON ROOKIE MODE. FAM IF THE JANITOR SHAKES A DB AND GETS IN THE END ZONE HE'S CATCHING A TD PASS. AS OF TODAY THAT FUCKIN MANIAC HAS THROWN FOR OVER 70,000 YARDS—THAT'S VIDEO GAME SHIT. BREES BEAT PEYTON MANNING, A DUDE WHOSE PARENTS SHOULDA JUST SAID "FUCK IT, NAME THIS NIGGA 'QUARTERBACK,' LOOK AT HIM" *CAMERA PAN TO NEWBORN IN UNI WITH BALDNESS AND OD LARGE FOREHEAD.*

SO YEAH IF YOU FROM NEW ORLEANS AND AREN'T A SAINTS FAN, YOU CAN ABANDON THE BENGALS/RAVENS/LIONS WHOEVER FOR THE SAINTS. I GUESS YOU CAN ALSO MAKE A LATERAL MOVE TO YOUR HOME TEAM IF YOUR FAVORITE TEAM AND YOUR HOME TEAM ARE EQUALLY GOOD. THAT'S MAD RULES BUT SPORTS IS SERIOUS BUSINESS. ESPECIALLY WHEN YOU'RE $85,000 IN THE HOLE TO AN ALBANIAN BOOKIE WHO WILL BREAK ALL YOUR LIMBS AND YOU HAVE NIGHT TERRORS ON THE RARE OCCASION YOU CAN SLEEP.

"WHERE AM I—"

"WHERE ARE YOU GONNA GET 85 G'S IN A WEEK?"

"THAT'S NOT POSSIBLE I—"

YOU'RE DEAD.

No. This is all wrong. The idea of switching team loyalty is so foreign to me, I don't even have anything to say about it. If you move somewhere, you can't just switch to that team. That's not how it works. You also can't just start cheering for a team because they're winning; that's wild corny. I mean maybe that works for you but I wasn't raised that way. Hell. It broke my heart switching from my Android to an iPhone. But switching teams? HELL no. And some people will say, "Easy for you because you're a Yankees fan and they have 27 rings," which is true (27 rings, bro!), but also the Yankees haven't won it all since 2009 and you don't see me out here tweeting "Let's go Mets" or rocking a Boston Red Sox jersey (yuck).

I DO AGREE THAT THERE IS A NOBILITY ATTACHED TO REMAINING LOYAL TO A TEAM, WIN OR LOSE. OR MAYBE I JUST TELL MYSELF THAT AS AN OBSTINATE KNICKS FAN. IF YOU'RE A NY JETS FAN OR A SACRAMENTO KINGS FAN, SPORTS PEOPLE GENUINELY FEEL FOR YOU LIKE "DAMN BRUH, MY CONDOLENCES." IF YOU TELL A NIGGA YOUR TEAM AND HE SAYS "MY CONDOLENCES," YOU JUST GOTTA HOLD THAT L IF IT'S FACTUAL. IF THE DUDE IS JUST BEING A HATER BECAUSE HE'S A CELTICS FAN AND THEY WERE SUPPOSED TO BE GOOD AND ENDED UP IMPLODING, THEN FIGHT HIM. GORDON HAYWARD CAME BACK AND IS PLAYING LIKE AN ACTUAL WHITE GUY. IF YOU STICK BY YOUR HOMETOWN TEAM THICK OR THIN YOU CAN ALSO ACT HOLIER THAN THOU IN SITUATIONS WHERE A DUDE FROM QUEENS IS A PACKERS FAN AND THEY LOSE TO THE GIANTS IN THE FIRST GAME OF THE PLAY-OFFS. YOU CAN TALK A METRIC TON OF CASH MONEY FINANCIAL SHIT B, YOU

GOTTA TAKE ADVANTAGE OF THAT 24-HOUR WINDOW TO SLANDER THEY TEAM AS MUCH AS POSSIBLE. AFTER A DAY THEY'LL BE LIKE "U A CORN THAT WAS MAD LONG AGO!! NEXT!!" WHICH IS PRECISELY WHAT I SAY ABOUT THE 2018 WORLD SERIES.

People believe there's a limit on how long one can bring up old stuff in sports, but if it's good old stuff, you can mention it forever. For example, I love mentioning the Yankees having 27 World titles (27 motherfuckin rings, bro!!!!!!). Now, if we're being honest, my black self couldn't attend a bunch of those games because of segregation or just regular racism/not wanting to be called "boy." But I still mention those wins because they're great moments for my Yankees. If you're not a Yankees fan, you're like "That's bullshit, Desus," and I'm like "Um, 27 rings, bro." See how easy deflecting is? As a sports fan you need to learn how to jump in front of possible slander people are going to throw at your team and take away their ability to insult you.

Also—and this is completely up to the reader—you can always bring up an athlete's criminal record (unless your team has more criminals, in which case, maybe you don't).

THIS IS REAL: IF YOUR HOME TEAM IS GOOD FOR A STRETCH BUT THEN WACK AND YOU SWITCH TEAMS, YOU CAN'T SWITCH BACK TO YOUR HOME TEAM IF THEY BREAK OUT AND BECOME REALLY GOOD. NO BACKSIES, EVER.

THERE IS ANOTHER THING THAT MOST PEOPLE WOULDN'T ALLOW BUT I'LL GO ON THE RECORD AS NOT ENCOURAGING IT BUT NOT BREAKING YOUR BALLS IF YOU DO. THAT THING IS BEING A FAN OF AN INDIVIDUAL PLAYER. LIKE SAY IF YOU'RE A LEBRON FAN, YOU CAN BE A LAKER FAN. THEN IF HE GOES BACK TO CLEVELAND AGAIN, YOU CAN BE A CAVS FAN. MAD

PEOPLE ARE AGAINST THAT, BUT I'M PRETTY SURE IF JORDAN WENT TO THE KNICKS, THEN THE SONICS FROM THE BULLS, YOU'D HAVE 3 JORDAN JERSEYS, MY GUY. IMAGINE HOW MANY JERSEYS THE KOBE STANS WOULD HAVE IF HE GOT TRADED AROUND. IT IS OKAY TO BE A FAN OF AN INDIVIDUAL PLAYER AND ALSO YOUR HOMETOWN TEAM, BUT IF YOUR FAVORITE PLAYER IS PLAYING YOUR HOMETOWN TEAM, YOU GOTTA BE ON YOUR HOMETOWN TEAM'S BENCH.

THEM'S THE RULES, MY GUY. GOT IT? YOU CAN ALWAYS REFER BACK TO THIS TEXT BECAUSE I'M SURE A COUPLE OF YOU ARE GONNA COME REREAD THIS WHEN TOM BRADY RETIRES. I KNOW THAT'S WILD CONTRADICTORY BUT WHAT THE FUCK YOU WANT, BRO. I'M LIKE 3 L'S DEEP LISTENING TO PLAYBOI CARTI ON REPEAT. MAN, I CAN'T WAIT TO BE RICH RICH. THANKS FOR HELPING, GUYS. FOR REAL, I'M GONNA DO SOME COOL SHIT LIKE RENT A MANSION IN THE HAMPTONS AND JUST LET Y'ALL PARTY AND DESTROY THE SHIT AND FOOT THE BILL. WHO CARES? JESUS THAT'S TERRIBLE FINANCIAL ADVICE. THANK GOD FOR STEVE (SHOUT-OUT TO STEVIE P) . . . YOU SHOULD BE FINISHED IN THE BATHROOM BY NOW. YOU CAN PUT THIS DOWN AND GO BACK TO WHAT YOU WERE DOING. I'LL BE RIGHT HERE WHEN YOU GET BACK.

CHAPTER 5

WHAT THE FUCK IS AN "ALPHA" ANYWAY?

CUCK

KAG

In theory, a man should be able to cry whenever he feels like it. But in reality, FOH. Let your girl randomly catch you crying a few times and see if she doesn't pull that out like the Big Joker during your next argument. Men who cry look weak (that's not me talking, that's toxic masculinity).

WOW HOW FRAGILE IS YOUR MASCULINITY? GUYS, LISTEN TO ME. YOU CAN CRY WHENEVER YOU WANT.

Even John Boehner, who has the skin of a tanned crocodile suitcase and chain-smokes like 4 packs of cigs a day, looked wild pussy anytime he cried.

NAW, LOOK AGAIN AT JOHN BOEHNER! THAT NIGGA CRIED 13X A DAY AND STILL HAD LOVELY TAN PERNIL SKIN AND WAS MAD SUCCESSFUL. CRYING IS CATHARTIC. CRY IF YOU STUB YOUR TOE. CRY IF MELO AND LALA ACTUALLY BREAK UP. CRY IF CEL-

LINO & BARNES NOT BEING A THING ANYMORE IS TEARING YOU APART INSIDE. IT DOESN'T MATTER!! FUCKIN CRY!! I CRIED WHEN MY FIRST SON WAS BORN. IT FELT GREAT!! I GOT INTO A FIST-FIGHT WITH A DUDE MY EX GIRL WAS CHEATING ON ME WITH, BEAT THE NIGGA'S ASS, WENT HOME, AND CRIED. IT FELT SO GOOD. IF I COULD BOTTLE THAT SENSE OF [EVEN TEMPORARY] RELIEF AFFORDED TO YOU BY RELEASING THE PRESSURE VALVE ON YOUR TEAR DUCTS, I WOULD, AND TARGET WOULD CARRY IT, RIGHT NEXT TO THE WOMEN'S HAIR CARE IN B23. I'VE BEEN CONDITIONED NOT TO CRY SO I DON'T REALLY CRY OFTEN, BUT WHEN I DO, THE SHIT IS UGLIER THAN KIM KARDASHIAN'S UGLIEST UGLY CRY.

I'll concede there are times a man can cry and not get looked at sideways by others. Here are some examples:

1. The ending of *Saving Private Ryan*
2. The ending of *The Iron Giant*
3. When Mufasa dies in *The Lion King*
4. When a man realizes it's not his barber's fault, his hairline is really gone
5. When you order spicy chicken at Popeyes and get home and realize they gave you mild
6. Birth of a child & you can immediately tell it's not yours & you didn't want it (these are tears of joy and immediately followed by a night at a strip club or a seafood restaurant)

I guess there are a few other times when a man can cry. When your team wins it all, for example. But it would have to be an underdog team like the Pittsburgh Pirates or my aforementioned beloved New York Knickerbockers. Not the Cowboys or Warriors or something. You can't cry when the Yankees win again. Let the Knicks win an NBA Final—shit, even a random Thursday night game in November—and I'll cry in front of Madison Square Garden like a newborn baby fresh out the womb, I swear to Jah.

THERE'S NO INAPPROPRIATE PLACE TO CRY UNLESS YOU'RE AT YOUR EX'S WEDDING (BUT WHY WOULD YOU BE?) AND EVEN THEN THEY CAN BE TEARS OF JOY! YOU AVOIDED MAKING A HUGE MISTAKE! CRYING DOESN'T ALWAYS HAVE TO BE NEGATIVE. SHANE SMITH FROM *VICE* HAD ME IN LAS VEGAS AND I'M NOT GONNA SAY HOW MUCH MONEY I WALKED OUT OF THAT PRIVATE CASINO WITH BUT I DID WAKE UP THE NEXT MORNING, LOOK AT MY BAG, AND CRY TEARS OF JOY. RELAX DOG, LET THE TEARS FLOW IF YOU'RE FEELING IT. JUST DON'T BAWL . . . DO THAT QUIET SNORTING CRY SO YOU DON'T LOOK LIKE A FUCKIN WEIRDO SOBBING ON THE 4 TRAIN AT 10AM. I'M ON BOARD WITH CRYING FREELY, BUT UNLESS YOU WANNA END UP ON SOMEONE'S INSTAGRAM STORY, YOU'RE GONNA HAVE TO FIND A LESS PUBLIC VENUE TO CRY.

THE BEST PLACE TO HAVE A GOOD CRY IS IN THE SHOWER BECAUSE YOU CAN ALWAYS PRETEND YOU WEREN'T CRYING IF SOMEONE RUNS UP ON YOU WHILE YOU'RE IN THERE EXORCISING YOUR DEMONS. CRYING? ME? HAHA NO WAY BRO, I WAS JUST LETTING THE HOT WATER HIT ME DIRECTLY IN MY EYEBALLS, THAT'S WHY THEY SO RED. I'M CHILLIN HAHA!!

There are different forms of crying. The very stoic "all my friends are dead so I'll let a single tear roll down my cheek" is always a respectful way to show emotion. Snorting like a baby with wild snot bubbles in your left nostrils and moaning is never a good look (again, this does not apply if my Knicks win).

Also (and most painfully) the loss of a pet is one of the worst feelings you'll ever have and it never goes away, so you'll have to get used to not crying in public when you see another dog take a shit the way your pooch used to. I guess if you lose a kid you'll cry over that as well.

IF YOUR PLANT DIED; IF YOUR CAT DIED; IF YOUR CAR GOT TOWED, CAUSING YOU TO BE LATE, AND YOUR BOSS SAID ONE MORE LATENESS AND "YOUR ASS IS GRASS" (WHAT A FUCKIN DWEEB), FUCKIN CRY BRUH. IF YOU DON'T AND YOU KEEP YOUR FEELINGS ALL BOTTLED UP INSIDE, NEXT THING YOU KNOW YOU'RE DOING WEIRD SHIT LIKE HAVING SEX WORKERS STEP ON YOUR BALLS.

HYPOTHETICAL JERKOFF: *MERO, WHO MADE YOU THE AUTHORITY ON MASCULINITY?! HUH?! YOU TWEETED ABOUT LAMBORGHINIS!! ON SEVERAL OCCASIONS!!*

YEAH, SO THE FUCK WHAT? FIRST OFF, WATCH YOUR TONE. I WAS GONNA SAY "LET'S PEEL BACK THE LAYERS OF MY LOVE FOR EXPENSIVE CARS" BUT THERE'S ONLY ONE LAYER: I COULDN'T AFFORD NICE SHIT AND NOW I KINDA CAN. FOR OTHER DUDES THERE'S DEFINITELY SOMETHING PHALLIC ABOUT A EUROPEAN SPORTS CAR THAT COSTS MORE THAN A HOUSE IN TAMPA. FOR ME? I GREW UP NOT BEING ABLE TO ACQUIRE THE SHIT I WANTED WITHOUT RACKING IT OR FINESSING A WAY TO IT AND . . . *LIL UZI VOICE* NOW I DO WHAT I WANT! NOW I DO WHAT I WANT!

CARS ARE THE ANTITHESIS OF AN INVESTMENT AND DEPRECIATE AS SOON AS THE FIRST PISTON FIRES OFF AND THE ENGINE REVS UP, BUT FUCK IT, BECAUSE LIKE DRAKE SAID IN SHAKESPEARE'S *KING LEAR:* "YOU ONLY LIVE ONCE, THAT'S THE MOTTO, NIGGA YOLO." MY PORTFOLIO IS BALANCED LIKE A

GYMNAST ON ADDERALL AND ALL MY OTHER FINANCIAL AFFAIRS ARE HEALTHY. SO I CAN BLOW SOME MONEY AND HELP THE AMERICAN AUTO INDUSTRY AT THE SAME TIME, THAT'S WILD NOBLE. IF YOU WANT A CAR TO PICK UP GIRLS, THAT IS ULTRA CORNY, MY PALITO DE QUESO. YOU SHOULD DRIVE A CAR BECAUSE YOU LOVE DRIVING A FINELY TUNED DRIVING MACHINE. FUCK THE MASCULINITY OF IT. RIGHT NOW I SOUND LIKE AN ASSHOLE WITH A BEARD AND A SEPTUM PIERCING TELLING YOU ABOUT HOW HE DOESN'T DRINK TO GET DRUNK AND ESCAPE REALITY AND THAT IT'S ALL ABOUT THE FLAVORS AND HOW "BALLGAG NUTZ IPA" IS "FUCKIN AMAZING SMALL-BATCH STUFF, MAN." THEN AGAIN, IF YOU NEED A CAR TO GET LAID, FUCK IT, GET IT HOW YOU LIVE PLAIR. HOPEFULLY THIS BOOK SELLS ENOUGH TO LET ME LEASE AN ASININE GROUND ROCKET WITH CONFIDENCE SO I CAN DRIVE IT 150MPH ON RT. 17 LISTENING TO PLAYBOI CARTI—"FOREIGN." LIKE I SAID, IF YOU'RE A BOZO WHO NEEDS A CAR TO GET LAID, THEN YOU'RE GONNA NEED TO KEEP UP WITH THE JONESES, AND THAT IS EXPENSIVE AS FUCK, SO YOU MIGHT AS WELL JUST PATRONIZE YOUR LOCAL SEX WORKER, WHICH IS BOTH CHEAPER AND SOMEHOW LESS OBVIOUS THAT YOU'RE PAYING TO GET LAID.

Back to man-crying. A great way to get away with it is being drunk. After enough drinks, you can become a blubbering mess and not get judged. Everyone just chalks it up to being wasted. But, and this is important, this only works if your friends are also hammered to the level you are. The caveat is you could end up shirtless fighting the best man at your wedding after shots of tequila. Or worse, after spending the night trying to hook up with a chick at the local bar, you spend the morning crying in her living room, half naked, about how your dead dog used to try to eat pigeons and would dart forward in the park to catch them in his mouth and "Oh god I miss you, Rocco! Is the sun coming up? I'm so sorry. What's the address here, I'll get an Uber."

Even more fun is when you really have unresolved issues and need to go to therapy, but therapy is expensive, and also who has time for that? So your issues stay hidden but you know on some level that they're just waiting to manifest themselves. And how do they do that? Yup, random tears at inappropriate times. So then you're at your desk at work, looking at Twitter, and you come across a video of a mother duck attempting to save one duckling that fell down a sewer grate, and someone rescues the duckling and now you're blubbering in your office and even *you're* like "what in the fuck is going on here?"

If the conversations we have about masculinity on Twitter are the litmus test for manhood, we're all fucked. One example is, "Real men don't wash their butts," and like fam, are you really walking around out here with swamp ass because you don't want to be judged? That doesn't sound (smell) weird to you?

I remember years ago I was trying to enter a bar in Manhattan wearing a pink polo (shouts to Cam'ron for teaching me early that black men look great in pink). As I was walking in, the bouncer checked my ID and said, "Pink shirt huh? You're braver than me!" I said, "You're missing out, I does numbers in this shirt," and he said, "Nah, not for me. Don't want to give people the wrong idea." This guy, whose job was to maybe get shot or stabbed defending a physical property that he did not own, was scared of wearing a pink shirt. Isn't the whole definition of masculinity to be comfortable as a man and just be who you are? Dude was a real weirdo. AND for the record, that shirt did numbers at that club specifically. Women loved the pink!

Knowing who you are as a man is extremely important in life because it affects even the little things, all the way down to what sneakers you wear (some of you don't have the swag to wear exclusive colorful kicks because you worry about what other people think about them). But it also affects bigger life issues, such as your ability to walk away from a dispute. I remember being younger and knowing if someone tried to punk me, disrespect me, or whatever, they were bringing disrespect to my hood (233RD STAND UP) and you couldn't let that shit slide. So a simple disagreement could easily lead to a stabbing or shooting. And now you're doing 10 years because someone called you a pussy. Stupid.

People think carrying an AR-15 into Walmart, just because your state has open carry, is a sign of masculinity, but that's almost the exact opposite of "being a man" or "being sure of yourself." It's someone else's dumb idea of manhood, not yours. Carrying a gun when it's legal doesn't require much from you, Brad. Try carrying a gun illegally in a city where, if you get caught, you're getting an automatic 3 years. That's real bravery. And real stupidity. And let me throw an umbrella "allegedly" in here just to cover all my bases, legally. Anytime you're carrying a long rifle around for show, you're being a jerk and a bully, straight up. In your head, you're the hero, because at any moment if something happens, you can "handle the situation." But the reality is: Ain't nothing happening while you're buying foot powder at Kroger, Bob. Now you're just a dick walking around scaring people. Congrats, big boy, you tough guy, you. (Sidenote: These people tend to have truck nuts on their cars and if buying a set of fake *genitals* for your *car* doesn't scream "masculinity issues," I dunno what does.)

Some people buy flashy cars to show they're the man and I didn't understand this until recently. I always thought buying a $600,000 car was super wasteful, but you have to remember how I was raised. My parents used to ration bacon when we were kids because there were a bunch of us (one strip of bacon per child, which led to me frying and eating mad bacon on the first night in my new apartment, which made me super sick but it was totally worth it because it symbolized my freedom). My parents have never had a new car, ever, so when my sister got a car straight from the lot, my parents nearly fainted.

Anyway, back to buying a car to floss . . . in many cases, it's exactly that. No one needs a Bentley or a Bugatti, but people buy and drive them all the time and they're definitely low-key shitting on you (by you, I mean us, because I don't have Bugatti money but one day . . . fingers crossed!). The 2019 Bugatti Chiron costs $3 million. Here's where the flex comes in: No one who buys a Bugatti only has $3 million, duh. So this person is telling you very loudly that they have a boatload of money. Life-changing money. Money that could help build a school or a library or start an after-school program for children. And this person said, "Nah I'm buying a fast car, suck it, poors." They have so much money that a $3 million car doesn't matter. That's a flex indeed. Is it a flex I'd make? Ask me again in like 5 years when I've sold out and have no morals and have 4 Bugatties or whatever the plural of them is. Am I writing about this to make Mero feel bad for thinking that sometimes wanting a nice car is just wanting a nice car? We may never know.

CHAPTER 6

SHOUT-OUT TO YOU IF YOU BOUGHT THIS BOOK FOR ACTUAL ADVICE, AND NOT FOR YOUR VIP 1 PERSON LAUGHING PARTY. I WROTE ALL MY SHIT SMACKED OUTTA MY WHOLE MENTAL SO IT'S DEFINITELY LIKE 55% GOOD ADVICE. I'M ABOUT TO TELL YOU WHY YOU SHOULD ALWAYS SHOPLIFT IN THE NEXT COUPLE PAGES. THAT'S PROBABLY NOT GOOD ADVICE. I HAVEN'T EVEN WRITTEN IT YET AND I CAN TELL YOU I'LL BE IN MY WEED CHAMBER AT THE CRIB DOING DABS SMOKING L'S AND JUST GOIN IN EXPLAINING HOW BOOSTING IS NOBLE. BUUUUT THEN ALSO I GAVE YOU REALLY GREAT ADVICE ABOUT RAISING YOUR KIDS AND SMOKING WEED. YOU TAKE THE GOOD YOU TAKE THE BAD YOU TAKE 'EM BOTH AND THERE YOU HAVE I'M FU-CKIN WASHED, I'M FU-CKIN WASHED. I'M 35 RIGHT NOW. BY THE TIME THIS SHIT COMES OUT I MIGHT BE 36.

SOMEBODY ON TWITTER TOLD ME 35 IS OLD. I RESPONDED SAYING I "JUST MADE THE CUTOFF, I'M A MILLENNIAL" AND IMMEDIATELY FELT LIKE A DICKHEAD RATTLING ON ABOUT WHAT I

—THIS HAS GOT TO BE INFURIATING TO EDIT LOL. BEN THE EDITOR SQUINTING LIKE, ***WHY*** DOES THIS MOTHERFUCKER INSIST ON WRITING 3,000 WORDS IN ALL CAPS, SPRAYING, COMMAS, ALL, OVER, THE, PLACE, LIKE HE PLAYING *GTA* AND DID THE GUN CODE. *FALLS ASLEEP SMACKED FOR 7 HOURS IN A CHAIR, WAKES UP NEXT MORNING* THIS IS BEAUTIFUL, THIS IS LIKE I'M WRITING ABSTRACT ART. YOU'RE FUCKING WELCOME. THAT CARTI SHIT DOES SLAP, THOUGH, *DIE LIT* IS SUCH A GREAT ALBUM TITLE. BY THE WAY, I REALLY DID FALL ASLEEP WRITING THIS PARAGRAPH AND WAS WOKEN UP IN MY BASEMENT BY MY DISGUSTED WIFE (LOVE YOU XOXO). *RELIGHTS BLUNT* SEE YOU IN A FEW PAGES, PAL.

Mero's high. Not like "Hey I'm kinda fucked up but I'm all good." No. If you think you know people who get high, you've never met Mero. You're like, "Nah Desus, this guy I know gets high all day every day, 24-7. I get it." No, you don't. There is nothing else like this. Right now inside of Mero's medulla oblongata, the little people running his body are panicking as red lights go off and an automated voice says, "Emergency! System shutting down!" and one of the engineers is screaming, "He's typing! We can't nod out now!" Another person at a different control panel yells, "He's moving! Everyone brace yourself!" and Mero goes head down on the Macbook for just a few moments, less than five seconds, but if you walked in on him during a shutdown, you'd be absolutely certain that he's dead. And then he pops back up and immediately starts smoking again. I've seen this happen literally thousands of times, and it never gets old. *Boom,* down he goes, full slump, aaaaand he's up again. It's unreal.

Anyway, what is this chapter about? Oh yeah, crime. Crime is trash because prison is so boring. You can't tweet in there, you can have sex but it's not free sex, and also the food is trash. And that's what I remember anytime someone asks me to commit a crime (like asking me to use my TV money to purchase a brick, which I immediately said no to because the price was a little high and felt disrespectful). Also not all crimes are crime-crimes. If you kill your whole family, you're a criminal. If I sneak some weed on a flight, I'm just trying to smoke good, my guy.

I WAS GONNA BE RESPONSIBLE HERE AND TELL YOU "YOU SHOULD LEAVE SHOPLIFTING IN HIGH SCHOOL. YOU CAN GET INTO OD TROUBLE AS AN ADULT" BUT FUCK THAT. I'M A GRAFFITI NIGGA AND A MAJOR PART OF THE GRAFFITI CULTURE I GREW UP IN WAS BOOSTING. WE CALLED IT RACKING AND NIGGAS WAS OUT HERE RACKING EVERYTHING. PAINT, $500 FUCKIN NORTH FACE SPELUNKING SPACE JACKETS, FOOD. WE HAD A SYSTEM AND DEALS IN PLACE WITH BODEGAS AND LITTLE INDEPENDENT SHOPS WHERE YOU WOULD RACK SOME SHIT THEY PAID MAD MONEY FOR WHOLESALE AND SELL IT TO THEM FOR HALF THAT. RACK AND RETURNS IS WHERE YOU RACK SOME SHIT AND GO RETURN IT LIKE "OH I DON'T NEED THIS TINY LIGHT SWITCH THAT COSTS $90, WHY WOULD ME RETURNING 10 OF THEM AT ONCE RAISE ANY ALARMS? SIR, ARE YOU RACIST?"

THE SAME WAY I CAN'T EVER SEE MYSELF NOT CREATIVELY WRITING MY NAME ON PUBLIC PROPERTY, I CAN'T EVER SEE MYSELF NOT AT LEAST RACKING SOME GOOBER GRAPE FROM TARGET. SERIOUSLY. IT'S LIKE A DISEASE I'M NOT MAD I HAVE. IT'S EXHILARATING IN A WAY THAT A ROLLER COASTER ISN'T, FAM. SOMETIMES I TEST MYSELF TO SEE IF I STILL GOT IT. *PRODIGY VOICE AND EMOTION* ALSO I'M JUST REALIZING THAT WHEN I WAS HITTING THE BUMPY I WAS HELPING THE COMMUNITY.

MERO, WHAT THE FUCK ARE YOU TALKING ABOUT?

"HITTING THE BUMPY" IS HITTING UP THE STORES YOU GOT DEALS WITH TO UNLOAD THE SHIT YOU RACKED AT PRICES BELOW WHOLESALE. YOU OBVIOUSLY AIN'T WALKING INTO WALMART LIKE "YO, I GOT 130 BOXES OF CREST WHITE STRIPS, 150 BOTTLES OF WHATEVER THE LATEST DIET PILL CRAZE IS, AND 125 OF THESE MAD EXPENSIVE HAIR PRODUCTS." BECAUSE WALMART IS A HUGE CORPORATION AND THEY WILL SNITCH ON YOU BEFORE YOU OPEN YOUR MOUTH. AHKI AT THE BODEGA IS DEFINITELY DOWN TO DO BUSINESS AND NOT SNITCH BECAUSE YOU HAVE A SYMBIOTIC RELATIONSHIP. YOU GIVIN HIM THE OPPORTUNITY TO G OFF AND SELL MAD CREST 3D WHITESTRIPS FOR THE LOW BECAUSE YOU GAVE HIM 100 BOXES FOR A G AND HE'S ABOUT TO MULTIPLY THAT BY THREE. HE'S GIVING YOU THE OPPORTUNITY TO PULL UP TO SHORTY CRIB WITH $500 WORTH OF WEED AND GET THE WILD TOPPY WHILE SMOKING 5 GRAMS OF WEDDING CAKE IN A BACKWOOD.

THE RIGHTEOUS PART IS THAT YOU ARE HELPING KEEP A MOM & POP TYPE ESTABLISHMENT OPEN IN THE FACE OF RAPID GENTRIFICATION AND "BUSINESS IMPROVEMENT DISTRICTS," WHICH JUST MEANS WHATEVER STORE CAN'T PAY THE RAISED RENT IS GETTING THE BOOT AND BEING REPLACED WITH A NATIONAL PIZZA CHAIN. YO, I DON'T KNOW WHAT'S IN THAT KIND OF PIZZA BUT ONE TIME I LEFT THAT SHIT OUT TWO DAYS IN A ROW AND NO VERMIN FUCKED WITH IT AT ALL. IF MY PALATE IS LESS REFINED THAN THAT OF A BRONX-DWELLING RAT OR COCKROACH, I REALLY NEED TO TAKE STOCK OF MY LIFE. CHAIN PIZZA IS EXACTLY LIKE UNPROTECTED SEX B. IT'S SO GOOD YOU DON'T CARE WHAT'S IN THAT SHIT AND YOU DON'T CARE IF THAT SHIT MAKES YOU PEE OUT YOUR ANAL HOLE FOR 48 HOURS. YOU DON'T RESPECT THE CONSEQUENCES OF EATING

THAT SHIT BECAUSE IT TASTES LIKE GETTING A BLOWJOB IF YOU HAD TASTE BUDS ON YOUR DICK. WOW. IF YOU WORK FOR ANY CORPORATE PIZZA CHAIN AND WANT ME TO CHANGE MY MIND ON TV FOR A COUPLE MILLION DOLLARS, I'M ALL THE WAY WITH IT.

ANYWAY, IF YOU OUT HERE RACKING AND HITTING MULTIPLE BUMPIES, YOU A MODERN ROBIN HOOD. IF YOU NOT OUT HERE DOING A TRISTATE AREA BOOSTING SPREE BUT STILL WANNA FEEL OKAY STEALING SHIT, LET ME ASSUAGE YOUR ANXIETY. IF YOU STEAL FROM, SAY, WALMART, YOU ARE GIVING A DOUBLE MIDDLE FINGER TO CORPORATE AMERICA, DEAD-ASS. YOU ARE A REVOLUTIONARY FOR STEALING THAT BOX OF BAND-AIDS FROM TARGET, FAM. YOU'RE CHE GUEVARA WITH BLING ON.

HAPPY RACKING Y'ALL. BE SAFE OUT THERE AND REMEMBER: THAT SECURITY GUARD ISN'T GOING TO CHASE YOU FOR A COUPLE OF G-STARS AND A FERRAGAMO BELT. AND IF HE DOES, HE'S GIVING UP AFTER A BLOCK. SO WEAR GOOD RUNNING SHOES WITH GOOD CUSHIONING JUST IN CASE YOU GOTTA TAKE FLIGHT OUTTA THERE.

The criminal justice system is trash but I don't really know a better way. Maybe freeze people like they did in *Minority Report*? The penal system is weird because you could get two years for killing someone, or forty years for breaking into a property. There doesn't seem to be any rhyme or reason for sentencing. Remember when they were giving more time for people selling crack vs. cocaine, even though you need cocaine to make crack? (NOTE: RACE *MIIIIIGHT* PLAY A FACTOR IN ALL OF THE ABOVE.)

American prisons are terrible. Maybe not as bad as prisons in some Latin American countries, but if you compare us to most other countries, we suck. Sweden's prisons are like 5-star

Airbnbs. You can get a degree while there or make wooden shoes or whatever. You learn. In American prisons you learn how to take showers in front of other people while hiding a razor in your foreskin JUST IN CASE.

America would be wild if we went old-school and back to Hammurabi's eye-for-an-eye shit as punishment for crimes because, in theory, you'd think it would stop rapists and killers, but I think it would just end up with a lot of us getting our arms cut off for not picking up dog doodoo or having our identities stolen by the government for using an ex's Netflix account. And what happens if evidence comes back that you were innocent? Now the state has to buy you a new arm. Very cumbersome process.

I think one day we're going to have an *American Idol*–style show where we, the viewers, vote for a prisoner on death row to be killed on TV and there's a number you can either text or call to vote. And every week someone gets voted back to death row until we get to our two finalists and people will be on Twitter like "I'm team #inmate1!" and wearing shirts in support of their inmate. The final episode will have a talent portion and the inmate that gets killed is going to perform an amazing version of "O mio babbino caro" that becomes the number one song on Spotify for months after his execution. Then you realize the record company that owns the song was sponsoring the show *the whole time*. Okay, that just turned into an episode of *Black Mirror*. Netflix, holla at ya boy.

IF YOU CAN'T KILL A MOTHERFUCKER IN THE COURSE OF THEM INVADING YOUR CRIB, WHEN ARE YOU SUPPOSED TO CATCH A BODY? I'M NOT SAYING THAT AS SOME "STAND YOUR GROUND" MANIAC WHO JUST WANTS TO HOMICIDE ANOTHER HUMAN,

BUT I GOT KIDS AND A WIFE B. IF YOU RUN UP IN MY CRIB WITH NO MASK, YOU GOTTA GO B. BRONX PHILOSOPHER FRENCH MONTANA ONCE SAID, "MASK ON, THEY COMIN FOR YA ICE. MASK OFF, THEY COMIN FOR YA LIFE." I UNDERSTAND BEING A "CELEBRITY"—I PUT THAT IN QUOTES BECAUSE I GENUINELY STILL HAVE THIS NOTION IN MY BRAIN THAT I'M NOT *AT ALL* IN THE PUBLIC EYE, LIKE I CAN JUST DO WHATEVER I USED TO . . . IN ALL HONESTY I SHOULDN'T HAVE SAID ANY OF THAT SHIT ABOUT BOOSTING—COMES WITH THE FEELING THAT I AIN'T AND WILL NEVER BE THE TARGET OF SOME SHIT, BECAUSE I HAVEN'T DEALT WITH "THE UNDERWORLD" FOR SEVERAL YEARS.

I WAS MORE WORRIED ABOUT GETTING ROBBED OR SHOT WHEN I WOULD OCCASIONALLY HAVE A GOOD NIGHT PUTTING DRUGS IN CAUCASIAN STUDENTS' HANDS. IF THAT DAY EVER COMES AND I'M IN THE CRIB, I'M SORRY, BUT I GOTTA LEAVE YOU LOOKIN LIKE BAKED ZITI THAT FELL OUT THE TRAY. WITH A REGISTERED FIREARM, OF COURSE. I'M NOT GONNA BUY AN AK-47 AT A GUN SHOW IN JACKSONVILLE AND DRIVE BACK HOME WITH THAT SHIT. I'D RATHER GET ROBBED THAN GO TO PRISON. HAVING NEVER DONE "HARD TIME," MEANING PRISON, AND BEING LUCKY ENOUGH TO HAVE DONE A LITERAL ZILLION THINGS THAT WOULD HAVE GOTTEN ME "HARD TIME" AND NEVER GETTING CAUGHT UP, IMAGINE I GET EMBROILED IN SOME SHIT NOW THAT I'M A PUBLISHED AUTHOR. WHY WOULD YOU RIDE AROUND WITH AN ILLEGAL GUN IF YOU GOT MAD MONEY? I'M NOT GONNA SAY MONEY DOESN'T GIVE YOU THE FEELING OF INVINCIBILITY, BECAUSE THERE ARE TIMES WHEN I REALIZE HOW MUCH MONEY I'VE MADE MAKING YOU LAUGH AND I'M LIKE, HOLY SHIT, THIS IS MORE MONEY THAN I EVERRRR MADE LEGIT OR SELLING NARCOTICS OR BOOSTING OR JUXING

COMBINED. I HEARD AN INTERVIEW WITH CASANOVA2X WHERE HE SPOKE CANDIDLY ABOUT ROBBING A CHECK-CASHING PLACE AND COMING OFF WITH $7,500, THINKING IT WAS A HUGE COME UP, AND HOW COMPARATIVELY HE'S MADE MUCH MORE IN ENTERTAINMENT. THAT'S OD RELATABLE TO ME CUZ I WOULD ALLEGEDLY DO SOME ALLEGEDLY ILLEGAL SHIT, ALLEGEDLY MAKE 2 GRAND IN 48 HOURS AND THINK I WAS DOOOOIN IT. ALLEGEDLY.

ANYWAY, IF SOMEBODY RUNS UP IN YOUR CRIB, IT'S A GREEN LIGHT TO RELEASE THE DRACO ON THEM, AS LONG AS YOU GOT PAPERS FOR THAT SHIT. BECAUSE IF YOU DON'T, YOU GOING TO JAIL, FAM. IT'S VERY DIFFICULT TO GET AWAY WITH MURDER. THAT'S WHY WHEN YOU DO SOMETHING WILD AND GET AWAY WITH IT, THEY SAY YOU "GOT AWAY WITH MURDER." ALL THIS SHIT THAT ROMANTICIZES MURDER AND MAKES IT ABOUT TRUNKS AND TARPS AND BONE SAWS FORGETS THE PART WHERE YOUR DNA AND/OR FINGERPRINT IS IN *SOME* DATABASE SOMEWHERE, EVEN IF YOU NEVER EVEN JAYWALKED. AM I SOUNDING WILD CONSPIRATORIAL? CAN YOU TELL AT WHAT POINT IN THIS LIL ESSAY I STARTED HITTING THIS BLUNT STUFFED WITH GORILLA GLUE? YO PLAYBOI CARTI—"FOREIGN" GOES SO HARD. I SAID IN 2015 THAT IF I WASN'T DRIVING A TOPLESS LAMBO DOWN FORDHAM IN 5 YEARS BLASTING SOME SHIT, I WAS GONNA QUIT THIS WHOLE COMEDY/WRITING/TV/MOVIE THING. I GOT LIKE 4 MONTHS LEFT ON THAT AND I WASN'T KIDDING. OH THE WHOLE REASON I SAID THAT IS BECAUSE THIS CARTI SONG IS PRECISELY WHAT I ENVISIONED PLAYING. I FEEL LIKE A JERK MAKING THIS LEFT IN THE MIDDLE OF HAVING TO EXPLAIN LIFE TO YOU, I'LL BLAME IT ON THE LOUD. I'M KIDDING, YOU SAW THE TEKASHI SAGA. 98% OF TIME PEOPLE GO TO JAIL BECAUSE SOMEBODY FLIPPED. FREE FREAKY!

Mero is high again, again. The wildest part of crime is that it's mad *easy* to get away with it, not hard. And you're probably like "Desus, what are you talking about? I watch *Law & Order* . . ." LET ME STOP YOU RIGHT THERE. *Law & Order* is NOTHING like real-life police investigations. They always have high-quality 4K footage of whatever crime they're investigating on that show. Living in NYC where's there a camera everywhere, let me tell you the reality: Most of those security cameras suck and have the photo quality of whatever flip phone came out 5 years before the iPhone. Yes, the StarTAC. New York has hit-and-run murders all the time and there's literally no footage to be found. I'm not saying this like we need more cameras (which will eventually be used by robots to learn our customs so they can infiltrate society without us realizing). I'm saying, don't trust the ones we have.

One time I got arrested and the detective asked me about a murder a few blocks away. I asked what that had to do with me, and he said, "Come on, I know you keep your ears to the streets." Low-key, I was flattered. He clearly knew your boy was out there in the streets. But that also showed me that if someone doesn't talk, a lot of crimes just straight up don't get solved, and in most cases it takes a tip to help the cops get the ball rolling.

I'm not saying you *should* commit crime, but I don't know. I guess keep the above in mind before you do.

I MET A DUDE ON A FLIGHT ONCE AND—LONG STORY SHORT—THE GUY WAS IN HIS THIRTIES AND SAID HE HAD NEVER HAD A SINGLE ENCOUNTER WITH POLICE. I WAS AMAZED. THEN I REALIZED THERE'S DEFINITELY MAAAAD OTHER PEOPLE WHO HAVE NEVER HAD A RUN-IN WITH POLICE. I HAD SO MANY GROWING UP IN THE STOP-AND-FRISK BRONX WHERE COPS

WOULD STOP YOU FOR BEING THREE BLACK/LATINO DUDES WALKING IN UNISON, I COULDN'T FATHOM NEVER HAVING BEEN HARASSED BY A COP.

I'M SUPPOSED TO TELL YOU HOW TO DEAL WITH COPS BUT THERE'S REALLY A VARIETY OF WAYS TO DEAL WITH COPS DEPENDING ON YOUR RACE, GENDER IDENTITY, ALL THAT. PERSONALLY THE WAY I DEALT/DEAL WITH COPS IS ONE-WORD ANSWERS AND A BUNCH OF PAPERS, LICENSE, REGISTRATION, INSURANCE, BIRTH CERTIFICATE, HIGH SCHOOL DIPLOMA, ALL THAT SHIT. RUN MY SHIT. I HAVEN'T GOT PINCHED FOR ANYTHING SINCE LIKE 03–04. NOWADAYS I PULL THE "I'M ON TV" SHIT ALL THE TIME. NO BULLSHIT—I WAS RECENTLY RIDING DOWN TREMONT IN THE OFFICIAL BRONX HOOPTY, AKA THE '05 ACCORD. I DID A WILD ILLEGAL U-TURN RIGHT ON THE AVE. I HAD NO IDEA THERE WAS A STATE TROOPER PARKED BETWEEN TWO CARS. HE PULLED UP NEXT TO ME, TOLD ME TO ROLL MY WINDOW DOWN, GRINNED LIKE A MUTHAFUCKA, AND WAS LIKE "YO, I LOVE YOUR SHOW, BRO!" THEN HE DID HIS OWN WILD ILLEGAL MANEUVER TO TAKE A SELFIE. I HAD HALF A ZIP OF ANIMAL COOKIES ON ME AND I WASN'T EVEN WORRIED BECAUSE THIS DUDE WAS FREAKING OUT OVER A PHOTO. AND BECAUSE OF THAT SINGULAR ENCOUNTER, I NOW TALK TO COPS HOWEVER I WANT. PROBABLY A BAD IDEA BUT FUCK IT, LIKE SPIKE JONZE SAID, "EVERYTHING IS FINITE." IF A COP RIDDLES ME WITH BULLETS, I'M FULLY CONFIDENT IN HEATHER'S ABILITY TO RAISE THE KIDS DOLO AND IF SHE REMARRIES, I'LL HAUNT THE DUDE AND BE LIKE "BOO!" WHEN HE'S IN THE SHOWER SO HE BUSTS HIS ASS.

EXAMPLE: AFTER THAT INCIDENT, I GOT PULLED OVER ON THE TURNPIKE DOIN' LIKE 110 AND SWITCHIN' LANES & SHIT. COP FOLLOWED ME FOR A GOOD TWO MILES WITH NO LIGHTS,

THEN THREW ON THE FLASHERS, GOT ON THE HORN, AND TOLD ME TO PULL OVER. I WAS INDIGNANT AS FUCK.

COPISHLY "YOUR VEHICLE IS REGISTERED IN NJ, YOU HAVE A NY LICENSE, BUT YOU LIVE IN NJ?"

"THAT IS FUCKIN CORRECT, OFFICER."

"WHY DON'T YOU HAVE YOUR NJ LICENSE?"

"BECAUSE I DON'T HAVE A JOB AND I JUST HANG OUT LIKE, FUCK Y'ALL, I'M NOT CHANGING MY LICENSE!!! I JUST FUCKIN MOVED HERE A FEW MONTHS AGO, AIN'T THERE SOME KINDA FUCKIN GRACE PERIOD FOR THIS SHIT? OR YOU JUST WANNA BE A FUCKIN DICK?!? DOES CHRIS CHRISTIE NEED MORE DONUTS FOR Y'ALL!?!? OR FOR HIM?!?!"

GUESS WHAT HE DID? HE DIDN'T DO SHIT. HE GAVE ME A TICKET THAT WAS LONGER THAN TAKING THE MCAT ON ANGEL DUST, TO WHICH I RESPONDED, "YOU GONNA FEEL LIKE AN ASSHOLE WHEN YOU COULD BE NAPPING IN YOUR CAR BUT NOW YOU GOTTA GO TO COURT WITH ME AND WATCH THIS SHIT GET THROWN OUT BECAUSE YOU FILLED IT OUT ALL FUCKED UP." THEN YOU KNOW WHAT I DID? I THREW THE TICKET OUT THE WINDOW AND PEELED OUT. IT WAS THE RUSH OF A FUCKIN LIFETIME. I HAD NEVER DONE ANYTHING EVEN *CLOSE* TO THAT REGARDING "LAW ENFORCEMENT." I FELT LIKE I HAD THE POWERS OF A CONNECTED RICH WHITE LADY. IN RETROSPECT, I COULDA EASILY GOT CLAPPED, SO NOW I FOLLOW STANDARD PROCEDURE. BUT EVEN STANDARD PROCEDURE DOESN'T WORK A LOT OF THE TIME IF YOU AREN'T THE WHITE SHADE OF EPIDERMIS.

I THINK I WAS TALKING ALL BRAZY TO THAT NJ COP JUST BECAUSE HE WAS AN NJ COP. NON-NYPD COPS DON'T GIVE ME THE INSTANT ANXIETY I ASSOCIATE WITH THE BLUE & WHITE PATROL CAR AND THE NYPD STANDARD ATTIRE. ALSO, HE WAS

WEARING A STUPID-ASS HAT. THIS IS A BOOK SO YOU WOULDN'T KNOW THAT I JUST SAID OUT LOUD: "IMAGINE IF VIRGIL DESIGNED COP UNIFORMS? SHIT WOULD BE LIKE 'STUPID HAT' ON A HAT THAT LOOK LIKE SOME RANGER RICK SHIT WITH THE LIL STRAP THAT SCOOPS UP THE BACK OF YOUR HEAD FAT." I SAID THAT TO MYSELF AND LAUGHED FOR TEN MINUTES.

BUT YEAH I GUESS DON'T DO WHAT I DID, IT WAS MAD STUPID. JUST LISTEN TO THE COP'S DIRECTIONS? I'VE HAD COPS THROW ME ALL OVER THE PLACE AND THOUGHT IT WAS STANDARD COP SHIT. IT'S NOT. I FIT EVERY DESCRIPTION SO MY MAIN PIECE OF ADVICE WOULD BE: DON'T MAKE ANY SUDDEN MOVES. COPS ARE JUMPIER THAN CATS OFF THE FIRE CATNIP. I HATE TO GENERALIZE—OF COURSE THERE ARE GOOD COPS THAT WILL PULL OVER, COME ON THE BASKETBALL COURT, SHOOT AN AIRBALL, AND LET YOU ROAST THEM WHILE THEY SIT IN THEY CAR. THERE ARE GOOD COPS THAT'LL BE LIKE "GOOD NIGHT SIR" AFTER THEY TOSS YOUR CAR FOR 45 MINUTES AND FIND NOTHING, LOOK HOW LOW THE BAR IS.

Growing up brown in NYC shapes your view of the cops in a totally different way. I was never raised to view the cops as helpful or friendly, or people to turn to when you have a problem. I remember my older sister got robbed at gunpoint right by our house and the cops accused the guy she was walking with of setting her up, because he was from the projects and so he clearly must have known whoever did the crime. Even as a kid I was like, "Oh wow, that's wild fucked up."

As I got older, I always saw the NYPD as just another rival gang, except they had permission to use their guns, so best to just avoid them altogether. We used to avoid walking on a major street at night so we wouldn't get stopped and frisked (East

233rd Street with its four traffic lanes, for example). The police used to cruise major streets and just harass people who were walking and pat them down. It was humiliating. So we learned to walk on East 232rd or East 234th Street because those blocks are narrower and you could spot the DTs (detectives) coming.

I've called 911 twice in my whole life and both times I felt like a snitch. The first time was because I witnessed a hit-and-run and the dispatcher got an attitude with me because I didn't want to give my name (no snitching!). But luckily an ambulance was passing by so I hung up and flagged them down. I was able to be a good human without breaking my street cred. Don't judge me.

I've actually had a cop point a gun at me while running at me, yelling, "FREEZE OR I'LL FUCKING KILL YOU," and that's not even in the top 5 scariest moments in my life. To be fair, I've lived a wild life, but that's kind of just what an interaction with the cops is like for me.

THE MOST POPULAR ARGUMENT PEOPLE LIKE TO THROW OUT THERE IS "WELL, IF YOU LISTEN TO THEM, NOTHING WILL HAPPEN!" THAT'S BULLSHIT. COPS AREN'T ROBOTS. THEY ARE PEOPLE AND THEY MIGHT BE HAVING THE WORST DAY THEY'VE HAD IN 5 YEARS, AND THEN THEY SEE YOU CASUALLY DRINKING A BEER ON YOUR STOOP, THEN DECIDE THEY ARE GOING TO DECOMPRESS BY COMPRESSING YOUR HEAD ON SAID STOOP OR, AT THE VERY LEAST, WRITING YOU A SUMMONS, MOST LIKELY TAKING YOU IN BECAUSE YOU "FIT A DESCRIPTION," AND AT WORST, MERKING YOU OR SCARING THE SHIT OUT OF YOU.

ROLL THE DICE, PAL. I'LL BE IN MY BASEMENT MINDING MY BUSINESS AND NEVER MAKING EYE CONTACT WITH LAW ENFORCEMENT AGAIN. BECAUSE IF YOU DO SOMETHING FUCKED UP YOU GO TO JAIL. ONCE THEY FIGURE OUT HOW FUCKED UP

THAT THING WAS, ACCORDING TO OLD WHITE MEN THAT MAKE THE LAWS, YOU EITHER FINISH OUT YOUR TIME IN JAIL OR THEY SEND YOUR ASS TO PRISON.

That eye contact comment is hilarious because it's true. To this day, I still don't make eye contact with law enforcement because you never know! I was at Yankee Stadium a few months ago, working on this book, and a cop saw me and yelled, "Hey you! Come here!" I immediately turned into Stop-and-Frisk Desus and had a split-second decision to make: Do I walk over to him or turn the other way and run? I had just smoked a blunt in the street but that's neither here nor there. So I head over to the cop, no sudden movements, and keeping my hands exactly where they should be. And the cop goes, "You're Desus, right? Do that cop voice you do," and I was like, oh shit, I'm about to get beat up for mocking NYPD and it's going to happen in front of Yankee Stadium, and that's literally an intro for our podcast. So I do the whole Italian, Staten Island, "Whoa whoa whoa, put your hands up against the wall, asshole," voice, and the cop turns to his partner and says, "I TOLD YOU. HE SOUNDS JUST LIKE FRANKY!" and the other cop is like "Oh wow, he really does!" And that's my new experience with NYPD, because I'm on TV and I think that changes everything, but then again Jay-Z, Puffy, and J-Lo all have been arrested, so anything is possible.

Shit, that's how life works: One day you're just chilling in your living room, then a couple of decisions later you're in the penal. And now you're sitting in bookings like "Damn, who's gonna water my plants."

JAIL IS CHILL BECAUSE IT'S SHORT-TERM. IF YOU'RE GOING TO JAIL, YOU MIGHT BE DOING A YEAR OR LESS. IF YOU'RE DOING REAL TIME, YOUR ASS IS GOING TO PRISON. GOING TO JAIL VS.

GOING TO PRISON IS LIKE GOING TO LA MARINA VS. GOING TO PUNTA CANA. YOU CAN HOP ON A TRAIN TO LA MARINA AND YOU PROBABLY WON'T BE THERE THAT LONG, BUT IT'S A "BEACH." MEANWHILE, IF YOU GO TO DR, YOU FLEW MAD HOURS TO GET THERE, AND YOU AREN'T GONNA LEAVE ANYTIME SOON BECAUSE YOU PAID HELLA MONEY AND THE BEACH IS LIT. THE CORRELATION I'M TRYING TO MAKE HERE IS THAT YOU DON'T REALLY NEED A "SURVIVAL GUIDE" FOR JAIL. JAIL IS SUMMER VACATION. IF YOU SPEAK SPANISH AND/OR ARE OKAY AT SPADES, JAIL IS BASICALLY JUST A REALLY FUCKED-UP CHAPTER OF THE EAGLE SCOUTS OR SOME SHIT. YOU DO MAD ACTIVITIES ALL DAY, EAT SHITTY FOOD, AND GET TALKED DOWN TO BY THE STAFF.

PRISON, ON THE OTHER HAND, IS TOTALLY LIFE-CHANGING AND IS LIKE SKIPPING UNDERGRAD AND JUMPING RIGHT INTO YOUR MASTER'S IN THAT YOU ARE GOING TO BE ON THIS FUCKING CAMPUS FOR THE FORSEEABLE FUTURE. THE BEACH METAPHOR WAS FUCKED UP BECAUSE PEOPLE WOULD RATHER GO TO PUNTA CANA THAN LA MARINA. CAMPUS METAPHOR IS FUCKED UP, TOO, I'M SMACKED. YOU KNOW WHAT? THIS MAKES NO FUCKING SENSE. UNLESS YOU THINK IT DOES, IN WHICH CASE I'M A GENIUS.

You're in jail. The key things to remember are: 1) none of these people are your friends, 2) anyone listening to you is trying to use whatever info you tell them to their own advantage, and most importantly, 3) grab as much food as you can when you get a chance because you will get into savage mode.

Most people like to sit on the benches in bookings like civilized human beings. Sorry, pal, those days are over. You need to let people know you're with the shits, literally. Sleep on the floor or even under the bench. If you're asleep you can't get into trouble (smart, right?). But you also have to do that not-really-asleep-I-see-you-motherfucker sleep to make sure you don't get your pockets or butthole taken.

Next you have to figure: Can I get out? Remember, it's never what you did, it's what they can prove. Don't talk to any cops, just your lawyer. They already got you and there's nothing you can say to get those cuffs magically taken off you, so just clam all the way up and save it for the judge.

The sandwiches they give you are usually bologna or peanut butter, two flavors no one wants, on dry-ass white bread. But this ain't a Michelin restaurant, my guy, you're in jail. So guess what? These sandwiches are also going to function as pillows. Leave 'em in the plastic, prop em up against your shoes (you will have taken your shoes off at this point, trust me), and *boom*. You got a bed. Did your chest just sink? Good, it should. Jail is wack and if you really get locked up for a long time, you're going to have to beat your meat in a dorm full of other dudes and rely on your spank bank for masturbation material. Then when you finally get released, the wild buzzkill is that the chick whose memory you beat your dick to nonstop for your whole prison sentence now looks like the grandmother from *Family Matters*.

My favorite bad prison advice (often told by people who post on Reddit) is to find the biggest person in the cafeteria and sneak attack them with a tray. In what world does this seem like a good idea? At best, you get beat to death by this goon and his crew (excuse me, "posse." Thanks, Phil Jackson). At worst? You have to ask your mother to send you sneakers that are clearly not your size and you're now making mascara using lubrication oil from door hinges and your very large cellmate (the same guy you attacked in the cafeteria) doesn't allow you to use your male name or pee sitting down while he's in the cell. Also he made you turn your bedsheets into a male romper. So, great idea, Tyler. Let me know how that works out for you.

TO SURVIVE IN PRISON YOU NEED TO MAKE ONE OF TWO DECISIONS. 1) DO I EVENTUALLY WANNA GET OUT OF HERE AND SMELL THE SWEET SCENT OF A HUMAN VAGINA EVER AGAIN? AND 2) DO I ACTUALLY CARE? PRISON IS PRETTY LIT EXCEPT FOR THE POTENTIALLY UNCOZY SEXUAL ENCOUNTERS. I GUESS I'LL STICK AROUND. LITERALLY NOBODY HAS EVER SAID THAT SECOND ONE. REMEMBER WHEN JADAKISS SAID, "I KNOW NIGGAS THAT GO TO JAIL JUST TO GET THEY TEETH FIXED" . . . JADA IS DOPE BUT THIS WAS DEFINITELY NOT TRUE. WHY THE FUCK WOULD YOU DO THAT? I'D RATHER BE FREE AND HAVE CROOKED TEETH THAN HAVE PEARLY WHITE CHOMPERS AND BE DRINKING ALCOHOL I PRODUCED IN THE SAME VESSEL I DO CAQUI IN. THERE REALLY IS NO DECISION HERE. YOU GOTTA GET THE FUCK OUT.

SO HERE'S HOW YOU SURVIVE IN PRISON . . .

FIRST OF ALL, STOP WATCHING MOVIES. MOVIES MAKE YOU THINK AS SOON AS YOU GET TO PRISON, IT'S ALL UNCUT COCKS FLYING UP YOUR BUTTHOLE AND MAKESHIFT WEAPON–BASED VIOLENCE. IT'S NOT EVEN LIKE THAT. MY UNCLE WAS IN PRISON AND HE SAID IT WAS A LOT OF NOTHING. THAT'S REALLY THE WORST THING ABOUT PRISON: FINDING WAYS TO PASS THE TIME. I'M TOTALLY ON THE PRISON ABOLITION SHIT BECAUSE PRISONS ARE A TREMENDOUS WASTE OF MONEY AND ALL THEY DO IS PROVIDE WHAT IS ESSENTIALLY SLAVE LABOR FOR PRIVATE COMPANIES. YES, THAT'S THE END OF WOKE RANT. ANYWAY, LEARN SPANISH, READ BOOKS, AND UNDERSTAND YOUR FOOD IS GOING TO FUCKING SUCK FOR THE NEXT HOWEVER MANY YEARS. PROTIP: IF YOU REQUEST KOSHER MEALS, IT

WILL BE LESS SHITTY BUT STILL NOT GOOD. DON'T WORRY ABOUT GANGS AND SHIT LIKE THAT IF YOU AREN'T IN ONE, AND DON'T LET ANYBODY KNOW YOU HAVE MONEY IF YOU DO. IF YOU HAVE MONEY AND A FAMILY THAT LOVES YOU AND KEEPS YA COMMISSARY FATTER THAN BLAC CHYNA'S ASS, YOU ARE FOOD FOR OTHER BROKE INMATES WITH FAMILIES THAT ABANDONED THEM. THEY STILL HAVEN'T GOTTEN OVER IT. THEY REALLY LIKE YOUR CIGARETTES AND THAT SMALL COLLECTION OF HONEY BUNS THAT YOU'VE AMASSED. ANOTHER EASY WAY TO BLOW THROUGH YOUR PRISON SENTENCE IS TO JUST GET REALLY FUCKING HIGH ALL THE TIME. IF YOU HAVE ACCESS TO DRUGS, PRISON IS JUST A CONTROLLED ENVIRONMENT TO GET HIGH IN WITH ABSOLUTELY NO ACCESS TO CISHET SEX AND/OR SMASHBURGER. PRISON SUCKS BUT IF YOU GO, YOU WILL SURVIVE BY READING AND NOT TAKING SHIT FROM ANYBODY THAT DOESN'T HAVE "KILL NIGGAZ" TATTOOED ON THEIR FACE. GOOD LUCK, PALITO BRIGANTE.

If you're white with money, feel free to get belligerent and yell at the corrections officers. Make sure to mention any politicians you know and how your tax dollars pay their salaries. Your team of lawyers is probably on the way so you'll be fine. I got arrested once with a guy who owned a French restaurant on the Upper White Side and it was hilarious. He knew he was getting out. He used one of his phone calls to tell his assistant what food he wanted waiting for him at the courthouse. His crime? He was hosting a dinner in his restaurant and somehow got into a fight in which he SWUNG AT A COP. Yeah, most people get shot for that. My man caught one punch from an officer and then kept saying he was going to sue the city. It was amazing to watch. The rest of us were in some weird New York undercover prison and he was reenacting an episode of *Brooklyn Nine-Nine.*

When it was time to see the judge he had three attorneys waiting for him and that case got thrown way the fuck out. He still said he was going to sue the city and it turned out he was friends with Mike Bloomberg (allegedly).

Keep in mind I said prison was cool if you were white with money. Without money it won't turn out well for you. You'll either end up in a white power group or become a really bad rapper with mad tattoos. Or both?

CHAPTER 7

ON THE INEVITABILITY ...OF BECOMING WASHED

I know we've discussed being washed in terms of relationships, but let's go deeper. What is washed? Is it a state of mind? A state of being? An adjective? An insult? Something to aspire to or something to avoid? Scientists have no idea. We are breaking new ground here.

AHHH YESSSS COME, FOLLOW ME, *PLAYS OPENING NOTES OF ALY-US "FOLLOW ME"* FOLLOW ME INTO THE LAND OF THE WASHED. IF WE'RE GONNA BE REAL, I WAS WASHED BEFORE I TOOK MY LAST HAPPY BIRTHDAY SHOT OF PAUL MASSON AT 30. BEING WASHED HAS NOTHING TO DO WITH NUMERICAL AGE. YOU COULD BE WASHED AT 20. I WAS CREAMED BY THAT AFOREMENTIONED FORD BRONCO IN MY EARLY TWENTIES AND BY THAT TIME I HAD ALREADY BEEN EVERYWHERE AND SEEN EVERYTHING THERE IS TO SEE IN NYC. I WISH I WAS KIDDING BECAUSE I DIDN'T *WANT* TO SEE *ALL* OF IT. BEING

WASHED IS GETTING SUPER HIGH AND BROWSING HOUSEWARES. BEING WASHED IS WHEN, AN HOUR INTO A PARTY, YOU SUDDENLY REMEMBER THE HALF A BLUNT AND THE EGGPLANT PARM FROM EMILIO'S THAT ARE WAITING FOR YOU TO COME HOME AND HAVE A MÉNAGE À TROIS, AND SMILING. IT'S "POWER WALKING" AS AN EXERCISE. IT'S HAVING LACTAID AND A PEN AND SOME PAPER ON HAND AT ALL TIMES "JUST IN CASE" YOU NEED TO EAT ICE CREAM OR WRITE SOMETHING DOWN IN ANALOG FASHION. BEING WASHED IS WAKING UP ON A FRIDAY MORNING AND THINKING ABOUT HOW YOU ARE GONNA DITCH PLANS YOU PRETENDED TO BE HYPED FOR ALL WEEKEND BECAUSE YOU WOULD MUUUUCH RATHER EAT AN EDIBLE AND WATCH THOSE NBA TV SHOWS WHERE A BUNCH OF PLAYERS HAVE A GROUP DISCUSSION ABOUT RANDOM SHIT LIKE "WHO WAS THE BEST REBOUNDER OF EACH DECADE, STARTING FROM THE '70S." IF NOT BEING WASHED IS AN EDM FESTIVAL AT AN ALL-INCLUSIVE IN CANCUN WITH CHAD AND THE BROS WHERE YOU ARE DODGING VOMIT AND THE POOLS ARE MURKY AND WARM, BEING WASHED IS A PRIVATE VILLA IN THE MALDIVES WHERE THE ONLY PEOPLE YOU COME INTO CONTACT WITH ARE EITHER HELPING YOU ACHIEVE CLIMAX OR BRINGING YOU WINE AND BURRATA (AND LACTAID) FLOWN IN FROM SOMEWHERE SO IT'S DELICIOUSLY FRESH.

IN OTHER WORDS, BEING WASHED IS FUCKING AMAZING. I WENT TO TURKS AND CAICOS WITH HEATHER A LIL WHILE BACK AND DID NOTHING BUT SMOKE WEED, FUCK CONSTANTLY, EAT THE STUPIDEST FOODS EVER (IN A GOOD WAY), LAY ON THE BEACH, AND OCCASIONALLY GO FUCK AROUND WITH GIANT FISH ON A LITTLE AQUA MOTORCYCLE BABY JET SKI THING. NO MASSIVE CROWDS, NO SERATO-FACED DJ PLAYING THE WORST DUBSTEP TONI BRAXTON REMIXES YOU HAVE EVER HEARD IN

YOUR FUCKIN LIFE. JUST YOU AND PERHAPS YOUR PARTNER ENJOYING THE BEAUTY OF TRANQUILITY. BEING WASHED IS THE PINNACLE OF LIFE.

Being washed is a state of matter much like solid or liquid or plasma. Anything or anyone can be washed. The only known Law of the Washed Universe is that it happens to everyone. Every club demon, party monster, and social butterfly has their day. That moment when you're in the club and the lights are right, drinks are flowing, everyone is having a wonderful time . . . and all you want to do is go home. Suddenly you view invitations to leave your home as a personal insult. In your head you start thinking: "How much is it going to cost to get there? Is there a cover? I have alcohol here at home. I have weed. There's Netflix and a PS4 as well. Why would I leave this place?"

And now instead of heading out to the club, you're in your bed wrapped in a duvet looking at bread-making machines on Williams Sonoma (you can't afford them but it's still fun) or maybe you're googling recipes for a nice hearty pumpkin chowder to make in the a.m. because it is, after all, a bit crisp out.

These are the thoughts of the washed.

Washedness crept up on me. One Saturday morning I tweeted about the lack of whole bean coffee in my neighborhood. In retrospect, that was probably the first sign. WASHED. Fast-forward a few months and I'm in Rite Aid testing which version of Icy Hot has the least potent smell because I stood up too fast while watching a Knicks game. WASHED.

Being washed is in the details. The Lactaid pill I now have to consume before eating a chopped cheese sandwich (pronounced *sang widge*) is a blink-and-you'll-miss-it washed moment. What happened to my glory days of eating a whole box of Taco Bell tacos with my guy G-steel and then getting up and running out the house like it was nothing? Those days have disappeared in the fog of washedness.

Being washed is different than getting older. No longer playing basketball because you're scared you'll tear your ACL is part of getting older. Saying new rappers names have too many symbols and misspellings for you to keep up with is being washed.

Here's a true story about being washed. On our illustrious late-night show, we filmed a scene where we played basketball against Cory Booker. We didn't warm up before filming, and in fact, I drank a Beck's before hitting the court. Not to get an advantage, but to numb my body from the pain I was about to feel. Unbeknownst to us, Cory Booker is not just a ballplayer, but a gym ballplayer, which means there's a lot of body contact and hip checks and such. Also, we were in his gym, in front of his people, and they were rooting for him, so what should've been a causal game now felt like Game 7 of the NBA Finals. So I was going hard and trying to block shots and then Cory Booker tried to dunk on me. I absolutely could not allow that. I left it all out on the court, and he never dunked on me, but it hurt. I was trying to summon 15-year-old Desus but he's long gone. The next morning when I started to get up, my body just said "Nah." I have no idea what I did but my back was locked up like a Chick-fil-A on a Sunday. I literally had to crawl to the bathroom for painkillers and the whole time my body was screaming, "That's what you get, stupid! We only play basketball on video game consoles now. What's wrong with you??"

My best advice is to just let go and embrace the washedness. It's called washed because it's wavelike. You want to be like the sand and allow this force of nature to cover you while you submit to its demands.

Imagine washedness as the fictional characters from Stephen King's *The Langoliers,* but not the book, I mean the ones from the 1995 TV miniseries.

If you had to google that reference, you're still okay.

If you knew what I was talking about. . . . Welcome to Club Washed.

THE MOMENT I REALIZED I WAS A FULL-GROWN WASHED ADULT WAS WHEN I FINISHED HIGH SCHOOL AND ENTERED THE WORLD OF LEGAL WORK. ACTUALLY THAT'S BULLSHIT. MY DAD HAD ME ON ROOFTOPS GUIDING INDUSTRIAL-SIZE AC UNITS INTO PLACE WHILE HE MANUALLY CRANKED THEM UP ON WHAT LOOKED LIKE SOME FLINTSTONES FORKLIFT/CRANE HYBRID. WITH A FRAYING CABLE. I WISH I KNEW WHAT THE FUCK THAT THING WAS CALLED. I HAVE NEVER SEEN ONE BESIDES THE ONE MY DAD OWNED. I THINK HE INVENTED THAT SHIT. HE LITERALLY WELDED BUNK BEDS FOR ME AND TITO (MY BABY BROTHER) OUT OF THREE TWIN BED FRAMES LIKE THE MOVIE *STEPBROTHERS*. I KNOW HE DID IT BECAUSE I WAS THERE WITH A FUCKIN MASK ON LIKE "THIS NIGGA CAN BUILD ANYTHING, HOLY SHIT."

YOU KNOW HOW CARS GOT SIZES & SHIT? LIKE YOU CAN GET A 2-DOOR COUPE IF YOU WANNA DRIVE FAST AND BE THE COOL FLEXGOD? THEN THEY GOT THE SEDAN OR SUV FOR WHEN IT'S LIKE, AIGHT, THERE'S GOING TO BE MORE THAN TWO PEOPLE IN THIS CAR? THERE MIGHT EVEN BE A BABY SEAT OR TWO YOU GOTTA PUT IN THAT MOTHERFUCKER. YOU HAVE TO BE PRACTICAL AND YOU MUST "BECOME THE SUV," YOU MUST BECOME WATER . . . I THINK BRUCE LEE SAID THAT SHIT. I'M NOT 100% POSITIVE AND I HAD A PIÑA COLADA W EXTRA BRUGAL FOR BREAKFAST BECAUSE ALL MY KIDS ARE AT SCHOOL AND ME AND THE MRS GOT THE DAY OFF, WHAT DOES THAT HAVE TO DO WITH "BECOMING AN SUV"? I HAVE NO IDEA BUT REMEMBER

THAT MOVIE WHERE BRUCE WENT TO SOMEBODY'S TRAINING FACILITY . . . I WAS GONNA SAY DOJO BUT I'M NOT SURE THAT'S THE CORRECT WORD AND I'M NOT TRYNA OFFEND MY ASIAN GANG . . . ANYWAY BRUCE GOES TO THEY TRAINING FACILITY OR SOME SHIT IDK I'M SMACKED AND THERE'S A SIGN THAT SAYS "NO DOGS AND CHINESE ALLOWED" (BRUCE PLAYED A CHINESE DUDE IN THE MOVIE). THAT SIGN WAS DUMB HIGH IN THE AIR AND BRUCE JUMPED UP AND KICKED THAT SHIT TO PIECES, SHIT WAS WILD, SHOUT-OUT TO BRUCE RIP.

PLEASE NOTE I SAID SUV AND NOT MINIVAN. MINIVANS ARE CORNY AS FUCK. MINIVANS ARE THE SIGN THAT BRUCE LEE KICKED, TO ME PERSONALLY, THEY ARE THAT OFFENSIVE. IT HAS NOTHING TO DO WITH THE "SOCCER MOM" STIGMA AND MASCULINITY OR WHATEVER (NICE TRY, I'M NOT SPEWING ANY TOXIC MASCULINITY IN THIS SHIT B, I GOTTA PAY FOUR FUCKIN COLLEGE TUITIONS). I JUST THINK THOSE SHITS LOOK LIKE A FUCKIN GUINEA PIG ON A SPIT IN PERU IN THE YEAR 3042. I DON'T GIVE A FUCK IF YOU PUT RIMS ON THAT SHIT, MY GUY. THAT'S ACTUALLY KINDA WORSE. THAT'S LIKE PUTTING EXTRA EARS ON YOUR HEAD, YOU KNOW WHAT I'M SAYIN? IT'S LIKE OH BOOM I PUT THIS SOUND SYSTEM IN THIS TOYOTA SIENNA! NIGGA I DON'T CARE. YOU JUST PUT AN EXTRA NOSE ON YOUR BUTT. WHICH IS A TERRIBLE PLACE FOR A NOSE BTW. FAM IF YOU HAD A BAD HEAD TO BEGIN WITH, NOW YOU'RE JUST DRAWING ATTENTION TO THE SHIT WITH THEM EXTRA EARS. I DON'T KNOW EXACTLY WHAT CONSTITUTES A "BAD HEAD" AND LOOK, GIMME A BREAK THIS STRAIN IS CALLED "ANIMAL COOKIES." MAYBE YOUR HEAD'S MAD POINTY OR SOME SHIT? MAYBE YOU GOT THE WILD DENT IN YOUR SHIT. WHO KNOWS. POINT IS YOUR HEAD IS TRASH. MINIVANS ARE LIKE, YO, I CONCEDE TO MY OPPONENT "SWAGGERLESSNESS."

SO YEAH, FUCK MINIVANS. AN SUV LETS YOU CHOOSE YOUR

DESTINY. YOU CAN LOW-KEY IT IN THE HONDA PILOT OR YOU CAN SWAG IT OUT IN THE GLK BENZ OR SOME SHIT. I KNOW THOSE ARE IN QUITE DIFFERENT PRICE RANGES BUT IT IS WHAT IT IS, YOU COULD GET LIKE AN ACURA MDX OR A FORD EXPLORER OR SOME SHIT AND STILL SWAG IT OUT. THERE'S NO HOPE FOR THE SLIDING DOOR ROTISSERIE-CHICKEN-LOOKIN ASS BABY BUSES WE CALL MINIVANS, THO.

WHAT I WAS TRYING TO SAY WAS THAT I FELT LIKE AN ADULT THE FIRST TIME I HAD BILLS IN MY NAME, BUT EVEN THEN, IT WAS LIKE I WAS JUST PAYING MY BILLS BECAUSE I WAS SUPPOSED TO DO IT. I DIDN'T REALLY "FEEL" LIKE AN ADULT. I JUST FELT LIKE A KID WHO HAD MORE RESPONSIBILITIES. MY THOUGHT PATTERNS WERE THE SAME WHEN I WAS 26 AS THEY WERE WHEN I WAS 21, WHICH IS KINDA WILD DEPENDING ON WHO YOU WERE AT 21. IF YOU WERE A HERB THEN YOU'RE SAFE, BUT IF YOU WERE OUT HERE SCHEMIN, DOIN SHIT OF QUESTIONABLE LEGALITY WITHOUT A SECOND THOUGHT, THEN THAT'S PROBABLY NOT THE BEST LIFE STRATEGY APPROACHING YOUR 30S.

You should also be able to recognize the washedness in other folks. It's the most human and caring thing you can do. For example, if I'm washed, don't invite me out on Monday night, because those days are over, and you should know it. Or if you know I get winded watching TV, don't invite me rock climbing. These very simple observations are necessary to keep friendships and relationships going. Sometimes it's as simple as checking another person's Instagram. If all the photos I've posted are sneakers still in their boxes and a few plates of hot wings, would it make sense to invite me to run the New York Marathon?

Washed can also relate to the amount of money you have in your account or your current status in life. If you're too broke to go out, you're financially washed. If you have mad kids and no babysitter, you are full-out washed and can't be invited to any event. Often your washed status has nothing to do with what you've planned for life but rather what life gives you to work with.

One of the worst crimes one can commit is rejecting the washed label. Sometimes people call you out and say "Hey, you washed bastard" and your instant reaction is definitely to say "no" and get defensive. But I know you're washed. You know you're washed. Let's all get together and admit this washedness in a safe space, like a Ben & Jerry's or the TV section of Target.

EVERYBODY IS DIFFERENT SO THAT SWITCH THAT TURNS YOU FROM A LUXURY CHILD (SHOUT-OUT MY GUY TOPSHELF TYSON FOR THAT ONE LOL) TO A FULL-BLOWN "I GOTTA JUGGLE SOME SHIT" ADULT CAN VARY WILDLY. FOR SOME PEOPLE IT'S SOMETHING AS SIMPLE AS FINISHING COLLEGE AND/OR GETTING A FULL-TIME "I CAN PAY RENT DOLO . . . KINDA" JOB AND "ADULTING" FOR THE FIRST TIME. MEANING PAY YOUR OWN BILLS, HAVE TO KEEP A SCHEDULE OF SHIT, YOU KNOW. NOT JUST WAKE UP AT 5PM, FIND OUT HOW TO FINAGLE WEED AND BEER AND A PLACE TO HANG OUT.

FOR SOME PEOPLE IT'S BEING RESPONSIBLE FOR SOMEBODY ELSE. I BECAME AN ADULT WHEN I SAW MY FIRST CHILD BE BORN. THAT WAS SOME BRAIN-MELTING SHIT. IT TOOK ME A SOLID 30 SECONDS, I'VE ALWAYS BEEN GREAT AT BIOLOGY AND ANATOMY AND SHIT . . . TOOK ME A SOLID 30 SECONDS TO PROCESS THIS BRAND-NEW HUMAN WAS CREATED BY HEATHER AND ME. I BURST INTO TEARS. THEY WERE HAPPY TEARS BUT THEY WERE ALSO "HOLY SHIT I GOTTA GET MY SHIT ALL THE WAY TOGETHER, I HAVE A WHOLE-ASS HUMAN BEING TO INFLUENCE" TEARS. SO I AUTOMATICALLY BECAME AN ADULT

AND A BETTER PERSON . . . AND WASHED. IT WAS CHEMICAL. IT JUST HAPPENED.

IF YOU REALLY THINK ABOUT IT, HAVING A KID IS ABSOLUTELY NUTS. IT'S WILD EXPENSIVE, IT'S SLEEP DEPRIVING, AND IT'S A LIFETIME COMMITMENT. SO WHY DO YOU DO IT, ASIDE FROM THE WHOLE "IF PEOPLE STOP HAVING KIDS ALTOGETHER HUMANS WILL DIE OUT" THING? BECAUSE, WARNING THIS IS GONNA SOUND HELLA CORNY, THE LOVE YOU GET FROM YOUR CHILDREN IF YOU AREN'T A TRASHBAG PARENT IS WORTH EVERY SINGLE ONE OF THOSE REASONS TO NOT HAVE KIDS. SUPER HARDCORE DOG PEOPLE POINT TO THAT SAME THING AS TO WHY THEY BELIEVE BRINGING THEIR 80LB HUSKY TO APPLEBEE'S SHOULDN'T BE AN ISSUE. BUT THE MOST THAT MOTHERFUCKER IS GONNA DO WHEN YOU DIE IS WHINE, PAW AT YOUR CORPSE, THEN EVENTUALLY GET HUNGRY AND EAT YOU FROM THE DICK UP. I SAY THAT AS A FRIEND AND A DECADE-LONG DOG OWNER.

WHEN YOU HAVE KIDS AND YOU KICK THE BUCKET YOUR KIDS WILL CRY OD, CONSOLE YOUR MOM, AND THEY'LL ALL HAVE A "THIS NIGGA DIED, WE'RE OD SAD, BUT HERE'S A FUNNY ANECDOTAL STORY ABOUT HIM BEATING MY BASKETBALL COACH WITH A BAG OF BALLS" COMMEMORATIVE EVENT WHERE YOUR KIDS EACH GIVE A ROUSING SPEECH ABOUT WHAT A GREAT DAD YOU WERE. BUT IF YOU HAVE NO KIDS AND YOU PERISH, YOUR DUMBASS FRIEND WILL GO UP THERE AND TRY SOME NEW MATERIAL IN HIS EULOGY, BOMB, AND ALL 7 PEOPLE THAT CAME TO SEE YOU GET UP AND LEAVE LIKE IT'S A BOTTOM OF THE 8TH BLOWOUT. I'M KIDDING, IT MIGHT NOT BE THAT BAD, YOU MAY HAVE SIBLINGS THAT LIKE YOU OR LIKE A COOL COUSIN OR SOME SHIT, MAN I DON'T KNOW, I DON'T EVEN KNOW YOU.

I MUST BE A NARCISSIST BECAUSE I JUST FEEL LIKE THE

WORLD NEEDS MORE MERO IN IT, AND IF INSTANTLY BECOMING WASHED WAS THE TRADE-OFF FOR THAT, THEN FUCK IT B. I'M KIDDING BUT I'M NOT. I'M PART OF MY FATHER'S LEGACY. WHEN THIS SHIT SELLS A ZILLION COPIES PEOPLE WILL GO UP TO MY POPS LIKE, YO THAT'S YOUR KID! AND MY DAD'LL BE PROUD UNTIL HE GETS TO THE HOW TO DO DRUGS PART, WHICH IS THE VERY BEGINNING. HE'LL STILL BE PROUD I SOLD A ZILLION COPIES. AND MY MOM AND HIM SMASHED AND MADE ME, THAT'S WILD B.

Sometimes being washed is a simple math formula. Maybe you met a hot 21-year-old, but you're 41. Sure it *sounded* like a good idea, until she's looking at you for that 4th order of cock at 2am but your heart is still racing fast from the last time you nutted . . . at 10pm. You might not see that you are now a Washed American but know this: You are definitely at the point in your life to stand proudly during the National Anthem for Washed People (aka some song by Sublime).

Washed sex is amazing because there are 2, *maybe* 3 positions, and that's it. And hopefully the person you're sleeping with is also washed so there are no surprise positions out of nowhere (unless it's after a brunch with unlimited mimosas). Washed sex is missionary, doggy, MAYBE some head if it's your birthday (or she paid the rent), and that's it. All that other stuff is out the window. Shower sex? Umm have you seen the heating bill, we can't afford that. Vacation sex? I came on this vacation to relax and sleep till 11am without the kids . . . also my bad back is acting up after that long flight because I got hit by a car when I was 18 and have a bulging disc.

The stakes are low with washed sex. The worst it can get is attempting something you saw in porn and having your partner not even say "no," but just hit you with a "what's wrong with you?" You walk in the room with some Dijon mustard, nipple clamps, and an XXL anal plug and just see your partner pick up the phone and very slowly dial 911 without breaking horrified eye contact with you.

Every so often with washed sex, you'll pitch a perfect game, meaning the sex was amazing and you have absolutely no idea why. Maybe it was the vitamin B you took before breakfast, maybe you switched to vegan food, maybe you had two Stellas at the Rangers game and came home asking your wife if she wanted to feel your ronkonkoma and it just worked. Either way, please proceed with caution because 1) your heart could explode and then we'll immediately roast you on Twitter, before the official cause of death is even known, or 2) your partner might get used to the STRONG COCK and now you gotta try super hard every time, no matter how tired you are or if your acid reflux is acting up because you had jerk wings at happy hour after work.

Washed sex for women is wild easy because you can just say *Ugh men suck,* and become the wild pillow princess, but dudes don't even care and will eat you out OD and get mad excited when you let out the simplest moan or even a fart if you're nasty like that. So don't even stress it Ma, it's all good.

HAVING KIDS WARP-SPEEDS YOUR WASHEDNESS. OKAY, FUCK IT B, I OFTEN MAKE THIS MISTAKE ACCORDING TO MY THERAPIST, MY MOM, AND MY WIFE. ALL VERY INTELLIGENT WOMEN. YOU SHOULDN'T PLACE THE SAME EXPECTATIONS THAT YOU HAVE FOR YOURSELF ON OTHER PEOPLE, BUT GUESS WHAT? I'M NOT PERFECT SO I DO IT ANYWAY AND MY WEST INDIAN ROOTS MAKE ME GENETICALLY JUDGMENTAL. SO HERE IT IS: IF YOU *WANT* TO HAVE KIDS, YOU GOTTA BANG 'EM ALL OUT BEFORE 35. YOU DON'T WANNA BE ULTRA ULTRA ULTRA WASHED

BY THE TIME YOUR KID IS A TEEN. IMAGINE YOUR KID GOES FIRST IN THE NBA DRAFT AND SHOUTS YOU OUT AND THEY PAN OVER TO YOU IN YOUR CHAIR AND YOU LOOK LIKE STROM THURMOND'S CORPSE'S CORPSE. YOU MANAGE A WEAK "I SHOULD PERISH ANY DAY NOW" SMILE, THE CROWD CHEERS, AND YOU SHIT IN YOUR PAMPER BECAUSE THE APPLAUSE WAS SO JARRING. HOW SAD IS THAT?

MY OLDEST IS 8 RIGHT NOW AND I'M 36. I'M NOT GOOD AT MATH AND THE CALCULATOR APP IS ACROSS THE ROOM BUT I'M GONNA GO AHEAD AND SAY BY THE TIME HE'S IN HIGH SCHOOL I'LL STILL BE ABLE TO TOSS HIM BP OR PLAY HORSE OR SOME SHIT. I'LL BE WASHED BUT NOT WASHED BEYOND RECOGNITION. I WON'T BE HOOKED UP TO A SHITBAG OR AN OXYGEN TANK.

The other warp speed to washedness has to do with our beloved hairlines: If you're bald, or even balding, you're immediately auto-washed.

Balding is such a slow process. At first you might notice that your hairline doesn't come down as low as it used to. And that's okay, maybe your barber "pushed your shit back," it will grow back. And maybe you skip a few cuts and let it grow out. But it never quite returns to where it was before, and then little by little, you start to think it may be closer to the back of your head than the front.

There are lots of signs that your hair days are on their way out. Your barber taking a little longer to shape you up, for instance. If your barber stops, looks at you, and attempts to balance your head by turning it slightly side to side, you are in danger.

No one is safe from hairline creep. Even one of the greatest sports players in world history (no, not Serena) has been fighting a very personal and public battle against a receding hairline: King James. A man that both Beyoncé and Rihanna are in love with. And yet: washed. A man who will probably retire with more shots, points, and assists than Jordan. And what does Twitter love to focus on? His hairline. Full disclosure: I was probably one of the worst offenders of roasting LeBron's hair until I got famous and now the karma is killing me. I deserve it.

Imagine hitting a game-winning shot in the play-offs or making an amazing block and then some guy who hasn't been on a basketball court in a decade makes a hilarious meme showing how your hairline is now the same shape as a lunar eclipse. SAD!

(Again, full disclosure, that guy was me.)

Losing your hairline is very traumatic and not to be made light of. There's probably no greater moment of anxiety in human life than walking up to a nightclub and seeing a "no caps" sign. That warm flash of embarrassment that runs through one's (my) chest as you (I) weigh your (my) options. Do you make a scene about dress codes being racist? Do you say "Fuck that, we're going to find a different spot" and ruin the night? Or do you dare take your hat off and go, as we call it in the hood, "urban topless"?

Many an evening will be spent in the bathroom mirror staring at one's scalp and suffering from the follicle oppression created by hair loss. Again, the sad truth is one's hairline doesn't leave all at once—it ebbs and flows like a wave reaching the shoreline, like washedness itself. Maybe you'll end up with a smooth recession that's even and balanced. But NOT LIKELY. The reality is, you're probably going to get the dreaded George Jefferson aka the Mr. Bozo half-bowl look, and that's just sad. Hairline looking like the old Yankee stadium (27 rings, bro!).

At this point, there are two options to "deal" with this hairline erosion. The first, and maybe the more professional option, is to grow out dreadlocks. However, in order to rock dreads with a receding hairline, you have to ask yourself two questions: 1) Am I Stevie Wonder? and 2) Am I a professor of African American studies, a writer, or perhaps a pundit for political television (hello MSNBC)? If the answers were no, then no dreads for you, my guy. Although, dreads with a bald spot screams a monumental lack of concern for external appearances, which is also the best way to be an academic success.

Your final move is the blade. Cutting it all off and going Michael Jordan bald. If you cut all your hair off and people don't immediately ask if you have cancer, then this chop has been a long time coming. Now that you're bald, people are going to be looking at you differently. Think about the friendliest bald person you know. Mr. Clean? Daddy Warbucks? Montel Williams? You're now in the same category as these people. Feel free to invest in high-collared sweaters and turtlenecks because that's your new look. If one is attempting to go full uncle, now would be the time to grab a simple hoop earring. Two hoops might be too much, so start slow.

Now that you've shaved and have your scalp out, you have to determine how to protect said skin. Perhaps it's time to invest in a paperboy-style hat or go full Samuel Jackson and rock a Kangol backwards. SWAG! Maybe a porkpie hat and pretend you're a famous Harlem Renaissance musician. Do you like to troll people online and mess with Rotten Tomato ratings because a comic book film got recast with a female lead? This way to the fedoras, my good washed sir!

Kinda related, but there's no real reason to ever cut off one's facial hair unless it's part of intake protocol for a correctional facility. Growing a beard is a responsibility and if one can grow a proper beard, you owe it to society to let that shit flourish.

There are little weasel-faced dudes out right now who wish their facial hair connected and I need you to recognize and empathize with them. It's no different than being 7'11" and having no interest in basketball. Sometimes you choose the game, sometimes the game chooses you.

SORRY I'M STILL ON MY JUDGMENTAL SHIT. IF YOU DON'T HAVE A CAREER AND YOUR OWN PLACE AND SOME KINDA EQUITY BY THE TIME YOU ARE 35, YOU GOTTA REJIGGER YOUR FUCKIN PLAN, MY PAL. YEAH, YOU WENT TO COLLEGE? THAT'S DOPE. YOU GOT 12 DEGREES? I'M SUPER PROUD OF YOU. BUT GET THE MOTHERFUCK OUT OF MY HOUSE! YOU ATE THE LEFTOVERS FROM CHEESECAKE FACTORY I WAS GONNA SMASH AFTER I BLEW YOUR MOM'S BACK OUT, BUT NOW GUESS WHAT? I CAN'T DO THAT BECAUSE YOU ATE MY FUCKING BANG BANG SHRIMP AND YOUR ROOM IS ACROSS THE HALL, YOU IMMATURE DICKHEAD. NOBODY TOLD YOU TO GET INTO A GAZILLION DOLLARS OF DEBT THAT YOU'LL BE PAYING THE INTEREST ON UNTIL YOU ARE OUTSOURCING YOUR BREATHING TO A GIANT BEEPING BOX IN HOSPICE CARE. THEN YOUR KIDS THAT YOU HAD TOO LATE GOTTA TAKE ON THAT BURDEN. *I* PAID OFF MY WIFE'S *UNDERGRAD* STUDENT LOANS IN THE YEAR OF OUR LORD TWENTY SEVENTEEN, AS PENANCE FOR SELLING WHITE FORDHAM KIDS COKE SO STEPPED ON I CALLED IT SAVION GLOVER. ALSO BECAUSE I HAD THE HOT HAND AT A BLACKJACK TABLE AT THE BELLAGIO IN VEGAS (I'M NOT KIDDING). SHE GRADUATED IN TWO THOUSAND AND FUCKING FIVE. SO SHE WAS PAYING INTEREST ON A LOAN AND NOT TOUCHING THE PRINCIPAL FOR OVER A DECADE. IS THAT WHAT YOU WANT? SOMEBODY TOLD ME IT WAS A BAD IDEA TO GO TO YOUR LOCAL COMMUNITY COLLEGE WHERE YOU'LL PROBABLY GET YOU A FREE RIDE IF YOU HAVE EVEN SEMI-DECENT GRADES OR IF YOU'RE

BROKE. DO YOUR "CORE CLASSES" THERE, THEN GO SOMEWHERE ELSE AND PAY AN EXORBITANT AMOUNT OF MONEY TO DRINK BOXED WINE, EAT SHITTY PIZZA, AND PRETEND LIKE IT'S A LIFE-CHANGING EXPERIENCE. YOU KNOW WHAT WAS A LIFE-CHANGING EXPERIENCE FOR ME? OFFING G-PACKS OF E. THAT WAS A REAL TEACHABLE MOMENT. TELL ME ONE SUPER IMPORTANT THING YOU LEARNED IN THE FIRST 2 YEARS OF UNDERGRAD. I'LL WAIT . . . *DECOMPOSES*

EXACTLY. YOU KNOW HOW MANY TIMES I'VE USED "MLA FORMATTING" OR "APA FORMATTING" IN ANYTHING I EVER WROTE AND GOT PAID FOR? ~ZERO TIMES. OBVIOUSLY THESE ARE THINGS YOU SHOULD LEARN JUST TO HAVE GENERAL KNOWLEDGE, BUT YOU DEFINITELY DON'T HAVE TO FALL INTO THE BOOBY TRAP THE BABY BOOMERS SET UP FOR YOU TO PUNISH YOU FOR BEING YOUNG AND NOT HAVING TO WORRY ABOUT DYING FROM POLIO. I TYPICALLY ONLY USE "SMDFTB" FORMATTING WHEN I WRITE, AND I DAMN SURE WASN'T PAYING 10 RACKS A WEEK OR WHATEVER THE FUCK PRIVATE 4YR COLLEGES ARE CHARGING NOWADAYS.

MY 40-SOMETHING SISTER-IN-LAW—WHO IS SO PROGRESSIVE SHE BE AT BLACK TRANS WOMEN'S MARCHES AND SHIT GETTING LOCKED UP AND WANTING TO COMPLETELY ABOLISH PRISON AND SOME OTHER SHIT. SHIT JOE SHMOE ON TALK RADIO WOULD CALL AN "EXTREMELY RADICAL LIB"—WENT TO A CC, THEN FORDHAM, THEN PRINCETON. DO YOU THINK ANYBODY GIVES A SHIT SHE TOOK ENGLISH 120 AT A COMMUNITY COLLEGE? THEY DO NOT. THEY LOOK AT THE RÉSUMÉ AND "PHD FROM PRINCETON" JUMPS OFF THE PAGE AND KARATE KICKS THEM IN THE FACIAL. SAVE SOME MONEY AND GET SOME GIMME CREDITS AT A COMMUNITY COLLEGE, THEN CONTINUE ON YOUR JOURNEY, YOU DOPE. I WOULD GO AS FAR AS TO SAY GOING TO A COMMUNITY COLLEGE FOR THE FIRST YEARS

GIVES YOU A VERY "BOOTSTRAPS" LOOK ON A RÉSUMÉ. BUT HEY, WHAT DO I KNOW? I JUST DID THAT EXACT THING, THEN I WROTE THIS BOOK THAT YOU BOUGHT THAT IN TURN HELPED ME BUY AN ITALIAN SPORTS CAR.

ANYBODY THAT TELLS YOU TO GO INTO WILD DEBT FOR COLLEGE IS TRYING TO FLEX THEIR SCHOLARSHIP/LUCK/ABILITY TO BREAK DOWN A DEFENSE, OR JUSTIFY THEIR LACK OF FORESIGHT, OR THEY GOT THE MOMMY-AND-DADDY DOLLARS. OR THEY HAVE SOME WEIRD LOYALTY TO A SCHOOL, WHICH UNLESS THEY GOT A FREE RIDE, NEVER MADE SENSE TO ME. MY WIFE'S COLLEGE HITS HER UP FOR MONEY PRETTY OFTEN AND I FEEL LIKE WE'RE PAYING A CRACK DEALER AFTER WE ALREADY PAID FOR AND SMOKED THE CRACK. LIKE HEY YOU MADE SOME PRETTY GOOD CRILZ MY GUY, WE ENJOYED IT, SO HERE'S EXTRA MONEY SO YOU CAN CONTINUE TO MAKE GOOD CRACK AND REPLACE SOME LAPTOPS FROM 2018 TO 2019 MODELS? THAT DOESN'T MAKE ANY SENSE. I'M NOT AN EXPERT IN THIS SHIT BUT IT FEELS LIKE A SCAM, AND MY MOMS ALWAYS TOLD ME, "IF IT LOOKS LIKE A SCAM, IT'S A SCAM" EVERY TIME I STOPPED AND WATCHED MUTHAFUCKAS PLAY 3-CARD MONTE ON FORDHAM ROAD BACK IN THE DAY. YOU PLAYING 3-CARD MONTE WITH YOUR FUTURE B. GO TO COLLEGE.

TO BE CONCISE: DO YOUR FIRST TWO YEARS AT A COMMUNITY COLLEGE AND CONTINUE ON YOUR JOURNEY THROUGH ACADEMIA. YOU WILL SAVE A SHIT TON OF MONEY. TAKE MY WASHED-LIFE ADVICE. PLEASE NOTE ABSOLUTELY NONE OF THIS APPLIES IF YOUR PARENTS HAVE MONEY, OR YOU SECURE A FULL RIDE. THEY ARE GONNA FOOT THE BILL SO DEFINITELY TAKE THE OPPORTUNITY TO DO BONG RIPS FROM NOVELTY BONGS AND WASTE THEIR MONEY BECAUSE REBELLION!! IF DECIPHERING THIS IS MAKING YOUR HEAD HURT GO BACK TO YOUR COLLEGE AND ASK FOR A REFUND.

Okay, I'm not going to lie, I'm pretty confused by what Mero just said, but I'm imagining him just slurring it to me and I'm like "word word" and "that deep" and "true" because as a true friend sometimes you have to be able to let your boy ramble and say things that he thinks are mad deep but they sound like wild after-hours coke talk that have nothing to do with the subject at hand (washedness), and you're like: "Fuck, I gotta take the train home with this person and I need him to sober up." Then he comes back from the bathroom sniffing his nose and he yells at you: "HOLY SHIT. YOU KNOW WHAT? WHAT IF I MADE A CLOTHING LINE FOR CELEBRITIES' MONKEYS? THAT'S AN UNTAPPED MARKET, BRO! WE COULD OWN THAT! FRENCH MONTANA HAS A MONKEY, THAT GUY FROM RAE SHRHUMDER HAS A MONKEY, I THINK MICHAEL JACKSON'S MONKEY MIGHT STILL BE ALIVE BUT HE MIGHT BE A SEX OFFENDER BUT FUCK IT FUCK IT FUCK IT HE NEEDS PANTS AND THEY ALL NEED PANTS AND WHAT IF WE MADE COOGI SWEATERS FOR THEM AND THAT WOULD BE CRAZY BECAUSE THAT'S SUCH DRIP WHOOOOOOOOOO OH MY GOD IS THIS TV ON THE RADIO I FUCKING LOVE THIS TRACK." And you realize you're not going home till like 6am and, as a washed gentleman, you can't live like this.

CHAPTER 8

HOW CAN YOU BALL OUT WHEN YOU'RE BROKE?

THERE ARE TWO WAYS YOU CAN GO ABOUT THIS: YOU CAN BREAK THE LAW OR YOU CAN NOT. IF YOU WANNA BE A LAW-ABIDING CITIZEN, YOU CAN GOOGLE "FREE STUFF TO DO IN [CITY]" AND TRY YOUR LUCK. BUT IF YOU HATE THE LAW AND WANNA BREAK IT, THERE'S OD WAYS TO BALL OUT WITH NO MONEY. HERE IS A SMALL, ITEMIZED LIST OF POSSIBLE STRATEGIES FOR YOU TO GET SOME PAPER IN YOUR BINDER.

1) ROB A NIGGA: THIS SOUNDS EASIER THAN IT IS. YOU COULD JUST SNATCH A PURSE BUT THAT'S SOME GRIMY 1980S SHIT AND YOU MIGHT SNATCH A PURSE THAT HAS NOTHING IN IT BUT SOME PENNIES AT THE BOTTOM AND A CRUMPLED-UP SEPHORA RECEIPT. ALSO, DON'T SNATCH A PURSE BECAUSE THAT'S A VERY MISOGYNIST ACT, UNLESS YOU ARE A WOMAN YOURSELF, IN WHICH CASE YOU ARE JUST A BROKE SCUMBAG. ROBBING SOMEBODY AT GUNPOINT IS MUCH MORE EFFECTIVE BECAUSE GUNS SCARE THE SHIT OUT OF MOST NIGGAS. AS A PER-

SON WHO HAS DISCHARGED MANY FIREARMS—COMPLETELY LEGALLY!!!!!!!!—YOUR AVERAGE STAY-IN-THE-HOUSE JOE AIN'T GOT THE STONES TO BUST A FUCKING SHOT AT ANOTHER PERSON. YOU MAY NOT BE BUILT FOR THIS, SO GO AHEAD AND SKIP TO 3. I THINK THERE'S A WILD MANDATORY MINIMUM SENTENCE FOR ROBBING A NIGGA AT GUNPOINT, GOOGLE IT. SO FOR REAL, DON'T ROB A NIGGA, MY GUY, IT WILL GET YOU IN ALL SORTS OF TROUBLE. NOT WORTH THE HASSLE. BUT IF YOU'RE A FUCKIN GOON AND YOU DON'T GIVE A MUTHAFUCK ABOUT *ANYTHING,* THEN BY ALL MEANS, ROB A NIGGA. ALSO TANGENTIAL BUT VERY RELEVANT: LISTEN TO YOUR OG'S. NOT THE WRONG PLACE/WRONG TIME GUY IN THE BARBERSHOP CONSTANTLY RELIVING THE ONE FELONY CHARGE HE CAUGHT WALKING OUT OF A BODEGA. I MEAN THE ACTUAL OG. THEY WILL GIVE YOU INSIGHT INTO A LIFE OF CRIME AND WHETHER OR NOT IT IS SOMETHING YOU ACTUALLY WANT TO PURSUE. IT IS ASSUREDLY NOT FOR EVERYBODY.

2) BOOST SHIT: I FEEL LIKE I AM THE BOOSTER POSTER BOY AT THIS POINT BUT YOU CAN GO TO MOST STORES, WALK OUT WITH SHIT, COME BACK AND RETURN IT WITH NO RECEIPT. GO TO A DEPARTMENT STORE AND THROW ON A JACKET. IN MOST OF THE TRISTATE AREA, THEY GOT THE WILD ROBOCOP DICK VEIN WIRES SECURING THE COATS TO THE RACK, SO YOU NEED THE HEAVY WIRE CUTTERS. BUT BE CAREFUL BECAUSE SOME PLACES GOT LOSS PREVENTION NIGGAS THAT TAKE THEIR JOB OD SERIOUSLY AND WILL DEAD-ASS TRY TO TACKLE YOU FOR THROWING SOME TRUES UP THE BACK. STROLLERS ARE LIT BECAUSE YOU CAN THROW MAD SHIT IN THE LIL UNDER-PART AND IF YOU HAVE AN ACTUAL KID IN THE SHIT YOU CAN BLAME IT ON THEM IF YOU GOT PINCHED.

3) THIS IS GONNA SOUND CRAZY . . . GET A FUCKIN JOB?? WHAT ARE YOU FUCKING 17 YEARS OLD? WHY THE FUCK WOULD

YOU DO EITHER OF THOSE OTHER THINGS I JUST SUGGESTED? WHY DO YOU EVEN HAVE A GUN, YOU JERK? YOU GET IN MAD TROUBLE FOR THAT SHIT MY GUY! CHILL. YOU'RE A HOTHEAD, YOU MIGHT SHOOT A NIGGA FOR CUTTING YOU IN LINE AT THE ICE CREAM TRUCK. AND IT'S A NEW GUY, NOT THE USUAL GUY, SO HE'S DEFINITELY SNITCHING ON YOU WHEN YOU RUN DIRECTLY BACK IN THE BUILDING LIKE A WINGDING. GO GET A JOB MY GUY. I KNOW THAT'S EASIER SAID THAN DONE BUT LET'S KEEP IT FUNKY—SOME OF Y'ALL AIN'T REEEALLLYYY TRYING FOR EMPLOYMENT. YOU MAY BE BEING KEPT AFLOAT BY A PARENT OR PARTNER, BUT YOU DON'T HAVE MONEY TO BALL OUT AND TO BE HONEST IF YOU ARE TRYING TO MAKE AN HONEST LIVING (I'M SPEAKING AS AN NYC RESIDENT). IT'S OD HARD TO KEEP YOUR BILLS PAID AND BALL OUT IF YOU'RE A REGULAR NIGGA. LUCKILY I'M NOT A REGULAR NIGGA ANYMORE [OBNOXIOUS CHUCKLE] AND I'M OUT HERE BUYING MULTIPLE RECLINERS TRYNA KEEP MY LIMBS COZY, WORD TO YAMS (RIP). IF YOU ARE A REGULAR NIGGA, JUST GET SOMEONE YOU DON'T CARE ABOUT TO COSIGN YOU ON A CREDIT CARD AND RUN THAT SHIT UP. YOU DO THAT SHIT FOR A COUPLE MONTHS UNTIL SOMEONE COMES KNOCKIN, NAH SMASHINGGG ON YOUR MOM'S APARTMENT DOOR, STARTLING YOU OUT OF YOUR RESTLESS COUCH SLEEP. YOU OPEN THE DOOR LIKE WHAT THE FUCK NI—!!! AND BEFORE YOU CAN GET THE SECOND SYLLABLE OUT, OFFICERS PETROZULLI AND PROSCIUTTO BOTH GOT THEIR KNEES IN YOUR HERNIATED DISC AND IMMEDIATELY CUFF YOUR DUMB ASS CUZ YOU WANTED TO SMOKE HOOKAH WITH A GIRL WITH A FAKE BUT VERY AESTHETICALLY PLEASING BUTT. GET A FUCKIN JOB AND WORK SOME OT.

Balling out when you're broke sounds difficult but it's wild easy, especially if you live in the greatest city in the world (NYC). I say this because this city is expensive as fuck and you can spend $100 within 20 minutes of leaving your crib, so being frugal is an essential life skill.

Here's a very easy way to ball out while broke without breaking the law: art galleries! They give free wine away and all you have to do is look at some weird photo or painting and say something like "Wow, the Dickensian aspect really jumped out at me," or "Incredible. So powerful and moving at the same time." And if you really want to make your mark, look at the price and put your hand under your chin as if you're seriously thinking about purchasing it, but then say "My funds aren't liquid enough right now." This works especially well if you're a minority because people will assume you're a rapper or athlete.

Focus groups are the main source of income for many New Yorkers, including myself at one time. Where else can you get $250 CASH for sitting in a room with strangers and lying about some product you don't use, won't use, and will never see again? I've done focus groups for strap-ons, baby strollers, deodorants, whatever. As long as the cash flows and I don't have to take a photo, let's go. If you're a G and become an expert-level focus grouper, you'll get good enough to schedule multiple groups in the same night. *CHING CHING* BABY.

Another tried-and-true way to make money: LAWSUITS! Listen, if you're broke, you know from watching daytime TV (*Jerry Springer, Judge Judy,* etc.) that the most frequent advertisements are for lawyers. And guess what, these lawyers are wild shady and will help you sue anyone you want! Maybe your belt loop got snagged while leaving the subway. That's a lawsuit! Someone misspell your name at Starbucks? Lawsuit for pain and suffering! The world of lawsuits is limitless. You ever see those subway grates in New York City? We New Yorkers call those insurance grates because all you have to do is stand on one and have it fall in and now you're a millionaire. Yeah, you won't be able to walk but I mean that's a better problem to have than extreme brokeness.

IF YOU ARE BROKE, WHAT DO YOU DO IF . . .

YOU ARE GOING ON A DATE?

IF YOU ARE SUPER OD POPPED AND NEED TO GO ON A DATE, I HOPE YOU LIVE IN A CITY THAT HAS COOL PUBLIC SHIT BECAUSE THAT'S BASICALLY YOUR ONLY OPTION. I KNOW "NETFLIX AND CHILL" IS FUNNY AND EVERYTHING, BUT TRY PULLIN THAT SHIT ON A FIRST DATE. THE OTHER PERSON IS GONNA BE LIKE "SO YOU TRYNA SMASH BASICALLY?" LET'S BE HONEST HERE, IF YOU INVITE SOMEONE TO YOUR CRIB, YOU'RE CROSSING A LOT OF LINES. THE PERSON NOW KNOWS WHERE YOU LIVE AND EVER SINCE THAT GABRIELLE UNION MOVIE (WHICH SHE WAS GREAT IN, BTW) WHERE THESE CREEPY MUTHAFUCKAS DO A HOME INVASION, I'M SUPER WEIRD ABOUT THAT SHIT. MATTERFACT THE DUDE THAT SOLD ME MY CAR SAID "DON'T EVER PUT YOUR ACTUAL ADDRESS AS 'HOME' ON YOUR GPS." I WAS LIKE "LOL, WHAT A PARANOID CREEP." THEN I WENT HOME, SMOKED AN L, AND WAS LIKE "OH SHIT WAIT, HE'S RIGHT, WHAT IF . . ." THEN I VERY SMACKEDLY CHANGED "HOME" TO A RANDOM BUSINESS IN MY GENERAL AREA AND MEMORIZED THE ROUTE HOME FROM THERE. NOW THAT I THINK ABOUT IT, THAT EXPLAINS WHY I'VE GOTTEN SMIZZY AT SOME FUNCTIONS AND ENDED UP BEING MIND-BENDINGLY CONFUSED FOR 5 MINUTES IN FRONT OF A CLOSED SALON ON SEVERAL OCCASIONS.

IF YOU LIVE NEAR RELIABLE TRANSIT, GOT UBER MONEY, OR GOT PARKING MONEY, YOU GUCCI ON TRANSPORTATION. BUT YOU'RE BROKE SO YOU GOTTA SUGGEST MEETING AT THE VENUE YOU PLAN TO ATTEND. THINK ABOUT HOW AWKWARD A

40-MINUTE TRAIN RIDE IS IF YOU GOT NOTHING TO TALK ABOUT. THE INVERSE OF THAT *IS* POSSIBLE SO FUCK IT, TRY IT. LET ME KNOW HOW IT WORKS OUT FOR YOU. YOU MIGHT BE A SUPER OD CONVERSATIONALIST, WHO KNOWS? OR MAYBE YOU SAY SOMETHING WILD AND THE DATE IS OVER BEFORE IT EVEN STARTED, CONGRATULATIONS YOU WENT ON A DATE FOR 40 MINUTES ON THE 6 LOCAL NEXT TO EARTH ANGEL (GOOGLE HIM, YOU'RE IN FOR A TREAT) BECAUSE YOU CAME OUT THE GATE WITH SOME DUMB SHIT.

IT'S 2020 MY GUY. THERE'S NO HIDING THAT YOU ARE BROKER THAN PAUL GEORGE'S LEG WHEN IT COMES TIME TO LIVE IN THE ANALOG WORLD. YOU CAN FRONT AND STUNT ALL OVER THE PLACE ON SOCIAL MEDIA BUT ONCE YOU SECURE A DATE WITH SOMEONE, THEY ARE GONNA FIND OUT YOU ARE BROKE AS SHIT.

BUT MERO, HOW THEY GONNA FIND OUT? I'MA JUST DO SOME COOL FREE SHIT LIKE YOU SAID AND MAYBE GO FOR A WALK IN CENTRAL PARK ON A NICE DAY OR GO TO A MUSEUM OR SOME SHIT.

HEY, GUESS WHAT, JERK. EVERYBODY KNOWS THOSE ARE BROKE DATE IDEAS. IF YOU GOOGLE "CHEAP DATE IDEAS," MUSEUMS ARE LIKE THE SECOND RESULT NOW THAT BACKPAGE .COM IS NO LONGER WITH US (IN RETROSPECT I SAY RIP BACKPAGE A LOT FOR A DUDE WHO NEVER ACTUALLY UTILIZED IT). MUSEUMS AND PARKS AND SHIT LIKE THAT IS A RED FLAG ON A FIRST DATE. IN FACT IT'S A GIANT RED FLAG THAT HAS "I AM OUTSTANDINGLY POPPED" WRITTEN ON IT IN ARIAL BLACK FONT. UNDERLINED, BOLDED. UNLESS OF COURSE YOU'RE WHITE. IF YOU'RE WHITE, YOU CAN BE LIKE "HEY, MEG, LET'S GO ON A DATE! LET'S GO HIKING! WE CAN HIT THE NOVICE TRAIL SO WE CAN TALK ABOUT OUR FAVORITE INTERPOL SONGS WHILE WE ENJOY NATURE!" GO AHEAD AND TRY TO TAKE YES-

ENIA HIKING ON A FIRST DATE AND SEE HOW FAST YOU GET CURSED OUT.

I HAVEN'T DATED IN LIKE A DECADE PLUS SO I BEEN OUTTA THE GAME, I'M GIVING YOU OLD ADVICE. MAYBE NOWADAYS FACETIMING SOMEONE AND HAVING A CHAT IS CONSIDERED A FIRST DATE, WHO THE FUCK KNOWS? I'M NOT OUT HERE LIKE THAT. I'M IN THE HOUSE LIKE CHANCLETAS MINDING MY BUSINESS AND WRITING THIS BOOK SO I DON'T HAVE TO GOOGLE "CHEAP DATE IDEAS" AND TAKE MY WIFE TO A MUSEUM. I ALREADY PUT THAT WORK IN AND GUESS WHAT? I DIDN'T HAVE AN EXTREMELY ERUDITE DOMINICAN GUY TO HOLD MY HAND THROUGH THE PROCESS. I KNOW YOU BOUGHT THIS TO DO THE KNOWLEDGE BUT THE ANSWER HERE IS THAT THERE'S NO ANSWER. YOU GOTTA SPEND MONEY TO MAKE MONEY, OR IN THIS CASE, GET LAID. UNLESS YOU ARE INCREDIBLY CHARMING. *SMILES*

If you're broke and going on a date, it's going to take a lot more effort to accomplish what you want. But if you're careful, it's fully doable. First off you have to tell the person you're dating that you're either a musician or a poet. Either of those jobs is perfect for being broke and, worse comes to worst, you can say "Oh, I don't really fuck with capitalism" and low-key that's hella sexy because now yeah, you seem wild woke, but also political and like a young Obama.

Sticking with this lie, I suggest taking a date to a good book reading or author night at a bookstore or library. Now, this is probably boring af (unless it's me reading this book) but it's an easy date and you can either act super into whatever's being read or just completely shit on it afterward and by then, the other person shoulda kinda figured out there's no money being spent tonight.

Here's another hint: Walking. Walking sucks but just lie and say you enjoy walking. Now it's suddenly a magical mysterious event where people reveal their soul to you, tell you how many kids they want, and maybe drop a hint about the time their father walked out. So as long as you keep the conversation going, they won't notice that a) they're walking and b) you're not spending any money.

Now, you'll have to spend *some* money, but the trick is to spend the least amount possible while making it seem like you're spending hella money. The answer: CARIDAD KING RESTAURANTS. I know that unless you're from the tristate area, you have no idea what a Caridad King restaurant is, so let me explain. Imagine a restaurant with no pretense, just delicious food for cheap. What type of food are we talking about? Rotisserie chicken, rice and beans, stewed oxtails, etc. And all of this for like $12 for two people! Now, this might sound too good to be true, but if you tell your date you "enjoy the down-home aspect of the restaurant and you also want to support local ethnic businesses" you should be good money in this situation. And if you don't have a Caridad King near you, move?

Also, and I'm sad to even offer this as an option: ROB THE PERSON YOU'RE DATING. Yes, I admit that this is extremely rude and immature but I'd like to remind you readers that I'm one half of the *sucio* boys and we are terrible people. There are plenty of ways to pull this off. My favorite is to physically take someone's phone and then Cash App yourself some money (sponsored sentence). Do this right before the date and they won't even know they're paying for themselves. Genius. Another trick is to have your homeboy stick you and your date up while leaving a restaurant, and then you and the robber divide the cash later. Genius again!

Listen, where there's a will, there's a way, and that way will make people pay!

IF YOU ARE BROKE, WHAT DO YOU DO IF . . .

YOU HAVE A HEALTH EMERGENCY?

IF YOU ARE BROKE AND HAVE A HEALTH EMERGENCY YOU CAN CALL AN AMBULANCE. THEY WILL COME LOAD YOU UP AND TAKE YOU TO THE ER DEPENDING ON THE SEVERITY OF YOUR EMERGENCY. DEPENDING ON THE HOOD YOU'RE IN, YOU EITHER GONNA SIT THERE FOR 19 HOURS OR GET RUSHED INTO A CURTAINED-OFF AREA WHERE AFTER A FEW MINUTES A DOCTOR WILL COME ASK YOU A BUNCH OF QUESTIONS, CHECK YOU OUT, AND TAKE APPROPRIATE ACTION. EASY PEASY, RIGHT? WE LIVE IN THE UNITED STATES OF AMERICA B, A VERY DEVELOPED NATION OR SUPERPOWER OR WHATEVER. OBVIOUSLY IF YOU FALL DOWN THE STAIRS GETTING OFF THE 6 TRAIN AND INJURE YOURSELF, YOU ARE GOING TO GET THAT TAKEN CARE OF FOR FREE BECAUSE YOU PAY TAXES AND SHIT RIGHT? **ENH!! WRONG!!**

AT THE END OF IT ALL, MY BROKE PAL, NO MATTER WHAT, YOU GETTING A MOTHERFUCKING BILL SO BIG ITS LAST NAME SHOULD BE RUSSELL. FAM I TOOK AN AMBULANCE FROM EAST TREMONT & DEWEY AVE IN THE BRONX TO JACOBI HOSPITAL (ALSO IN THE BRONX) AND THE SHIT WAS $1,800. FOR $1,800 AN UBER DRIVER WILL PARTICIPATE IN A DRIVE-BY SHOOTING WITH YOU, NO MASK. OR FOR THAT SAME 1,800 U.S. DOLLARS, A BABY SCHOOL BUS WITH SIRENS AND AN OXYGEN TANK CAN TAKE YOU TO THE HOSPITAL TO MEET YOUR FATE. IT AIN'T A RUMOR THAT HEALTHCARE IN THE U.S. IS FUCKED ALL THE WAY UP. DO YOU KNOW HOW MUCH IT WOULD COST YOU TO HAVE A BABY OUTTA POCKET, NO INSURANCE? ENOUGH TO BUY A MID-LEVEL LUXURY SEDAN WITH A TECH PACKAGE B. MAD FUCKIN MONEY. I'M NOT EVEN GONNA PRETEND I KNOW HOW THE

FUCK MEDICAL BILLING IS DONE BUT THEY MUST BE DOING VISUAL BUDGETS USING MONOPOLY MONEY. I LOOK AT THOSE RECEIPTS AND I'M LIKE, "THAT NIGGA WITH THE HAIRNET WHO WAS STANDING IN THE CORNER "JUST IN CASE" COST 10 RACKS?!" YOU KNOW HOW FUCKIN IRATE THAT MAKES ME B?

FOR A WHILE I WAS PAYING MORE FOR MY HEALTH INSURANCE THAN MY RENT. IN PLAIN SPOKEN ENGLISH, I WAS DEADASS PAYING MORE TO HAVE THE ABILITY TO INJURE MYSELF AND NOT COME OUT OF POCKET THAN I WAS FOR A **PLACE TO LIVE**. HOW FUCKIN STUPID DOES THAT SOUND? I GOT HEALTH INSURANCE NOW AND IF I DIDN'T I WOULD BE ABSOLUTELY FUCKED B. 4 KIDS, 3 IN SCHOOL, GERMS GALORE, MAD DOCTORS VISITS.

I DIGRESS, YOU'RE BROKE. YOU CAN APPLY FOR LOW-INCOME INSURANCE BUT IT MIGHT BE QUIET FOR YOU. OTHER THAN THAT YOU GOTTA BE HEALTHY. YOU CAN'T PREVENT AN ACCIDENT BUT YOU CAN PREVENT SHITTING IN YOUR PANTS BC YOU ATE TOO MUCH NUTELLA. TRY TO KEEP A HEALTHY DIET, WHICH IS EASIER SAID THAN DONE CONSIDERING YOUR ETHNICITY AND SOME OTHER FACTORS. AS A DOMINICAN, HAVING A TRADITIONAL DOMINICAN BREAKFAST CONSISTS OF FRIED CHEESE, FRIED SALAMI, AND MASHED-UP PLATANOS WITH A STICK OF BUTTER IN IT. YOU CAN TAKE OR LEAVE THE 2 FRIED EGGS. LISTEN, I'M NO NUTRITIONIST, BUT THAT'S NOT THE HEALTHIEST BREAKFAST. I FEEL LIKE A GENERAL RULE THAT HOLDS TRUE IS: IF THE SHIT IS FROZEN AND YOU HAVE TO MICROWAVE IT, IT'S PROBABLY NOT GOOD FOR YOU. SO NO 3AM BODEGA SPINNING-WINDOW MICROWAVED ATROCITY BECAUSE YOU'RE DRUNK AND WANNA EAT. ALSO DRINKING A LOT IS BAD AND DEFINITELY NOT HEALTHY.

IF YOU'RE REALLY BROKE YOU SHOULD BE KINDA IN SHAPE BECAUSE YOU WALKIN EVERYWHERE. OH WAIT YOU DON'T ALL

LIVE IN THE NY METRO AREA: (DAMN I HOPE YOU GOT A CAR B.) THIS IS KINDA HARD TO ANSWER CUZ IT'S LIKE IF YOU LIVE IN A CITY THAT'S WALKABLE, BEIN BROKE IS WAY MORE DOABLE THAN IF YOU LIVE IN A DRIVING CITY. I GUESS I'LL BUST IT DOWN BY THOSE TWO FACTORS . . .

I DONT EVEN NEED A CAR, I LIVE A BLOCK AWAY FROM 72ND ST ON THE 1: FIRST OF ALL, YOU DON'T NEED TO BRAG B. I'M IN A HOUSE NOW. HAVING A PARKING SPOT OR LIVING A BLOCK AWAY FROM THE TRAIN MEANS NOTHING TO ME ANYMORE. I PARK MY CAR INDOORS. ANYWAY, THIS IS NOT ABOUT ME DOING A LIL BABY FLEX (*SCREAMS* YES HAVING A GARAGE IS A FUCKING FLEX IF YOU WENT FROM A 2-BR APARTMENT THAT HOUSED ANYWHERE FROM 6 TO 8 PPL AT A TIME!!!). THIS IS ABOUT YOU STAYING HEALTHY AND BEING BROKE. HONESTLY BEING BROKE SHOULD KEEP YOU HEALTHY. I KNOW I HAD THIS WHOLE SETUP FOR DRIVING CITIES VS. NON-DRIVING CITIES AND YOU WERE LIKE, "WHERE IS HE GOING WITH THIS?" BUT IF YOU BROKE, YOU NOT OVEREATING AND YOU WALKING A LOT OR STANDING ON PUBLIC TRANSIT, AND IF THE CITY'S NOT WALKABLE, YOU EITHER STAY IN YOUR TOWN, EAT RIGHT, AND WORK OUT, OR SAVE UP AND GET A MAAAAD CHEAP, RELIABLE 4-CYLINDER VEHICLE, DRIVE TO HIKING TRAILS, AND DO OTHER WHITE PEOPLE SHIT LIKE CROSSFIT OR WHATEVER, BUT A CHEAP VERSION. THIS MIGHT BE A LATE TAKE WHEN THIS HITS SHELVES, BUT LET IT BE KNOWN ON SUNDAY, 30TH OF SEPTEMBER 2018, I'M CALLIN' IT: CROSSFIT IS THE KABBALAH OF FITNESS. MADONNA STARTED IT, SHE'S USING IT TO STEAL YOUR YOUTH B.

YOU COULD ALSO THUG IT OUT AND WORK OUT AT YOUR LOCAL PLAYGROUND. THEY GOT MONKEY BARS AND SHIT FOR YOU TO DO PULL-UPS. JUST MAKE SURE IT'S NOT THE MIDDLE OF THE DAY AND IT'S NOT CRAWLING WITH KIDS. WAKE UP AT 6AM, DRINK A ROOM-TEMP GLASS OF WATER, THEN GO WORK

OUT TILL YOU GOTTA TAKE A SHIT OR YOU FEEL LIKE PASSING OUT, WHICHEVER COMES FIRST. IF YOU DO THAT CONSISTENTLY, YOU SHOULD BE OKAY. LOOK, I TOLD YOU I'M NOT A NUTRITIONIST AND I'M ALSO NOT A PERSONAL TRAINER. THIS IS PRETTY COMMON SENSE SHIT THOUGH. DON'T EAT GARBAGE AT 3AM AND GET AN APPROPRIATE AMOUNT OF EXERCISE IN. YOU'LL BE AIGHT, YOU TOUGH RIGHT?

If you're broke and you have a health emergency, that could possibly be the easiest thing you'll ever have to handle. When I was uninsured, I lived in constant fear of injury or sickness because I didn't want to get that big-ass bill from the hospital. But one day I realized something deep: "Fuck that bill." Like what kinda shitty society do we live in where you have to have a fat bank account for attempting to survive? So I say to you, go to the hospital if you're sick, even if you don't have insurance, and when you fill out that intake form be sure to, ummmmmm, forget your actual social security number. Yes they might find you, but you'll be alive and can tell the bill collector to suck ya dick from the back because you're alive, with fucked-up credit, but alive.

But let me backtrack. What if you're broke but not sick enough for a hospital visit? Simple hood solution guaranteed to work 1,000% of the time: egg drop soup from your nearest Chinese food shop (or Chinese takeaway if you're across the pond). It's a lifesaver and will cure you no matter what ails you. Sore throat? Pregnancy? Cancer? Egg drop soup will cure any of these. It's a scientific fact. Don't debate me or quote me.

Another proven remedy for sickness is ginger ale. Yes, the lowly official beverage of Canada isn't just for upset stomachs. In the West Indies we use this drink for everything. Dirty clothing? Ginger ale. Headache? Ginger ale. Ugly baby? Rum and ginger ale. Nothing that golden bubble juice can't cure and it's available everywhere for like a dollar.

Last but not least, if you're really sick there's one more all-the-time solution: ALCOHOL. Rubbing alcohol, Wray and Nephew, vodka, whatever. As long as it stings on a cut, it's good for you. Drink a strong cocktail and pass out until you feel better (or if that doesn't work, have more when you wake up). Rub some rum on your head if you have a fever. You got an infected tooth? Rinse with cheap vodka. Alcohol solves a shitload of problems and also creates a shitload of problems but also solves those same new created problems.

IF YOU ARE BROKE, WHAT DO YOU DO IF . . .

YOU NEED TO PAY RENT?

YO YOU MIGHT BE BETTER SERVED READING DESUS'S ACCOUNTS OF NEAR EVICTION. I NEVER FRONTED ON MY RENT. MY PARENTS DRILLED THAT SHIT SO INTENSELY INTO MY HEAD, I THOUGHT IF YOU WERE ONE DAY LATE ON YOUR RENT YOU WERE OUT ON THE STREET. THAT'S NOT ACTUALLY WHAT HAPPENS. I HAVE BEEN A DAY OR TWO LATE ON RENT HAVING PANIC ATTACKS ABOUT DROPPING OFF A CHECK BY HAND BEFORE THE MANAGEMENT OFFICE CLOSES BECAUSE I'M IMAGINING MY XBOX SITTING IN FRONT OF THE BUILDING ON A PILE OF NORTH FACE JACKETS AND HALF A BOX OF DUTCHES. IF YOU GOT A MONTH OR TWO PILED UP THOUGH? THE LANDLORD IS COMING FOR YOUR ASS B.

FIRST COME SOME LETTERS, THEN HE SENDS HIS MINION THE SUPER UP TO DELIVER THE MESSAGE. I'VE SEEN THIS HAPPEN TO FRIENDS AND THE SECONDHAND EMBARRASSMENT WAS FUCKIN INTENSE. WE SITTING THERE PLAYING HALO SMOKING MAD WEED ORDERING OFF THE MENU AT KENNEDY FRIED AND MY GUY AIN'T PAID THE RENT? I KNOW THERE'S

SOME PART OF THE FRONTAL LOBE OF THE HUMAN BRAIN THAT HANDLES IMPULSE CONTROL AND DECISION-MAKING AND I KNOW IT ISN'T "FULLY DEVELOPED" UNTIL YOUR LATE 20S (TYPICALLY), BUT I ALWAYS PRIORITIZED SHIT IN ORDER OF FINESSABILITY. FOR EXAMPLE, IT'S WAY EASIER TO FINESSE A QUARTER ZIP OF WEED THAN IT IS TO FINESSE A CAR OR SOME SHIT. BY THE WAY, THIS IS ALL ASSUMING YOU LIVE IN A BUILDING WITH MORE THAN 3 UNITS. IF YOU ARE RENTING AN APT IN A 3-FAMILY HOUSE YOU CAN BUILD A RAPPORT WITH THAT PERSON AND MAYBE YOUR RENT FINESSABILITY GOES UP. IF YOU LIVE IN A BUILDING-BUILDING, YOU MIGHT NOT EVEN SEE YOUR FUCKIN LANDLORD. HE MIGHT NEVER LEAVE WESTCHESTER. YOUR ONLY LINE OF COMMS IS THE SUPER AND THE MANAGEMENT OFFICE. YOU CAN BUILD A RAPPORT WITH THE SUPER BUT IMA BE REAL WITH YOU, CHIEF: THE LANDLORD GIVES ABOUT AS MUCH OF A FUCK ABOUT THE SUPER AS HE DOES YOU. SO THE SUPER CAN'T CALL IN A FAVOR FOR YOU. YOU CAN TRY THE MANAGEMENT OFFICE, BUT I'M NOT EVEN SURE ALL BUILDINGS HAVE THAT, AND ALSO I WAS NEVER LATE ON MY RENT. THAT'S NOT A BRAG OR NOTHING; IT'S JUST A MEANINGLESS STAT LIKE "RJ BARRETT NOW HAS 30 GAMES IN A ROW WHERE HE HAS HIGH-FIVED A TEAMMATE WITH HIS LEFT HAND!" EXCEPT IT'S KINDA NOT SO MEANINGLESS BECAUSE YOUR CREDIT AND WHATEVER.

BUT FINESSABILITY IS IMPORTANT TO UNDERSTAND B. YOUR WEED GUY COULD BE SUPER CHILL AND BE LIKE "YEAH I'LL OPEN UP A TAB FOR YOU" LIKE A FUCKIN BARTENDER. YOUR LANDLORD DOESN'T WANNA HEAR SHIT ABOUT SHIT. THEY JUST WANT THEY MUTHAFUCKIN MONEY ON THE 16TH BECAUSE YOU ALREADY EXPLAINED HOW YOU GET PAID BIWEEKLY BUT SOMETIMES IT TAKES X AMOUNT OF HOURS TO CLEAR AND BULLSHIT YADIDADI DA. THEY DON'T CARE. YOU

CAN ALWAYS RANDOMLY CARTWHEEL INTO A BLUNT CYPHER AND BE A FUNNY CHARMING INDIVIDUAL AND NOT HAVE TO SPEND A DIME. BUT YOU AREN'T GONNA CHARM YOUR LANDLORD INTO LETTING YOU NOT PAY FOR YOUR 1-BEDROOM THAT YOU SHARE WITH THAT FUCKING MOUSE THAT IS ALWAYS IN THE FUCKIN STOVE AND I SWEAR TO GOD IF I WASNT NERVOUS ABOUT GLUE TRAPS BEING FLAMMABLE I WOULD LINE THE ENTIRE SHIT WITH GLUE TRAPS AND THEN FUCKIN FRY 28 PANCAKES ON ALL 4 BURNERS, YOU LITTLE PIECE OF VERMIN SHIT. YOU CHEWED A HOLE IN MY FUCKING CEREAL, YOU ASSHOLE. IT WAS BAGGED AND COST A DOLLAR BUT I WAS LOOKING FORWARD TO EATING IT BY THE HANDFUL IN WHAT MY WIFE CALLS A "HIGH MANIA." NOT ONLY DO YOU VIOLATE ON THAT LEVEL, YOU THEN HAD THE AUDACITY TO TAKE 4 LITTLE TINY CYLINDRICAL SHITS ON THE STOVETOP. THEY LOOK LIKE THE WORLD'S TINIEST BACKWOODS. I WAS STARVING, I'M LATE TO WORK, AND THIS IS WHAT I'M WAKING UP TO, SO NOW I AM A FLAMING BALL OF FURY. FUCK MICE. I'M GONNA WATCH 500 SNAKE-FEEDING VIDEOS NOW. *OPENS YOUTUBE TAB*

My father was a property owner and landlord so I grew up with the totally twisted viewpoint that tenants were all scammers. To hear my pops tell it, "they're always complaining and never paying their rent." I remember people calling at 3am complaining about not having heat and I was like, "I can't really help you with that ma'am, I'm 7." My father constantly had tenants running out and leaving him holding the bag, so I always felt bad like, "Wow, my poor father with these terrible tenants!"

That all went out the window as soon as I became a tenant and saw how life really works. The notion that every person will have their rent on time every month is wild ridiculous, especially with the way rent goes up every year. You could be a perfect taxpayer and never late on your rent, and then you get into a medical accident or lose a job, or even just your rent or power bill goes up, and now you're in the quicksand of late rent.

Even the very concept of "late rent" is mind-blowing when you really think about it. You work your ass off to pay your rent and try to have something left over after paying your bills (nothing for savings because let's be real here, savings are for rich people). If you have one hiccup (fired, medical, etc.) and get just one month behind in your rent, you now have to double your monthly income to make enough for 2 months' rent. HOW? HOW DO YOU DO THAT? Even if you apply for a new job, you're not going to get a paycheck for weeks in the best-case scenario. Shit is wild unfair. So you're gonna have to get your brain into extreme grind mode.

OKAY, I'M BACK. I WATCHED 3 MICE GET EATEN BY SNAKES AND IT WASN'T NEARLY AS CATHARTIC AS I HOPED IT WOULD BE. BUT LISTEN, MAKE SACRIFICES ELSEWHERE B. STAY THE FUCK HOME AND SAVE MONEY. SELL SOME SHIT. PICK UP HALF A PACK. I WAS A DIRTBAG, FAM. I DIDN'T HAVE CREDIT FOR SHIT. I GOT MY FIRST CREDIT CARD BECAUSE THEY SET UP BOOTHS OUTSIDE HUNTER COLLEGE AND PREYED ON MY DESIRE FOR A WATER BOTTLE AND A T-SHIRT. MY CREDIT LIMIT WAS $250. MY BALANCE WAS NO LESS THAN 400 SOMETHING DOLLARS A MONTH, EVERY MONTH. I WAS BLOWTORCHING MY CREDIT NOT KNOWING THAT YOU NEED GOOD CREDIT TO LIVE LIFE IN THE USA. IF YOUR CREDIT IS TRASH, YOUR LIFE IS FUCKED, IT'S WILD. I TRIED TO GET A TV ON CREDIT AT BEST BUY AND THEY WERE LIKE "FUCK OUTTA HERE, YOUR CREDIT IS WORSE THAN THE SOUND OF ORPHANS CRYING." IF YOU A YOUNG PERSON AND YOU AREN'T THE WISEST CREDIT CARD USER, PAYING YOUR RENT ON TIME AT LEAST PUTS A CHECK IN YOUR "THIS NIGGA

PAYS ON TIME" COLUMN. NONE OF THIS CREDIT ADVICE APPLIES IF YOU'RE DEDICATED TO LIVING A LIFE OF CRIME AND SCAMMING, IN INTERMITTENT SQUALOR, OR IF YOU'RE DISGUSTINGLY RICH. FOR THOSE OF YOU WHO ARE REGULAR DEGULAR WORKING PEOPLE LIVING LIFE, IF YOU WANT TO BETTER YOUR LIFE AND EVENTUALLY ELEVATE TO "I AM A GROWN-UP!" YOU NEED CREDIT (OR VERY RICH GENEROUS PARENTS TO PUT DOWN ALL THAT UP-FRONT MONEY YOU'RE GONNA NEED BECAUSE YOUR CREDIT IS LOWER THAN PAUL GEORGE'S HAIRLINE.) I KNEW I COULDN'T BUY A HOUSE, OR A CAR, OR OTHER ADULT NECESSITIES LIKE, SHIT, I DON'T KNOW, CHAIRS? BECAUSE MY CREDIT WAS TERRIBLE. HAVING GOOD CREDIT LITERALLY SAVED ME TONS OF MONEY ON MY HOUSE. I COULD GET INTO MORTGAGE RATES AND SHIT LIKE THAT BUT IF YOU READING THIS AND YOU'RE 19 YOU'RE LIKE "CHILL FAM YOU'RE GIVING ME ANXIETY." LISTEN DOG JUST DON'T THROW BLEACH IN YOUR CREDIT'S FACE IN YOUR YOUTH. IT WILL HAUNT YOU. MERO DID THAT SO HOPEFULLY YOU WON'T HAVE TO GO THROUGH THAT. IF YOU RENT AND THINK WHEN YOU TRY TO GET THAT APARTMENT THEY AREN'T RUNNING YOUR CREDIT TO FIGURE OUT HOW HEFTY THAT DEPOSIT + (x)MONTHS RENT UP FRONT IS GONNA BE? YOU ARE FUCKIN BUGGIN. I WAS GONNA SAY "DON'T TAKE CREDIT ADVICE FROM ANYBODY WHO DOESN'T OWN PROPERTY." BUT THEN I REALIZED THERE'S KIDS STUDYING THIS SHIT WHO KNOW ABOUT IT SO I TAKE IT BACK. ALSO *A LOT* OF THIS IS INFORMATION PASSED DOWN TO ME BY MY ACCOUNTANT AND MY MOM WHOSE MASTER'S IS IN ACCOUNTING. PROUD OF YOU MOM. SHOUT-OUT TO STEVIE P!

Credit is wild overrated and this is me keeping it a hundred percent trill and real with you: If you are from the hood, you figure you'll probably be dead or locked up by 30, so buying a house or a car seems like some dumb shit to save up for. And the idea of buying a house in 2020 when you aren't on TV might as well go in our drug chapter. So you gotta look at your credit card like your shot at greatness. Basically what I'm saying is, run up what you need right now on your card so that you have actual cash to attempt to pay rent. When I was super broke and it was just me, my cat, and dog, I immediately bought the biggest bags of pet food I could and threw them on my Visa because, worse comes to worst, I'd always be able to find a meal for myself but I couldn't let my babies starve. Did I worry about paying back that credit card? If you're about to live in the streets, you don't give a flying fuck about credit. You have much more pressing issues than something that can be handled at creditscore.com.

THAT'S RIGHT. SACRIFICE SHIT NIGGA! SOME OF YOU READING THIS NEVER HAD TO SACRIFICE SHIT. YOU ARE VERY LUCKY SO BE VERY GRATEFUL. I SOUND LIKE JAY-Z SCOLDING YOU EXCEPT NONE OF THIS SHIT RHYMES LOL. DO WHAT YOU GOTTA DO BUT GET THAT RENT MONEY ONDECKI MATSUI. HUSTLE IF YOU GOTTA HUSTLE AND THAT DOESN'T MEAN COOK UP A QUARTER AND POST UP IN FRONT OF WESTERN UNION. HUSTLING MEANS GETTING YOUR ASS TO WHERE THE MONEY'S AT. IT DON'T EVEN HAVE TO BE TANGIBLE CASH MONEY, IT CAN BE ANYTHING. FIND A NEED AND FULFILL IT ALL WHILE EXPENDING LITTLE TO NO LIQUID CASH. EAT AT YOUR AUNT'S HOUSE AND FRONT LIKE YOU WENT TO SAY HI BUT GET THAT GOOD COOKING. AND GAS IT TOO, LIKE, "DAMN THIS IS THE BEST FUCKIN LOCRIO DE SALAMI I EVER HAD, TITI!" AND TAKE A PLATE HOME. BOOM YOU JUST MEAL PLANNED NIGGA! LITTLE SITUATIONS LIKE THAT WHERE YOU CAN TUCK A COUPLE DOLLARS ARE SUPER IMPORTANT. MY POPS USED TO TELL MY MOMS, "WHAT THE FUCK IS 20 DOLLARS?" THEN SHE STARTED PUTTIN

$20S IN A STASH. NEXT THING YOU KNOW, OH SHIT WE NEED $1,200 CASH, BOOM THERE IT IS. SAVE FOR A RAINY DAY IF YOU HIT A LICK MY GUY, MORE ON THAT LATER, I LOVE Y'ALL, MAN, YOU KNOW THAT? I BOUGHT A HOUSE BECAUSE OF Y'ALL. I COULD FUCK AROUND AND BUY A LAMBO BECAUSE YOU BELIEVED IN A GOLD-GRILLED GRIMEBALL WITH STRAIGHTBACKS WAY BACK WHEN. THANKS MY GUYS. BUT YEAH, LEMME TELL YOU ABOUT WHAT TO DO IF YOU SUDDENLY COME UP ON WILD GUAP IN A FOLLOWING CHAPTER.

Not having rent money is torture because it's constantly on your mind. That late rent is just hanging over your head and always in the back of your throat and every little purchase, stuff that you need day to day, has "this should be going toward my back rent" written on it.

First off you have to calm down and breathe deep. Yes, you're in a difficult situation, but you can fix this, you just have to take steps to survive first. Now take inventory of your life. Do you have a credit card? You do? That's fantastic. You need to stock up on everything you need for the month before you run out of money, so stock up on basic meals like noodles and potatoes because that's what you're going to be eating to save money, unless you play your Auntie like Mero did.

Next you need to see where you're spending money and dead that shit. Spotify gotta go, cable (even our show!) gotta go. Save all your money fam. Even stop paying your light bill because it's better to sit in the dark inside your apartment than to be homeless. You gotta really fucking grind if you're trying to make this money. Fuck it, suck up your pride and collect cans (seriously, I did this).

Look around your apartment and see if you can sell anything. Xbox, sneakers, even your meals. EVERYTHING GOTTA GO! Don't be afraid to sell anything, even your smoke detectors.

Okay, now you've sold everything and collected cans and you've maybe raised 1/10th of one month of the rent needed. Here's my best advice for you: MOVE IN WITH YOUR BOO.

Now you might be thinking, "Desus, I don't have a boo." That doesn't matter. Find the first person who has an apartment and looks at you long enough and turn that shit into a relationship. Fast-track it. Tell them you love them after knowing them for two days. Start planning vacations and stuff. Ask to meet their parents. Involve yourself in their friendships. As soon as they start believing in you, start moving your stuff into their house. Even if things don't work out, you'll have a new place to live for at least like 3 months. It's legitimately a flawless plan.

IF YOU ARE BROKE, WHAT DO YOU DO IF . . . YOU GOTTA EAT?

IMA GO OUT ON A LIMB HERE AND SAY THAT GIVING YOU STEP-BY-STEP DIRECTIONS ON HOW TO COMMIT A CRIMINAL ACTIVITY IS ITSELF A CRIMINAL ACTIVITY, SO IMA SAY THIS IS ALLEGEDLY HOW YOU ALLEGEDLY EAT IF YOU ARE A BROKE BOY. LISTEN MAN, THERE AREN'T A LOT OF MID-ASS—GOOD—GREAT-PAYING JOBS OUT THERE. THERE'S THAT GAP BETWEEN QUALIFYING FOR SNAP BENEFITS WHICH ARE FUCKIN LIT AND NECESSARY, AND GETTING THE "NAH YOU GOOD" LETTER. ALSO SHOUT-OUT TO THE COLLEGIATE ACADEMIA GANG, Y'ALL EAT SOME WILD SHIT IN THE NAME OF FRUGALITY. DO YOU HAVE ANY IDEA HOW MUCH SODIUM IS IN A CUP O' NOODLES, FAM? THAT'S WHY MY UNCLE PABLO HAD A HEART ATTACK AT 43. NIGGAS GOTTA EAT RIGHT, WHICH IS DAMN NEAR IMPOSSIBLE IF YOU ARE IN THAT REALM BETWEEN BEING ABLE TO BUY SHIT ON YA EBT AND BALLIN AT TRADER JOE'S NOT EVEN

LOOKIN AT PRICES. ALSO AS AN ASIDE—SNAP LOW-KEY GETTING THE SHAFT BECAUSE A LOT OF THAT HEALTHY ORGANIC SHIT IS $19 A LB. AND YOU GOT $212 TO BUY FOOD FOR AN ENTIRE MONTH FOR YOU, YOUR MATE, AND YOUR OR "YOUR" KID.

BACK TO THE QUESTION AT HAND AND RECALLING THE OPENING STATEMENT: THE ONLY THING I DID WHEN I WAS HUNGRY AND HAD NO MONEY WAS BOOST. I RECOGNIZE IT MIGHT SEEM LIKE BOOSTING IS MY ANSWER TO EVERYTHING. I RECOGNIZE THAT AND YET HERE WE ARE.

MY MAN MIKE ONCE REACHED OVER THE COUNTER AT TWIN DONUT AND SWIPED A BEAR CLAW WHILE THE CASHIER TURNED TO GET CHANGE. THAT WHOLE PLACE WAS MIRRORS SO I HAVE NO IDEA HOW HE FINESSED THAT. BUT YEAH, FAM, GET A NORTH FACE STEEP TECH JACKET, THEY HAVE ZIPPERS IN THE ARMPITS AND ARE BULKY. UNZIP THE ARMPIT AND START TOSSIN. BEFORE YOU DO MAKE SURE YOUR WAIST ELASTIC IS DUMB TIGHT. GET WHATEVER YOU NEED. CARRY A BASKET SO YOU DON'T LOOK SUSS. THEN DUMP IT IN AN AISLE AND EXIT THRU THE REGISTER CLOSEST TO THE DOOR. BOOM U JUST RACKED PORK CHOPS, A CAN OF BEANS, AND A BAG OF RICE. SOMEBODY IN YOUR BUILDING GOT SAZON & ADOBO, IF NOT, THAT'S PROBABLY THE EASIEST THING TO BOOST OUT OF ALL THE INGREDIENTS. YOU CAN THROW THAT SHIT UP THE SLEEVE. NORTH FACE JACKETS ARE CRUCIAL TO THIS BECAUSE THEY HAVE MORE ZIPPERS THAN THE DUMB-ASS LIL "LEARN HOW TO USE EVERY CLOTHING CLOSURE" DOLLS. THE NORTH FACE EXTREME HAS WHAT IS ESSENTIALLY A BUILT-IN BACKPACK. THE SLEEVES VELCRO SO YOU CAN THROW MAD SHIT UP YOUR SLEEVE AND HAVE IT SECURELY VELCRO'D IN PLACE. THIS SHIT TAKES A LITTLE BIT OF COJONES THO MY PALS. IF YOU SCARED OF BOOKINGS DON'T EVEN BOTHER WITH THIS SHIT BECAUSE EVEN THOUGH THE SUPERMARKET IS SOMETIMES JUST LIKE,

YO, GTFOH, SOMETIMES THEY'LL CALL THE AUTHORITIES. NOW YOU GETTING BOOKED AND THE FRIDAY YOU THOUGHT YOU WERE GONNA BE DROWNING IN BUTT YOU ARE INSTEAD SPENDING SLEEPING UNDER A BENCH THAT SOMEHOW SMELLS LIKE BLEACH AND YET STILL FEELS FILTHY. HELLO MONDAY, HOW YA DOING? I SHIT IN FRONT OF 30 STRANGERS LAST NIGHT. I HELD IT FOR AS LONG AS I COULD. (NOTE: STAY AWAY FROM THE GUY WHO IS VERY CAVALIER ABOUT USING THE TOILET, HE'S A CERTIFIED JAIL NIGGA(tm). HE'S BEEN HERE BEFORE. THIS IS OLD HAT AND HE WAS JUST RECORDED IN 4K HD SHOOTING UP A BABY SHOWER, HE DOES NOT GIVE AN AIRBORNE FUCK ABOUT NOTHING. SO EITHER GET READY TO TAKE AN AGGRESSIVE DEFENSIVE STANCE IF YOU CROSS PATHS OR STAY OUTTA HIS WAY. WHEN THIS TURN INTO A JAIL TUTORIAL? SORRY. I'M ALSO NOT OD QUALIFIED TO GIVE A JAIL TUTORIAL BECAUSE THANK GOD OUT OF THE METRIC TONS OF DIRT I DID, I NEVER CAUGHT A SERIOUS CASE. IT'S ALL ACCUMULATED KNOWLEDGE FROM FAMILY AND PALS.

MY OTHER SUGGESTION ALSO TAKES A LITTLE BIT OF GUMPTION, AND NO, I DON'T CARE IF I'M USING THAT WORD RIGHT. DINE AND DASH MY GUY. THERE'S LEVELS, THOUGH. THE EASY WAY TO SKATE OFF WITH FREE FOOD IS TO STAND AROUND THE ORDER PICKUP AREA AND WAIT FOR A FRUSTRATED FAST-FOOD WORKER TO CALL THE SAME NUMBER TWICE. WALK UP LIKE, THAT'S ME SO SORRY AND JUST TURN TO BOUNCE IN A SWIFT MOTION. IF THEY CALL YOU BACK, HIT THE AHHH I CAN'T FIND MY FUCKIN RECEIPT *SUCKS TEETH.* 8 TIMES OUTTA 10 YOU WALK OUTTA THERE WITH FREE FOOD IF YOU DON'T LOOK LIKE A WILD SCUMBAG WITH A METH-SCARRED FACE.

THE OTHER WAY IS A LITTLE MORE RECKLESS AND I DON'T RECOMMEND IT UNLESS YOU ARE DESPERATE AS FUCK. JUST SLIDE OFF ON THE BILL. WHEN THE BILL COMES, PUT A BOGUS

CARD IN THERE AND ASK FOR THE BATHROOM. BY "BATHROOM" YOU MEAN "MY CAR," WHICH YOU THEN GET IN AND GET THE FUCK OUTTA THERE. THIS MAY GET YOU MURDERED BY POLICE IF YOU ARE A PERSON OF COLOR, SO DON'T DO THIS.

MY FINAL STRATEGY IS GROSS BUT MAD EFFECTIVE. WRAP A DEAD ROACH IN A TISSUE. GO WHEREVER YOU WANNA GO TO EAT. EAT WHATEVER YOU WANNA EAT. WHEN YOU'RE READY TO GO, DRAMATICALLY RUN TO A SERVER AND WHISPER TO THEM WITH OD URGENCY LIKE, "THERE'S A ROACH IN MY SALAD, I'M DEAD-ASS ABOUT TO THROW UP." IF YOU WHISPER THEY FEEL LIKE YOU TRYNA BE LOW AND THEY RESPECT IT. THE IMPORTANT PART IS TO REMEMBER TO ORDER A SIDE SALAD FOR THE ROACH. YOU GOTTA TOSS IT WITH SOME DRESSING. 9 TIMES OUTTA 10 YOUR MEAL IS COMPED AND YOU'RE CHILLIN. IN THIS AGE OF VIRAL BULLSHIT, WHEN THE REGIONAL MANAGER OF CHILI'S HAPPENS TO BE VISITING YOUR PARTICULAR ONE, THE ASSISTANT MANAGER WOULD GIVE YOU A FOOTJOB TO KEEP YOU QUIET.

TRY TO STAY OUTTA JAIL. OH SHIT I FORGOT YOU COULD GO TO A FOOD PANTRY . . . CHURCHES AND SHIT HAVE THEM. I'M NOT GONNA FRONT LIKE I KNOW WHAT GETTING FOOD FROM A FOOD PANTRY IS LIKE, I'VE NEVER DONE IT. MAYBE IT'S A HUGE PAIN IN THE ASS? IS IT REALLY JUST LIKE BOOM I PULL UP AND GET FREE FOOD? IS THERE A LIMIT? LIKE CHILL, YOU CAN ONLY GET 2 CANS OF TUNA AT A TIME? THAT WOULD SUCK CUZ YOU WOULD HAVE TO GET WACK SHIT LIKE CANNED FRENCH CUT GREENBEANS, THOSE SHITS ARE FUCKING CERTIFIED TRASH, BRO. YOU WOULD HAVE TO SACRIFICE GETTING GOOD CANNED SHIT AND MAYBE A LIL CEREAL AND GET CANNED DICED MUSHROOMS INSTEAD. FUCK THAT, GO ROB.

It's Desus's time to shine! Listen, let me put you on to hood food because I'm the king of making something out of nothing. First of all, there's always food around you if you keep your eyes open and your head on a swivel. Say you get to work and see there are free bagels or donuts in the conference room. Normal people take one. Hungry people know they gotta take a bunch to last them a while. In fact, stacking up on samples is something you have to learn how to do flawlessly. Try the food court at your local mall, the sample aisle at Costco, or even free food on the street. Take it all!

If you're broke and you want to cook for yourself, let me introduce you to your best friend, Ramen. Not the good ramen they sell in restaurants for $18.99, but the cheap shit you ate in college and got 34 packs for 4 dollars and is 90% sodium. Yes the amount of sodium is high, but fuck it, you're hungry, and I mean let's keep it funky, you're here for a good time, not a long time. There's worse ways to die than by ramen. The trick with ramen is even if you use your flavor packet there's a million things you can add to this meal, and they all work. Add cheese, add eggs, add an onion. Hell, you can add crushed-up Doritos and that shit tastes bomb af.

Up next cop some potatoes. Potatoes are the soul of hood eating. If you've ever worked at a bar or were lucky enough to watch *Bar Rescue*, you know that potatoes keep giving. You can boil the potatoes, you got mashed potatoes. Take the skins off and you got potato skins. Chop it up and fry it, you got French fries. So many options. Will you eventually get sick of eating potatoes? Maybe get off your high horse and enjoy these fucking starches, my guy.

Now, you might say "Desus, I don't have potato money," and I feel ya, so I'm going to put you on to another shortcut. Your friend, no matter where you are in life, is the dollar menu at your local fast-food joint. Look closely at the things being offered. Do you see it yet? That dollar menu is basically filled with cheaper versions of the more expensive items. For example, why buy a double quarter pounder when you can simply buy two cheeseburgers and combine them for half the price? Hell, live large and order a honey mustard sauce on the side, and suddenly you're the Guy Fieri of your local golden arches.

IF YOU ARE BROKE, WHAT DO YOU DO IF . . .

YOU WANT DRUGS?

WOW. HOW TO GET DRUGS WITH NO MONEY. THAT'S WHAT YOU ON RIGHT NOW, MY PAL? YOU NEED TO GET HIGH SO BAD YOU NEED MONEY STRATEGIES FAST? THIS COULDA BEEN THE SHORTEST CHAPTER IN THIS BOOK BECAUSE IT'S BASICALLY: DO YOU GOT A GUY THAT WILL GIVE YOU YOUR HIGH ON CREDIT? IF THE ANSWER IS NO, THEN YOU GOTTA GET OVER ON SOMEBODY.

THAT COULD BE A FEW THINGS. YOU MIGHT KNOW SOMEONE WHO IS ALWAYS GETTING HIGH SO JUST HANG AROUND THEM UNTIL THEY BUST OUT THE SUBSTANCES. MOST DRUGS ARE SOCIAL. NOBODY WANNA BE THE ONLY NIGGA AT THE PARTY ON MOLLY BRUH, TRUST ME. THEREFORE WHOEVER IS HOLDIN IS GONNA SHARE, UNLESS THEY A TRUE FIEND, IN WHICH CASE DOUBLE-CHECK YA WALLET AND BOUNCE BECAUSE YOU'RE GONNA GET FRUSTRATED. OR DUFF THE GUY, TAKE A MOLLY, AND THEN EITHER STAY THERE AND HAVE A DEEP CONVERSATION ABOUT THE DUFFING WHERE YOU SQUEEZE EACH OTHER'S SHOULDERS MAD TIMES IN REVERENCE, OR BE IN TRANSIT PEAKING LIKE A MUTHAFUCKA. IDC WHAT ANYONE SAYS, MAYBE IT'S A PRODUCT OF MY ANXIETY, BUT I *HATE* ROLLING ON THE TRAIN B. IT'S OVERSTIMULATING.

BEING SMIZZY OFF THE GAS THOUGH, CONVERSELY, MAD FUN. ESPECIALLY IF YOU GOT HEADPHONES AND SHADES TO ELIMINATE PARANOIA.

YOU GOTTA FINESSE YOUR WAY INTO WHATEVER YOU TRYNA GET HIGH ON; THE HARDER THE DRUG THE HARDER IT IS. WEED IS DUMB LEGAL MAD PLACES. NOT SUPER EXPENSIVE, AND YOU AREN'T HIGH FOR OD HOURS. IT'S STUPID EASY TO RUN INTO A BLUNT DEPENDING ON WHO YOU ARE. ARE YOU THE DUDE WHO ALWAYS GOT BUD? IS THERE A DUDE THAT IS ROLLIN FROM OUT A ZIP? I'M IN THERE. BEFORE YOU KNOW IT THERE ARE 7 DUDES IN THE STAIRCASE CYPHING. THERE ARE MANY FRUSTRATING THINGS IN LIFE THAT CAN HAPPEN TO YOU BUT SHOWING UP TO A STAIRCASE WITH A BATTALION OF NIGGAS AND YOU THE ONLY ONE WITH A BLUNT IS WILD DEFLATING. I'VE NEVER PLAYED ORGANIZED FOOTBALL BUT I CAN IMAGINE MY SCENARIO FEELS LIKE TAKING A FALCONS-LEVEL "L" IN THE SUPER BOWL. YOU LIGHT AND HIT THAT BLUNT TILL YOU ARE GOOD AND READY TO PASS IT BECAUSE IF YOU ARE UNFAMILIAR WITH THIS TYPE OF SITUATION, YOU AIN'T SEEING THAT BLUNT AGAIN (DEPENDING ON THE BABINESS OF YOUR CREWS' LUNGS). IT'S A DOVE AT A FUNERAL, FAM—YOU WERE HOLDING IT, IT WAS BRINGING YOU PEACE, THEN YOU HAD TO LET IT FLY AWAY. GETTING WEED WHEN YOU'RE BROKE IS JUST A MATTER OF TEXTING ENOUGH PEOPLE TO SEE WHO'S SMOKING WEED AND RUDELY INVITING YOURSELF OVER.

Getting high when broke isn't impossible but you gotta adjust your expectations. You might not be able to get coke, weed, or sweet lady H, but let me give you a few alternatives to get your buzz on:

Water: Yes, you can get high on water. Just keep drinking it till you're light-headed or something. I'm not 100% sure how it works but water can give you a little buzz (or kill you, I don't really know).

Another trick to get high is using regular drugs in your house. Rub some NyQuil on your chest after a hot shower and you'll definitely feel something (pain?).

These options suck, yes, and will probably only make you want drugs for real, so let's figure out how to get high.

If you're attempting to get weed, try either the closest college, Phish concert parking lot, or Jamaican nightclub (if there are any around you). Jamaican nightclubs are amazing spots, and the vibes will make people want to share weed with you (call everyone brother btw). Be sure to hum some Bob Marley or mention a trip you took to Jamaica, or even talk about the time you watched *Cool Runnings* if that's all you've got. People will gravitate toward you and give you some sort of weed or at least give you a few pulls. Another trick is keep telling some long, boring-ass story while you hold the blunt and keep ripping it. Take your time, draw out every syllable.

The irony of being broke is that it's when you'll need/want drugs the most. Adopt as your model the classic trope of the meth head. Their whole day is built around getting drugs. Every minute they're thinking about meth; every activity they do is to get closer to that sweet meth. You have to have that same mental state, but instead of turning the intensity dial all the way up to 11, just turn yours up to maybe a 4. You shouldn't be clawing at your skin, for example. I was gonna say not to offer sexual favors for drugs, but you know what? If that's what you got to do, let me just leave you with a quote from the illustrious Dark Man X:

> *I don't knock what a nigga do to get by*
> *Just make sure you gettin' by don't fuck with you gettin' mine*

CHAPTER 9

WE ARE GONNA USE THIS CLOSING SECTION TO GIVE YOU A LIGHTNING ROUND OF ADVICE ON ALL SORTS OF SHIT. ADVICE IS LIKE FOOD B. THERE ARE CERTAIN PLACES YOU GO TO FOR ADVICE ON CERTAIN THINGS, JUST LIKE THERE ARE CERTAIN RESTAURANTS YOU GO TO FOR CERTAIN FOODS. FOR EXAMPLE, IF SHE FUCK ME GOOD I TAKE HER ASS TO RED LOBSTER. OH SHIT YOU DIDN'T SEE THAT BEYONCÉ LINE COMING, DID YOU? THAT WAS ANOTHER TERRIBLE ANALOGY BUT FOR REAL, PEOPLE WITH EXPERIENCE ON THE ISSUE FOR WHICH YOU ARE SEEKING ADVICE ARE GENERALLY THE BEST PEOPLE TO ASK. ALSO, THE SKY IS BLUE. PREPARE TO HAVE YOUR FUCKIN WIG KNOCKED BACK WITH THE FAST ADVICE.

BEFORE WE START, THE BEST LIFE ADVICE I'VE EVER GOTTEN WAS "THIS TOO SHALL PASS," WHICH IS TATTOOED ON MY HOMEBOY'S ARM IN BETWEEN GANG SHIT. I SAW IT ONE DAY AND WAS LIKE, OH SHIT, WORD, THAT'S TRUE. NO MATTER HOW

WACK A SITUATION YOU FIND YOURSELF IN, "THIS TOO SHALL PASS." NOT TRYING TO BE PREACHY HERE BUT THE HUMAN MIND IS POWERFUL AND RESILIENT MOST OF THE TIME. IT TOOK BRITNEY SPEARS OD LONG TO LOSE HER SHIT, SHAVE HER DOMEPIECE, AND SMASH A CAR WITH AN UMBRELLA. YO REMEMBER WHEN YOU HAD TO SMASH THE CAR IN *STREET FIGHTER II* BONUS ROUND? THEY GOTTA MAKE ONE WHERE IT'S BRITNEY SMASHING A HONDA WITH A PARASOL. BUT YO YEAH THERE'S ALWAYS SOMEBODY DOING WORSE THAN YOU; IF YOU DON'T BELIEVE ME JUST GO TO THE BATHROOM AT PENN STATION. YOU MIGHT SEE A DUDE BATHING IN A SINK OR SHITTING INTO A BAG THAT HE THEN PUTS INTO ANOTHER BAG FULL OF SHIT BAGS. HOLD YOUR HEAD UP, MY PAL. THINGS WILL GET BETTER, TRUST ME, I USED TO HAVE 20 BAGS OF COCAINE IN MY BUTT WONDERING WHEN IT WOULD ALL COME CRASHING DOWN AND MY LIFE WOULD BE RUINED BECAUSE MY MOM WOULD DISOWN ME AND MY POPS WOULD BE ASHAMED I GOT KNOCKED. BUT INSTEAD OF THAT, YOU ARE READING A BOOK I WROTE AND FOR WHICH I GOT PAID MONEY TO WRITE HAAAAAAAAANNNNNN!!!! BEST ADVICE I EVER RECEIVED: "THIS TOO SHALL PASS."

Q&A 1: HOW LONG SHOULD BEEF LAST?

> *"Beef is forever. Fuck that. If I say it's on sight, that means it's on sight. I don't care if you're at church, if you're with your kids, if you're at your granny's funeral. When I see you, I see you for life."*
>
> —YOUNG DESUS, AGES 15 TO PROBABLY 22

> *"Hey Sheldon! How ya been? Wow! You got 2 girls now? That's a blessing, good to see. Remember when you tried to shoot me back in high school? Haha we were wildin. Anyway just picking up some vitamins and supplements. You be safe now."*
>
> —WASHED DESUS, NOW

Beef is one of those things that, in retrospect, feels way more serious than it really was. For example, me and my guy Devon almost got jumped on East 233rd one summer. That's all we obsessed about that whole year. The get-back, the retaliation, someone had to pay. We wasted a whole summer fighting and bucking at random guys from East 219th Street when we could have been getting money or chicks. A whole summer gone.

Those randos were our sworn enemies and there was even murder talk. And where did this beef stem from? Why had they jumped us in the first place? Someone slept with someone's baby's mother. I can't even remember who or why. And that's the usual truth behind the origin of a beef—it's so dumb you can't even remember it. Unless it's legit like Israel vs. Palestine, most beef is MAD stupid, or just an attempt to redirect fragile masculinity.

So should one hold on to a beef forever? The answer is no, but only if you have something else going in life. If you got a job, a family, moved off the block and have things going for you, why continue to live in the past, my dude? But if you're still out here on the block at 40 (ugh), you can't let beef slide. Sad reality.

Let it be known that street beef is *completely* different than Hollywood/Internet beef. Hollywood beef is about showing out for the cameras, timeline, IG. You want to go viral and/or get on TMZ to show what a tough guy you are by telling someone to suck your dick or that you'll fuck their mother, and it's all about the back-and-forth blustering. But there's almost never an actual physical interaction, let alone fisticuffs. Jay-Z, our Twitter father, said it best in his Rap City Freestyle:

They shootin', nobody dyin'
Somebody better put somebody body on somebody iron
Sometime soon or somebody lyin'

Meaning everyone talks lots of violence but it's all fake. Not advocating violence here, but I see through you. People who make the most threats of violence on Twitter are usually the softest, and real people can see it. You'll see two guys talking about let's drop a pin and settle this in real life, and it's like "dog, both of you have a mortgage and should be getting your prostates checked for polyps. Grow up, man."

PS: None of this chapter applies to [redacted], who attempted to jump and pepper spray me in 1st grade. My guy: When I see you I still am going to beat the brakes off you until you piss blood and I don't care about any of this Hollywood shit. Don't care if it's in Trader Joe's, or Coachella or Split Rock Nursing Home. If I have to beat you down with a colostomy bag on my side . . . so be it.

Q&A 2: IS PORN BAD FOR ME?

YO YOU DON'T WATCH P-NO MY GUY? YOU DON'T MAKE THE OCCASIONAL BATCH OF BEEF STROKINOFF? FUCK IS WRONG WITH YOU, FAM? AS A DUDE WHO IS PALS WITH SEVERAL ADULT FILM STARS I'M GONNA SAY NO, PORN IS NOT "BAD FOR YOU." MATTER OF FACT IMA SAY PORN IS ACTUALLY GOOD FOR YOU BECAUSE JERKING OFF IS DEFINITELY HEALTHY. THAT'S WHY ALL THOSE PLACES YOU GO TO GET YOUR COCK MASSAGED BY A NICE WOMAN ARE CALLED "HEALTH SPAS." MASTURBATING ISN'T WEIRD, EVEN ANIMALS JERK OFF, THAT SHIT IS BIOLOGICAL. HAVE YOU TRANSCENDED HUMAN NATURE? NO, YOU HAVEN'T, FUCK OUTTA HERE. YO IMAGINE BEING A MONKEY AT A ZOO AND YOU'RE STRESSED AF CUZ NO MATTER HOW HIGH YOU SWING ON THAT TREE THAT DRY MOAT THING IS KEEPING YOU IN YOUR ENCLOSURE. NOW IMAGINE THAT MONKEY BEING LIKE "FUCK IT ZOO WI-FI IS STRONG IMA JUST GO FIND MONKEY P-NO ON SPANKBANG OR SOME SHIT." THAT'S PRETTY LIT IF

YOU THINK ABOUT IT. HE JERKS OFF THEN HE'S CHILLING. I'VE SEEN VIDEOS OF MONKEYS AT ZOOS SMOKING NEWPORT 100S. I'M SURE THEY GOT ACCESS TO PORN. PORN IS JUST A TOOL IN YOUR "I NEED TO BUST A NUT AND CLEAR MY HEAD" TOOL KIT. ALSO IF THERE'S SOMEONE YOU KNOW YOU COULD NEVER SMASH IN A MILLION YEARS, YOU CAN JUST FIND A PORN STAR THAT KINDA LOOKS LIKE THEM AND SQUINT. VOILÀ YOU ARE SMASHING YESENIA FROM YOUR SOPHOMORE YEAR AT YOUR COMMUNITY COLLEGE THAT HAD A BOYFRIEND WITH A C-CLASS AND A DECENT COKE FLOW.

I GUESS IF YOU ARE SITTING HOME BEATING YOUR DICK TO SHREDS ALL DAY AND NEGLECTING YOUR ACTUAL LIFE, THEN PORN CAN BE BAD. BUT ALL THOSE "PORN RUINED MY SEX LIFE" NIGGAS ARE WEIRDOS BECAUSE FOR REAL, HOW MANY TIMES A DAY ARE YOU MAKIN HOT SALAMI? I GOT 4 KIDS SO I CAN BARELY JERK OFF IN THE SHOWER. YOU EVER JUST JERK OFF BECAUSE YOU'RE BORED? THAT'S THE TYPE OF LIFESTYLE I'M NOT TRYING TO LEAD. SO NO, PORN ISN'T BAD, BUT BEING OBSESSED WITH JERKING OFF IS PROBABLY BAD. YOU COULD HURT YOUR GENITALS. THAT WOULD BE TRULY TRAGIC. IMAGINE YOU IRREPARABLY DAMAGE YOUR DICK, BRUH? MA, IMAGINE YOU WENT SO HAMMER JILLING OFF THAT YOU SHATTER YOUR CLITORAL HOOD? THAT SOUNDS ABSOLUTELY AWFUL, MY GUYS. DON'T JERK OFF OD.

REMEMBER HOW MICHELLE OBAMA TOOK UP THE CAUSE OF GETTING AMERICA/KIDS TO EAT HEALTHY AND COORDINATED WITH EXPERTS ON NUTRITION TO COME UP WITH FOOD STRATEGIES? THEY WERE ON SOME HELPFUL FOOD PYRAMID SHIT. GOD BLESS THAT WOMAN. SINCE SHE DID THAT, MAYBE SOME JERKOFF IN THIS ADMINISTRATION CAN COME UP WITH A "HEALTHY MASTURBATING PLAN" AND LET US KNOW EXACTLY HOW MUCH IS TOO MUCH? ACTUALLY SCRATCH THAT, THOSE

NIGGAS ARE INEPT. MAYBE IN 2024 KANYE CAN TELL US HOW MUCH TO JER—YOU KNOW WHAT? NEVER MIND. P-NO IS CHILL THO. GAME CUBE NINTENDO, 5% TINT SO YOU CAN'T SEE UP IN MY WINDOW.

Q&A 3: WHAT IS THE PROPER WAY TO EAT A STEAK?

Twitter culture is savage and wild judgmental when it comes to preparing a steak right. There's no in between, either a steak has to be cooked until it's as hard as a catcher's mitt, or it has to be so undercooked it's still bleeding all over your shit. Nobody gives a fuck about cooking it "medium." (B)lacktwitter has been the number one proponent of the well-done steak, which I personally think is an insult to the legacy of the slain cow. I'm not Hindu but have some respect for that bovine that you're about to eat. Don't just flame it to death (again).

I enjoy a rare steak, which is a controversial stance in my world. But this is the hill I will die on. The rarer the better. In fact, if possible, I'd like to just eat the cow straight up in the field while it's grazing. Let's have a fair fight, give the cow a knife and let's go at it. Make me earn my meal.

Team Well Done has spread lies about bloody plates and other untruths in an attempt to slander less cooking time. But the longer you cook a steak, the less flavor you're going to get. Hopefully I'll soon reach the blessed stage of adulthood where I can enjoy a "black and blue" aka "Pittsburgh rare" (RIP MAC MILLER) named after steelworkers who would slap raw meat on their equipment because it was so hot (at least I think that's the definition . . . it also sounds like a porn clip I saw once). Black and blue is charred on the outside and cold/raw on the inside. Cooked for 1 minute on each side. One bite of a steak cooked this style will let you know what side of the Donner family you vibe with.

BONUS DARK DESUS DJ DROP:

Enjoy steak while you can. If any extinction level event ever occurs (nuclear bomb with fallout blocking the sun/Mass virus/Zombies/etc.), meat will be one of the first foods to disappear due to no one having the resources to raise cattle and all cattle being tainted. So meat will go from a staple in every meal to a very expensive and pricey one-time-a-year (if you live a whole year). For your wedding anniversary, or maybe a birthday, your remaining loved ones might surprise you with a sliver of beef thinner than a Steak-umm, and you'll find out it took them 3 months to trade enough crops to get this tiny morsel of meat. And you'll attempt to eat it but because of your forced plant-based diet, your teeth can no longer tear into this flesh, and you fall to your feet with tears in your eyes wondering why God would allow people to live like this, before you tragically and painfully succumb to an infection due to a hangnail that got wet.

Q&A 4: PUNCHING UP / PUNCHING DOWN

YO I WAS GONNA SAY THINK ABOUT JOKES LIKE THE OLD NES GAME *PUNCH-OUT!!* YOU'RE THE LITTLE GUY AND YOU REALLY DON'T GET G POINTS FOR FUCKIN UP SOMEONE IN YOUR REALM. BUT THAT GAME IS LOW-KEY PROBLEMATIC SO FORGET THE ANALOGY. OH YOU FORGOT? ABOUT "PISTON HONDA," THE JAPANESE BOXER THAT REALLY FUCKED WITH SUSHI AND TEA AND "JAPANESE" SHIT? OR "DON FLAMENCO," THE "LOL HE GAY" CHARACTER FROM SPAIN THAT WAS HYPER EFFEMINATE AND NOT IN A COMPLIMENTARY WAY? ALSO I'M PRETTY SURE ONE OF THOSE DUDES WAS A WILD NAZI OR SOME SHIT. AND L-O-FUCKIN-L AT THE LAZINESS OF THE NAME "VODKA DRUNKENSKI" FOR A RUSSIAN BOXER, THAT REALLY WAS HIS OG NAME, SO THEY CHANGED IT TO . . . "SODA POPINSKI," WHICH WAS

OFFENSIVE TO ME BECAUSE MY POPS GOT TYPE 2 DIABETES. SHOUT-OUT TO THEM FOR THINKING "VODKA DRUNKENSKI" WAS "TOO FAR" WHEN PISTON HONDA BASICALLY WALKS ON TO AN 8-BIT MIDI GONG SOUND. I SAY THAT TO SAY THIS: IF I WAS A MEMBER OF WU-TANG I WOULD SAY THE FACT THAT YOU CAN'T MAKE A LAZY JOKE SHOULD MAKE YOU SHARPEN YOUR SWORD GOD, WORD BOND, THE DAYS OF SAYING SHOCKING SHIT JUST TO SAY IT ARE OVER. IF YOU WANNA TOUCH ON A TOUCHY SUBJECT YOU BETTER HAVE A CLEVER, INTROSPECTIVE *AND* FUNNY WAY OF APPROACHING IT.

PEOPLE OFTEN GET CAUGHT UP SAYIN SOME WILD SHIT AND THEIR DEFENSE IS "I DIDN'T KNOW I COULDN'T SAY/DO THAT," WHICH YOU SOMETIMES KNOW IS A LIE AND YOU SOMETIMES KNOW IS TRUE. AS MY PAL D WOULD SAY, "GOTTA HEAR BOTH SIDES." FOR EXAMPLE, RAY J DROPPED AN F BOMB ON THE RADIO OBVIOUSLY EXTREMELY UPSET OVER A "FIGHT" HE HAD WITH FABOLOUS. I'M SERIOUS, YOUTUBE IT . . . AND BY F BOMB I DONT MEAN "FUCK" OR "FLEX BOMB." BUT HE CAUGHT AND CORRECTED HIMSELF AND FOLLOWED IT UP BY "I DON'T MEAN IT LIKE THAT! BE WHO YOU ARE, LOVE WHO YOU LOVE!" WITH EQUAL PASSION. THEN HE WENT ON TO TALK ABOUT "TOUCHING" FABOLOUS, SEVERAL POOLS, SEVERAL ROLLS-ROYCES . . . OH AND TWO BASKETBALL COURTS. IT WAS THE BEST RADIO I HAD HEARD IN YEARS. SHOULD WE FORGIVE RAY J'S F BOMB BECAUSE IT WAS A HEAT-OF-THE-MOMENT SITUATION AND HE APOLOGIZED IMMEJUTLY? CIRCLE YES OR NO AT THE BOTTOM SO YOUR FRIENDS CAN JUDGE YOU BASED ON YOUR ANSWER. LOL COOL PARTY GAME.

AT ITS CORE, THOUGH, THIS IS PUNCHING DOWN. *"MERO, YOU MILLENNIALS AND YOUR NEW PHRASES . . . WHAT DOES THAT EVEN MEAN?"* THANKS FOR ASKING BABY BOOMER READER (JK YOU PROLLY DEAD). PUNCHING DOWN IS WHEN

YOU MAKE A JOKE ABOUT A MARGINALIZED COMMUNITY. LIKE IF SEINFELD (NO SHOTS, JUST AN EXAMPLE) DID A 30-MINUTE SET ABOUT HOW PUERTO RICANS ARE LAZY, HOW WOMEN SHOULD MAKE SANDWICHES, OR TRANSWOMEN ARE "DUDES WITH TITS, BRO," IT WOULD BE PUNCHING DOWN BECAUSE SEINFELD IS A RIDICULOUSLY RICH WHITE MAN WHICH IS OD ADVANTAGEOUS AND COMES BUNDLED WITH ALL KINDS OF PRIVILEGES AND SHIT. BEING BORN A WHITE MALE WITH SOME MONEY IS LIKE GETTING THE NEW VIDEO GAME CONSOLE THAT COMES WITH A GAME AND THE 2ND CONTROLLER AND A LIL "6 MONTHS OF XBOX LIVE FREE" CARD. IF YOU FALL UNDER THAT UMBRELLA YOU CAN KINDA ONLY PUNCH LATERALLY. IF YOU WANNA MAKE IT IN THIS BIZ YOU BETTER LEARN TO PUNCH UP INSTEAD.

BUT MERO, WHAT DO YOU MEAN PUNCHING UP? IS THAT THE OPPOSITE OF PUNCHING DOWN? I'M SORRY I'M A FUCKING FOOL AND CAN'T USE CONTEXT CLUES!

YES IT IS, BUT NOT DIRECTLY. YOU CAN PUNCH UP AND STILL BE PUNCHING DOWN. OKAY, EVEN I'M TOO SMACKED TO EXPLAIN THAT WELL, BUT YOU SHOULD JUST KNOW, THERE ARE LEVELS. MY LITMUS TEST IS IF YOU SAY THE JOKE OUT LOUD AND IT SOUNDS KINDA CRINGEY, IT'S PROBABLY OFFENSIVE AND YOU SHOULD FIND ANOTHER ANGLE OR ANOTHER SUBJECT ENTIRELY. GROWING UP IN THE BRONX AND NOT REALLY LEAVING THE BLOCK MUCH, I DID NOT HAVE ONE SINGLE "WOKE" FRIEND, AND EVEN MY FRIENDS THAT WERE FROM EXTREMELY MARGINALIZED COMMUNITIES WEREN'T "WOKE." IF YOU GROW UP WITHOUT ACCESS TO SHIT, YOU HAVE TO LEARN FROM YOUR MISTAKES. WHICH SUCKS BECAUSE NOWADAYS WE LIVE IN THE "CANCEL CULTURE," WHERE IF YOU ARE POPPING AND AREN'T ON YOUR TOES AND KNOWING EVERYTHING ABOUT EVERY COMMUNITY AND SAY SOME DUMB SHIT, YOU

ARE "CANCELED." THAT MEANS PEOPLE WILL ACTIVELY BE LIKE, "DO NOT FUCK WITH SO AND SO, HE/SHE/THEY SAID XYZ."

SOME PEOPLE CALL SOMEONE OUT LEGITIMATELY, WHICH IS IMPORTANT WORK, AND SOME DO IT JUST TO LEAPFROG THE PERSON THEY ARE CALLING OUT FOR BEING "PROBLEMATIC," WHICH IS EXTREMELY DISINGENUOUS AND ALMOST WORSE THAN BEING OFFENSIVE (ALMOST!). YOU DON'T ACTUALLY BELIEVE THE "SMART, WOKE" SHIT YOU'RE KICKING, AND YOU DON'T PUT IT INTO PRACTICE IN YOUR DAILY LIFE. THIS IS WHY SOCIAL MEDIA IS TRASH NOW BECAUSE YOU CAN HAVE A DUDE FROM THE HOOD WHO IS FUNNY BUT HAS NEVER LEFT HIS STRIP AND HAS NO IDEA WHAT THE TERM "NON-BINARY" MEANS, MISGENDER SOMEONE, OR ASSUME SOMEONE IS OF AN ETHNICITY THEY ARE NOT. THERE'S PLENTY OF GAFFES THEY CAN MAKE, AND IT'S A WRAP FOR THEM. THAT'S VERY DIFFERENT FROM, FOR EXAMPLE, OH SHIT, THE PRESIDENT, WHO WAS BORN WITH A SILVER SPOON IN HIS MOUTH AND AMPLE ACCESS TO INFORMATION AND EXPOSURE TO ALL KINDS OF PEOPLE EUROSTEPPING ALL THAT SHIT AND LETTING OFF SHOTS AT ANY AND EVERYBODY THAT ISN'T HIS SPECIES (OLD WHITE GUY).

"BUT MERO, THERE'S GOOGLE NOW, THAT'S A COP-OUT, ANYONE CAN GET ANY INFORMATION."

THIS IS HALF TRUE. A LOT OF PEOPLE HAVE ACCESS TO INFORMATION, YET OFTEN DON'T EVEN KNOW WHAT THE FUCK THEY ARE EVEN LOOKING FOR. I CAN HONESTLY SAY I'VE LEARNED MORE OVER THE LAST 3–4 YEARS ABOUT PEOPLE I HAD NO IDEA EXISTED THAN I LEARNED IN THE PREVIOUS 20, SHOUT-OUT TO THE INTERNET. I KNEW WHAT I WAS LOOKIN FOR AND FOUND IT. IF YOU WOULD HAVE ASKED ME IN 2013 "WHAT DOES GENDER FLUID MEAN?" I WOULDA TOOK A WILD GUESS AND PROBABLY GUESSED RIGHT BECAUSE I READ VO-

RACIOUSLY AS A KID AND I LEARNED OD WORDS, SHOUT-OUT TO READING. YOU CAN FIGURE SOME SHIT OUT WITH CONTEXT BUT IT'S NOT AS SIMPLE AS IT'S MADE OUT TO BE. SOME PEOPLE ARE GONNA MISINTERPRET THIS AS LIKE "EVERYONE GETS ONE." THAT AIN'T IT, PAL. I JUST KNOW SOME PEOPLE CHOOSE TO BE IGNORANT AND SOME PEOPLE HAVE NO IDEA WHAT A PLUMBOB IS. I LITERALLY JUST FOUND OUT WHAT A STRAWBERRY HULLER WAS AND THAT IT EXISTED. YOU CAN APPLY THAT LOGIC TO MAD SHIT. BUT IF YOU ARE ONE OF THOSE DISINGENUOUS CLOUT CHASERS, YOU AREN'T TRYING TO HELP CHANGE PEOPLE'S MINDS. YOU'RE WAITING FOR A NIGGA TO SAY SOME WILD SHIT THEN GET TO VIRTUE SIGNALING. I THINK I'M GONNA BUY "PROBLEMATIC.COM" OR MAKE A "IS THIS PROBLEMATIC?" APP OR SOME SHIT FOR 99 CENTS. I'LL BE A BILLIONAIRE IN A MONTH. FUCK! I HAVE NO IDEA HOW TO MAKE APPS OR BUILD A WEBSITE AND I JUST GAVE THAT IDEA AWAY. OH WELL, AS LONG AS IT HELPS PEOPLE LEARN, I'LL BE HAPPY. NO VIRTUE SIGNALING, NO BACKSIES, NO CALLING SHOTGUN WITHOUT THE CAR IN SIGHT.

HEY, DO YOU FORGIVE RAY J? [YES] [NO]

Q&A 5: HOW MUCH IS TOO MUCH TO PAY FOR A PAIR OF SNEAKERS?

My relationship with sneakers has been, at best, a very strained one. There were four kids in my family and now as an adult I understand that's expensive as fuck. But as a kid, I assumed my parents were just cheap. No one explained to me that they were immigrants and didn't even have sneakers for a part of their lives.

When it was time to buy sneakers, I always hoped my mother would take me to Modell's because they had brand-name sneakers. But often we'd end up at Payless, Buster Brown, or Fayva (if you know these establishments, you are washed, congrats). Here my mother would buy me Skips or whatever name the kids in school would call them. They were perfectly functional sneakers, kept my feet dry, and looked decent, but they weren't Nike or Adidas. I stayed in a pair of Brooks.

My luck changed in junior high school when, while looking thru the discount bin, my mother pulled out a pair of blue and white Jordan 4's. I knew nothing about sneakers but I had seen all the cool kids at school rocking them and I had to have them. They were discounted because some of the lace holes were missing. Adding insult to injury, they were a full size smaller than my feet. But in my little head, I started devising my plan that would make me one of the cool kids.

I tried on the Jordans and immediately felt the wild tightness, but I crammed my foot in and walked around the store in agony. My mother asked, "How do they feel?" and I told her, "Perfect!" while hiding the pain of my toes curling over in the front of the shoe. She believed my lie (or, knowing her, knew I was lying and decided to teach me a lesson).

Anyway, I got home and grabbed my older sister's bottle of leather stretcher and dumped the whole bottle on them until both sneakers were soaking. I stuffed the inside with newspaper and hoped for the best.

The sneakers still hurt to wear but I looked fresh. There was a big class trip coming up where I wanted to premiere the Jordans. After wearing them at home for about a week, trying to stretch them out, the big day finally came. Our school went to Holiday Hill, a resort in Connecticut that had basketball courts and a pool and all types of outdoor activities for little New York street urchins.

I got on the bus and there was this relentless little snot kid named Richie (not his real name because I don't know what happened to his bum ass). Richie wasn't a bully or good at snapping, but what he did have was a huge, muscular sister in 8th grade who would beat up anyone who messed with her brother. And she was rough as shit, she had fought a teacher and a security guard, so no one was messing with her. She had behavior problems and had to be in a special classroom.

Anyway, back to Richie. Richie always had some slick shit to say to me and that day was no different. He saw my kicks and zoomed in, yelling, "Those are from two years ago." Now, in my head, I'm like "Whatever. They're still Jordans and when the reseller market takes off in 20 years, boy are you going to feel stupid," but surprisingly my fellow NYC schoolkids didn't feel the same way, and started cracking on me and my old Jordans. The trip was shitty. I was ruined. My plan had backfired.

Desus, what does that painful childhood memory have to do with the price of sneakers? Well, the answer is, my main hobby is now buying/collecting sneakers, mostly the retro Jordans that little Desus never had a chance to rock. Every time I order a pair, in my mind I just see little Desus telling Richie to suck his dick. My dick. Suck my dick, Richie.

As I've gotten more money, I've become a little more aggressive with my sneaker buying. It's not uncommon for me to come home to five pairs at my door. At this point, it's still an adrenaline rush to cop them. My parents make the same joke when they visit me: "Are you opening a Foot Locker?" which, not gonna lie, is pretty funny.

My father says I'm going to go broke buying sneakers but I reassure him it's harmless, that I'm saving money, and that at least it's not women or blow. He's had the same pair of sneakers for over 10 years, a pair of kinda bland basic white sneakers that people who rock All Lives Matter bumper stickers would rock. He doesn't see the point of buying a new pair of sneakers that he'd only wear while working on the car (being an older West Indian means he works on the car every day).

Sometimes I like to stand in my sneaker room (yes I have a room just for sneakers) and look at my collection like, "Fuck yes. I did this. I earned each and every one of these shoes with my natural fucking talent. I bought my way out of a schoolyard trauma by endlessly reliving it!" It's an amazing feeling, because 6 years ago when I worked for a wack-ass magazine, the only sneakers I owned were a pair of white Air Force ones, a pair of black Air Force ones (both required if you live in NYC), and a pair of black Chuck Taylors. That was my whole sneaker collection. Now? I got 'em all, baby. Sometimes I find pairs that still have the cardboard insert in even though I copped them years ago. It's not uncommon for me to accidental-purchase the same pair of sneakers twice. That's kinda of a flex, and kinda sad, too.

I, personally as a NKMDIA (No Kids Mad Disposable Income American), have no price point that I think is too high for a sneaker if I REALLY wanted it. But I'm still and forever the child of two people who moved to America with nothing and I hear my ancestors sucking their teeth when I make wasteful purchases.

We had a live show at Madison Square Garden (okay, the theater, not actual MSG, which is still major, but still) and I said to myself, "This is the big one." I was ready to cop the holy grail of sneakers: Kanye's Red October, the sneaker he dropped before he left Nike. The quick history of the Red October is: Nike released them as a surprise drop one Saturday afternoon and never restocked them. They now sell for about $6,000, and I almost copped them. I found a legit pair, I had my credit card number ready and . . . I couldn't do it.

$6,000 is a shitload of money for sneakers, and I ultimately felt that it could be spent in a better way. $6,000 is a life-changing amount of money for most people. I was one of those people literally a few years ago. As this celebrity happens, I hope I'll always remember that and not blow through my money on some dumb shit.

Also Kanye has been fucking wilding with the MAGA hat and my worst fear is I cop the Red Octobers, run into Richie, and he cooks me again.

Q&A 6: SHOULD I OWN A PET? WHAT KIND OF PET IS RIGHT FOR ME?

HERE'S THE MOST IMPORTANT QUESTION TO PONDER BEFORE YOU GET A PET: HOW ARE *YOU* LIVING? ARE YOU EATING HALF OF THAT CUP O' NOODLES FOR BREAKFAST AND THE OTHER HALF FOR DINNER? THEN NO, YOU SHOULD PROBABLY NOT GET A PET. IF YOU HAVE MAD DISPOSABLE INCOME AND FOR SOME REASON WOULD LIKE TO SINK IT INTO A LIVING FURBY THAT'S GOING TO EVENTUALLY PERISH AND MAKE YOU BOOHOO, THEN I GUESS A PET IS FOR YOU. I SAID IT BEFORE IN THIS BOOK AND I'LL SAY IT AGAIN BECAUSE FUCK IT, IT FITS. MY PARENTS ARE NOT FROM THE UNITED DOG KISSING OH NO THERE'S SNOW ON THE GROUND SO I HAVE TO GET BOOTS FOR MY DOMESTICATED WOLF STATES OF AMERICA. THERE ARE TWO TYPES OF DOGS IN DR: BLOODTHIRSTY GUARD DOGS THAT WILL RIP YOU LIMB FROM LIMB IF YOU TRY TO SNEAK INTO THE YARD AND STEAL MANGOES, AND STRAY DOGS. ACTUALLY SOME PEOPLE IN DR HAVE LITTLE SHOW DOGS. THOSE PEOPLE ARE VERY, DISPROPORTIONATELY RICH.

I HAVE A DIFFERENT POV ON PETS IN GENERAL. I'M NOT REALLY A PET KINDA GUY. WITH MY KIDS, A PET AT THIS POINT IS LIKE BEING AT WORK AND MY HYPOTHETICAL BOSS DUMPS A PILE OF FOLDERS ON MY DESK AND I'M LIKE "HEY, YOU GOT SOME MORE FOLDERS? I LOVE GOING OVER EXPENSE REPORTS

10 MINUTES BEFORE I'M SUPPOSED TO LEAVE ON A FRIDAY." MY KIDS BRING ME MORE THAN ENOUGH JOY, AND THEY DON'T EAT CIGARETTE BUTTS OFF THE GROUND AND THEY DONT SHED AND THEY DONT LICK THEIR OWN OR EACH OTHER'S ASSHOLES THEN GET IN MY FACE LIKE "GIMME KISS MUAH MUAH MUAH" ON SOME HYPERBOLIC PEPÉ LE PEW SHIT.

I'M NOT ANTI-DOG. IF YOU LIVE IN A RURAL AREA AND YOU WANT A BIG DOG, GO FOR IT. IF YOU REALLY LOVED DOGS YOU WOULDN'T OWN A DOG OVER 15 LBS WHILE LIVING IN AN APARTMENT. I REMEMBER CAREER DAY ON THE LAST DAY I WORKED AT MY FORMER JUNIOR HIGH (I WAS A PARAPROFESSIONAL THERE) AND THERE WAS A VETERINARIAN THAT WAS SUPER DEAD-ASS ABOUT HIS JOB AND HE MUSTA GOTTEN TIRED OF SEEING BIG DOGS THAT WERE SICK DUE TO LACK OF ACTIVITY, BECAUSE HE WAS WILDIN THE FUCK OUT ON PEOPLE. IF YOU HAVE A DOG WITH MEDIUM/LONG LEGS AND YOU DON'T HAVE A HALF ACRE LOT FOR THAT FURBALL TO RUN AROUND TOP SPEED AND GET HIS/HER WORKOUT IN, YOU ARE LITERALLY KILLING THIS PET YOU PURPORT TO LOVE SO MUCH. HE THEN WENT ON TO NAME APPROPRIATE BREEDS FOR INDOOR DOGS. SHOUT-OUT TO SHIH TZUS, WHICH IS WHAT MY DOG BROWNIE IS, WHICH IS WHY I STAN BROWNIE. SHE IS SUPER CHILL. NEVER TRIES TO LICK MY FACE, OR ANYONE'S, FOR THAT MATTER, EXCEPT LITTLE KIDS WHO LOVE THAT KIND OF SHIT. SHE KNOWS TO STAY OFF FURNITURE AND NOT JUMP ON PEOPLE. SHE GENERALLY MINDS HER BUSINESS UNLESS SHE IS CALLED UPON TO PLAY FETCH AND WHEN SHE DOES PLAY FETCH SHE PLAYS IT WITH ENERGY AND VIGOR SO SHOUT-OUT TO THAT OLD BITCH. WHEN SHE GOES, WE WILL PROBABLY NEVER OWN A DOG AGAIN BECAUSE BROWNIE IS THE ULTIMATE EXAMPLE OF "MAN'S BEST FRIEND." SHE IS THE PINNACLE OF DOMESTICATED CANINE EVOLUTION.

IF YOU HAVE ROOM AND ATTENTION TO GIVE, THEN GET A DOG. BUT IF YOU DON'T, YOU'RE A JERK THAT JUST GOT A LITTLE LIVING TOY TO SILENTLY TORTURE AND BORE TO DEATH. *"OH BUT MERO, I WALK MY DOG LIKE TWICE A DAY AROUND THE BLOCK. SOMETIMES WE EVEN GO TO THE STORE, THAT'S LIKE 3 WHOLE BLOCKS!"* MAN, IF YOU THINK THAT'S ENOUGH EXERCISE FOR FIDO, YOU ARE ABSOLUTELY TWEAKING. I GET SUPER SMACKED EVERY THANKSGIVING AND WATCH THE WESTMINSTER DOG SHOW BECAUSE IT'S HILARIOUS AND MY KIDS LOVE BEING LIKE "THAT DOG IS WEIRD!" IN MY WEED-ENTANGLED MIND, I'M JUST LIKE, "BRUH THESE ARE LITERALLY GMO'S THAT EAT TREATS AND DON'T MIND BLOW DRYERS." I SAY THAT TO SAY THIS, IF YOU HAVE A "WORKING DOG" OR SOME KINDA COLLIE OR SOME SHIT AND LIVE IN AN APARTMENT, SHAME ON YOU. I JUST WENT FROM "MEH" ABOUT DOGS TO SHAMING YOU FOR SLOWLY KILLING YOUR LIVING TOY, LOL WOW, WHAT STRAIN IS THIS?

MAD PEOPLE ARE ALLERGIC TO CATS, ALSO CATS AREN'T REALLY FUN? I MEAN THEY'LL PLAY WITH YOU BUT IT'S ON THEIR TERMS. DOGS ARE SUPER NEEDY AND CATS ARE THE POLAR OPPOSITE. A CAT WILL SIT ON A WINDOWSILL AND STARE AT YOU MENACINGLY, THEN LIFT ONE LEG UP, PERFORM ANILINGUS ON ITSELF, THEN HOP DOWN OFF THE WINDOWSILL AND RUB ITSELF ON YOU AND ALL YOUR FURNITURE. CATS ARE ASSHOLES. THEY WILL WAIT FOR YOU TO DO A LOAD OF DARKS AND HAVE IT OUT ON YOUR BED TO FOLD, THEN ROLL AROUND IN IT SO YOU PULL UP TO THE FUNCTION LOOKIN LIKE A DISHEVELED CAT LADY. ANOTHER THING TO CONSIDER IS THAT CAT SHIT DRIVES YOU NUTS. IT'S A SCIENTIFIC FACT THAT I SAW ON THE INTERNET SOMEWHERE. THAT'S WHY WHENEVER I WATCH *HOARDERS,* IT'S JUST MAD CATS. IT'S ALWAYS FUCKIN CATS. NOBODY IS EVER HOARDING COCKATIELS, OR GECKOS OR

SOME SHIT. I WILL CONCEDE THERE WAS ONCE A RAT GUY ON THERE, WHICH WAS FUCKING GROSS AS SHIT AND ALMOST MADE CAT PEOPLE LOOK SANE. BUT EVERY OTHER TIME IT'S LIKE "THE NEIGHBORS COMPLAINED OF A STRONG SMELL OF AMMONIA AND FECES, WE ENTERED THE HOME AND FOUND CLOSE TO 326 CATS, 85 OF WHICH WERE DEAD." CATS JUST WANNA FUCK OTHER CATS AND WAIT FOR YOU TO DIE. CATS DON'T EVEN ENJOY FUCKING. WHAT A MISERABLE EXISTENCE. YOU HAVE TO BATHE YOURSELF WITH YOUR TONGUE DESPITE BEING COVERED IN FUR AND YOU CAN'T EVEN ENJOY FUCKING BECAUSE YOUR DICK IS FUCKIN BARBS, MY DUDE. FOR REAL, CAT DICK IS NOT A REGULAR CYLINDRICAL DICK. I DON'T WANNA FUCK YOU WITH A BARBED PENIS, MA. THAT SOUNDS UNCOMFORTABLE FOR THE BOTH OF US.

OTHER SMALL MAMMALS LIKE FERRETS OR GUINEA PIGS AND SHIT, WAAAACK! FIRST OF ALL, EVERY TIME I GO TO PETCO TO GET BROWNIE FOOD, THE SECTION WITH THE FERRETS ALWAYS SMELLS LIKE I SLEPT ON MY SWEATY BALLS FOR A WEEK STRAIGHT. IT SMELLS LIKE A TEENAGE BEDROOM THAT HASN'T BEEN CLEANED IN 2 MONTHS AND IS BEING USED TO HOUSE EVERY CUM SOCK EVER. AND IT'S NOT LIKE THEY CAN DO COOL SHIT EXCEPT RUN AROUND, AND THEY NEED MAD ACCESSORIES EVEN TO JUST DO THAT. IF YOU BUY A HAMSTER OR GERBIL OR FERRETS AND GUINEA PIGS, YOU ARE PRESSING "OKAY" WHEN THE "THIS GAME CONTAINS IN-APP PURCHASES" BOX POPS UP. ALSO THEY CAN'T PLAY FETCH OR LEARN TRICKS B, THEY FUCKIN SUCK.

BIRDS. WHAT ARE YOU, FUCKING 89 YEARS OLD? THE ONLY PEOPLE THAT OWN BIRDS ARE ALSO THE PEOPLE YOU SEE AT MCDONALD'S EATING A FILET-O-FISH WITH A BLACK COFFEE AND VELCRO SHOES STARING INTO SPACE WAITING FOR THE COOL TOUCH OF DEATH. WHEN I WAS LITTLE WE HAD A PAR-

ROT INHERITED FROM MY AUNT THAT FLEW AWAY AND I SWEAR TO GOD, IT WENT AND MET OTHER PARROTS AND WOULD COME BACK IN THE SUMMERS TO SIT ON THE POWER LINES OUTSIDE MY BUILDING WITH LIKE 30 OTHER PARROTS. I DON'T KNOW IF IT WAS MY ACTUAL PARROT BUT IS IT CUSTOMARY FOR PARROTS TO JUST KICK IT ON POWER LINES IN THE BRONX? IT HAD TO BE HIM. SHOUT-OUT TO CUCA FOR GOING OUT IN THE AVIAN WORLD AND GETTING SOME BIRD BOX.

FISH ARE LITERALLY LIVING DECORATIONS AND ARE PROBABLY THE SINGLE MOST BORING PET YOU CAN HAVE. UNLESS YOU HAVE SOME WILD PIRANHAS AND ARE THROWING MEAT IN THERE AND THEY ARE WILD VICIOUSLY TEARING IT APART, THEN THAT WOULD BE FUN TO WATCH WHILE SMACKED. OTHERWISE ZZZZZZ.

REPTILES. IF YOU HAVE A PET SNAKE OR LIZARD OR WHATEVER, I GUESS THAT'S COOL. I'M ALSO WILLING TO GUESS THAT YOU HAVE NEVER HAD SEX IN YOUR LIFE OR IN AT LEAST A DECADE OR TWO. THERE'S ALWAYS A 40-YEAR-OLD PUERTO RICAN MAN AT ORCHARD BEACH WITH WHAT I ASSUME TO BE A PYTHON AROUND HIS NECK, OR MAYBE IT'S A BOA CONSTRICTOR, WHO KNOWS. POINT IS, YOU LOOK LIKE A CREEP. REPTILES ARE SMALL DINOSAURS AND I BET DINOSAURS FUCKIN STUNK.

THAT'S IT. THERE YOU HAVE IT, THE PROS AND CONS OF HAVING A PET. THEY ARE MOSTLY CONS BECAUSE I DON'T NEED ANY EXTRA RESPONSIBILITY, AND I CAN'T TELL A 3-YEAR-OLD TO GO TO THE DOG PARK BY HIMSELF. OH, I ALMOST FORGOT . . . YOU KNOW WHAT? I'M NOT EVEN GONNA TALK ABOUT BUGS CUZ IF YOU HAVE A PET COCKROACH OR SOME SHIT YOU'RE PROBABLY GONNA KILL SOMEBODY AT SOME POINT AND I DON'T WANT NO PROBLEMS SO I'M NOT GONNA TALK ABOUT BUGS.

Q&A 7: DO YOU HAVE A PROBLEMATIC FAVE?

Everyone has a problematic fave. It might be your homie or even your mother or boo, but they're problematic to someone. If your uncle makes homo jokes at Thanksgiving but you love him and miss him and read his racist email forwards, he's your PBF.

Some people's problematic faves are straight monsters to the rest of us, but to them, they're somehow okay. It's like R. Kelly fans, man, they love "Step in the Name of Love," "I Believe I Can Fly," and "Fiesta" so much that they're like "Well, he makes great music, so I can look past that other stuff." But as a rational person, I have to say those songs don't slap enough to let me rep a wild sex offender. Which is a pretty judgmental statement because I enjoy rappers who have shot (shouts to Jay-Z) or stabbed (shouts to Jay-Z) or even killed (shouts to Gucci Mane). But weirdly—killing someone isn't really problematic. It's what we call RNS territory and I don't want to say what the N stands for because white people are reading this. Hello, Brian! Thanks for buying the book!

As for my own problematic fave? I'm going to have to say: ME. Sorry. Is that classless? Perhaps, but that's also what a problematic fave would do. I'm my own problematic fave because I never expected to be famous or on television, but somehow I did, and if you look back through my life and the 5,000 jobs I've had (illegally and legally), you're gonna be like, "Wow this guy is kinda not a good person." Hopefully you look at my growth and how I've stopped making fake tweets for celebrities on Twitter and say "Well, maybe he's a better person now." But then you listen to the podcast and I'm asking about the current price of a brick of coke (is it still 41K like I thought in the beginning of this book? someone holla) and you're like, "Nah he's still garbage." But God's working on all of us and I once paid off a chick's back rent, so it's all goody?

ACTUALLY A BRICK IS ~21K BUT AS YOU MENTIONED BEFORE, I DO SPEAK SPANISH *SHRUGS*

AND YES, PICKING YOURSELF IS CLASSLESS. BUT I AM ALSO CLASSLESS, I PEED IN THE SINK AT A RESTAURANT LAST WEEK.

MY PROBLEMATIC FAVE IS EDDIE MURPHY. EDDIE'S CAREER TRAJECTORY IS ONE TO ASPIRE TO. MY MAN HAD SEVERAL DECADES ON SMASH. HIS STAND-UP SOLD OUT EVERY STADIUM. HE WAS THE LEBRON OF *SNL*. I COULD GO ON BUT GOT! DAMN! THIS NIGGA WENT IN ON GAY PEOPLE IN HIS STAND-UP. MY MAN HAD A TIGHT 5 ABOUT "FAGGOTS." YIKES!!!! YOU CAN'T SEE ME BUT I'M CRINGING JUST TYPING THAT. THAT SHIT DID NOT AGE WELL AT ALL. I DON'T EVEN KNOW IF HE'S SINCE APOLOGIZED OR WHAT BUT THAT'S DEFINITELY OD PROBLEMATIC. HE'S MY PROBLEMATIC FAVE BECAUSE HE GOT MAD CINEMATIC BANGERS. *HARLEM NIGHTS, BEVERLY HILLS COP, COMING TO AMERICA, THE NUTTY PROFESSOR,* ETC., ETC., ETC., AND HE DOES IT ALL. THE SCENE IN *BEVERLY HILLS COP* WHEN HE'S TRYING TO FINESSE A ROOM AT THE HOTEL AND CALLS THE FRONT DESK CLERK RACIST IS CLASSIC SHIT, IT WAS PROTO-WOKE. IN A HIT MOVIE!

EDDIE MURPHY IS RICH AS FUCK BECAUSE HE'S DYNAMIC AS FUCK. MY GUY IS COLLECTING *SHREK* CHECKS. I TELL YOU WHAT, IF I WAS GETTING *SHREK* CHECKS I WOULD CALL THEM CHREKS AND INSIST THEY BE BIG AS SHIT AND GREEN . . . YOU DIG *LIL WAYNE VOICE.* HE ALSO PLAYED LIKE EVERY(?) CHARACTER IN *THE NUTTY PROFESSOR,* WHICH HAD A POPPIN SOUNDTRACK AND PRETTY MUCH MADE A ZILLION DOLLARS AT THE BOX OFFICE. HE HAS MAD OTHER ICONIC MOVIES.

DID EDDIE DIRECT SHIT? I GOTTA GOOGLE THAT. I WOULD

RIGHT NOW BUT I'M LAZY SO I'M GONNA PRETEND HE DIRECTED SHIT AND WAS ALSO CRITICALLY ACCLAIMED FOR THAT. WOW EDDIE, YOU WERE FLAGRANTLY HOMOPHOBIC IN YOUR EARLY CAREER BUT THEN YOU DIRECTED *HARLEM NIGHTS* SO I FORGIVE YOU.

ALSO THIS NIGGA HAD A HIT SINGLE IN THE MIDST OF BEING A BONA FIDE MOVIE STAR. THAT'S WHAT HAPPENS WHEN YOU JUST CASUALLY CHILL WITH PRINCE AND RICK JAMES AND LEGENDARY MUSICAL NIGGAS LIKE THAT. YOU JUST ACCIDENTALLY PUT OUT A SMASH SINGLE. IT'S A SHAME THERE WAS NO AUTO-TUNE BACK THEN CUZ "PARTY ALL THE TIME" WOULDA PROBABLY WENT QUINTUPLE PLATINUM. I JUST LISTENED TO THAT SHIT AGAIN AND THOSE VOCAL RUNS BETWEEN VERSES WERE NOT IT, EDDIE. ALSO THE SONG IS KINDA SLUT SHAMING. BONG! MORE PROBLEMATICNESS!

THEN HE HAD THAT ERA WHERE HE HAD THE TINY TWIST BRAIDS. I'M NOT SURE WHAT HE WAS THINKING WITH THAT SHIT. GOOGLE IMAGE SEARCH "EDDIE MURPHY TWIST BRAIDS" SO Y'ALL NIGGAS KNOW WHAT I'M TALKING ABOUT.

WAITS CALMLY

LOOK AT THAT SHIT B. THAT SHIT IS ALMOST MORE PROBLEMATIC THAN HIM CALLING HIS GIRLFRIEND A COKEHEAD ON "PARTY ALL THE TIME." WHAT LOOK ARE WE GOING FOR HERE, EDDIE? "I'M ON A NATURAL JOURNEY BUT FIRST I'M GONNA PUT CHEMICALS ON MY HEAD SO I LOOK LIKE I'M IN ANIME"?? I DON'T KNOW, MAN. EDDIE HAS SAID AND DONE SOME FUCKED-UP SHIT BUT HE'S ALSO CONTRIBUTED OD TO THE CULTURE AND MADE STODGY HOLLYWOOD EXECUTIVE WHITE GUYS IN SUITS BELIEVE A BLACK PERSON COULD CARRY A MOVIE DOLO AND NOT CARRY IT BUT CARRY IT WELL AND STAR

IN A COUPLE FRANCHISES. DUDE JUST HAS THE WILD STAR POWER. HE OPENED A LOT OF DOORS FOR DUDES LIKE ME.

REASON 7843 THAT HE'S MY FAVE IS BECAUSE WHEN *SNL* DID THEIR REUNION SHIT, HE WENT UP THERE LIKE "YOU NIGGAS PLAYED ME WHEN I WAS ON HERE SO IMA STAND UP HERE STONEFACED AND READ THIS FUCKIN PROMPTER. YOU. ARE. FUCKING. WELCOME." THEN HE BOUNCED. THAT'S A MOTHERFUCKING LEGEND.

Okay, I'm jumping back in. My other problematic fave would have to be the one and only Lindsay Lohan. She's always doing crazy stuff in the news and getting popped in the mouth by homeless Syrian mothers for trying to take away their kids, but I have nothing but love for her. Me and my boy Black Pat shared a bottle in a club with her in like 2006 or 7 and the club had mermaids behind the bar and she and her crew were shook because Black Pat is big as fuck (he's a security guard) and we kinda sorta maybe stole their bottle. She was nice though. Also she made the most amazing song, "Bossy," which is a classic and you know what? Go turn it on right now. That's a fucking bop. Been a bop and will remain a bop. Every time she performs that you're like "Whoa, she's a queen."

Sorry if this choice makes you disappointed but then I wouldn't be your problematic fave. See how that came full circle?

Q&A 8: WHAT HAPPENS WHEN I DIE?

WOW, THIS WAS A TERRIBLE QUESTION TO ANSWER IN THIS STATE OF SMACKEDNESS. I LITERALLY JUST DID A DAB, I COULDN'T FILL OUT AN APPLICATION TO OLD NAVY RIGHT NOW. FUCK IT, BESTSELLER . . . I CONSIDER MYSELF A SPIRITUAL GUY. I WAS RAISED CATHOLIC AND I'M MARRIED TO A JEWISH

WOMAN SO OUR KIDS GET DOUBLE PRESENTS BECAUSE THEY ARE SPOILED LIL JERKS. OTHER THAN THAT WE AREN'T "PRACTICING." WE CELEBRATE HOLIDAYS. WE AIN'T UP AT TEMPLE OR CHURCH ON THE HOLY DAYS—WE HOME IN SWEATS. I DO BELIEVE IN SOMETHING BEYOND HUMANS. IDK IF IT WAS A PHILOSOPHER OR A STARTENDER OR BOTH THAT SAID, "IT'S ARROGANT OF HUMANS TO THINK THERE'S NOTHING BEYOND US." I'M KINDA IN THAT BOAT BUT I DON'T GIVE IT MUCH THOUGHT. BEST-CASE SCENARIO HEAVEN IS REAL AND I GET TO SMOKE WEED WITH BIG PUN AND CEET. WORST-CASE SCENARIO I GET CREMATED AND ALL THAT'S LEFT OF ME ARE OTHER PEOPLE'S MEMORIES UNTIL THEY PERISH, TOO. PICTURES & VIDEOS MY FAMILY PUTS IN A MAUSOLEUM WITH SPEAKERS THAT PLAY MY FAVORITE SONGS ON A LOOP. WATCH SOMEONE SWIPE THAT IDEA AND MAKE MAD MONEY. ACTUALLY THAT PROBABLY ALREADY EXISTS. IF IT DOESN'T, I CALL DIBS. THIS IS A LEGIT BOOK FROM A REAL PUBLISHER SO THIS SENTENCE IS A LEGALLY BINDING DOCUMENT.

YO I WAS JUST TALKING ABOUT JEHOVAH'S WITNESSES AND HOW TERRIBLE THEIR PITCH IS. CATHOLICS ARE LIKE, YO IF YOU FUCK UP YOU GO TO HELL WHERE YOU BURN FOREVER AND IT SUCKS AND THERE'S MAD MOANING AND DESPAIR AND SHIT. THEY GOT MAD CENTURIES OF IMAGERY DEPICTING THE SHIT. BUT IF YOU DON'T FUCK UP YOU CAN CHILL WITH YOUR DEAD PEOPLES UP IN HEAVEN. THEY GOT UNLIMITED SOFT SERVE WITH THE MAD TOPPINGS AND IT'S HEAVEN, SO YOU'RE NOT LACTOSE INTOLERANT ANYMORE. YES, OF COURSE YOU CAN SMOKE WEED. YEAH, YOU CAN KILL SOMEBODY IN A *CALL OF DUTY* MULTIPLAYER DEATHMATCH, BUT YOU GOTTA SAY HALF A HAIL MARY DURING THE KILLCAM. I LIKE THE IDEA THAT EVERYONE'S VERSION OF HEAVEN IS HEAVEN. ALSO SHOUT-OUT TO HINDUISM REINCARNATION AND MOKSHA SOUNDS LIT.

ANYWAY, JEHOVAH'S WITNESSES HAVE "PARADISE" BUT WHERE THEY FUCK UP IS THE IMAGERY. BRUH, I HAVE ZERO INTEREST IN SITTING ON A RIVERBANK DRESSED LIKE I WORK AT BEST BUY PETTING A TIGER. IF YOU SHOWED ME A GUY IN A RECLINER EATING POPEYES SPICY STRIPS WATCHING THE KNICKS WIN A CHAMPIONSHIP, YOU MIGHT HAVE MY ATTENTION. Y'ALL GOTTA REBRAND. HOLLA AT VICTOR, I'LL DO IT FOR THE LOW. ALSO WHEN YOUR GRANDPARENT OR PARENT DIES, AND YOU ACCOMPLISH SOMETHING THEY WOULD BE PROUD OF, PEOPLE SAY, "THEY ARE LOOKING DOWN ON YOU SMILING" OR SOME VARIATION OF THAT. THAT SHIT IS CREEPY WHEN YOU THINK ABOUT IT. IS MY GRANDMA IN A RECLINER WATCHING MY WHOLE FUCKIN LIFE? IS SHE WATCHING ME WRITE THIS RIGHT NOW? YO HOW EMBARRASSING . . . SHE'S FLIPPING THROUGH LIVING FAMILY MEMBER CHANNELS AND CATCHES ME JERKIN OFF IN THE SHOWER. WOW, THAT IS FUCKIN MORTIFYING.

LISTEN, MAN, FOLLOW YOUR HEART. IF YOU'RE LIKE "I'M ON SOME STRICTLY SCIENCE" SHIT "NEIL DEGRASSE TYSON IS MY JESUS" FLOW, THEN DO YOUR THING. IF YOU PRACTICE ISLAM, JUDAISM, HINDUISM, BUDDHISM, TAOISM, LYRICALISM, TWISM, WHATEVER YOU REP, DO YOUR THING. WHEN THEY TEACH YOU *HIS*STORY IN SCHOOL THEY SAY BOATS FULL OF DISEASE-RIDDEN PEOPLE ALLERGIC TO BOTH PEANUTS AND DANCING WELL SAILED HERE TO PRACTICE RELIGION FREELY. I REALIZE THIS SOUNDS LIKE IT HAS NOTHING TO DO WITH THE ORIGINAL QUESTION, BUT IT DOES BECAUSE, DUH, YOU PICK THE RELIGION WITH THE MOST APPEALING ANSWER TO "WHAT HAPPENS WHEN I DIE?" BONG, LINK UP WITH THEM AH AH AH NOW YOU ARE LOW-KEY HYPE TO BE REBORN AS AN ORCA. YOUR OWN MORTALITY IS NO LONGER SUCH A TERRIFYING CONCEPT. YOU COULD ALSO BE ON SOME BIOLOGICAL SHIT AND EVEN IF THAT'S YOUR WAVE, YOU GET BURIED OR WHATEVER AND FEED

THE EARTH, HELPING IT CONTINUE TO EXIST AS WE KNOW IT. *EXTINGUISHES BLUNT* THERE'S YOUR ANSWER, PAL. WHAT HAPPENS WHEN YOU DIE? WHATEVER YOU BELIEVE HAPPENS. BECAUSE THIS BODY, THE ONE THAT PERISHED, IS WEARING A SUIT IN A BOX, OR A DRESS OR WHATEVER ELSE DEPENDING WHERE YOU TRYNA BE DEAD ON THE GENDER SPECTRUM.

What happens when you die is a dark question but I'm Dark Desus so I'm down. The idea of heaven and hell are both laughable bullshit but let's break it down: So in theory Satan hated heaven and created a place where he runs shit, right? But then why would he be punishing people for following him? For all we know, hell is wild litty. Heaven definitely has to be trash. There's no weed, no Timbs, no chopped cheese sandwiches. And there are so many questions about how it works.

For example, here's a question I have about heaven: What if you have a dog and you die and that dog goes on to live with someone else and then they're driving and both the new owner and the dog die. The dog sees you at the pearly gates. Who does the dog spend eternity with? Also, are any dogs in heaven, let alone all dogs? Are cats in heaven? Do they have a separate heaven? Wouldn't a heaven full of dogs be hell for cats? What if there are really bad cats, like if Hitler's girlfriend had a cat? It would deserve to be in a bad place, I guess? But that place is dog heaven? Did Jesus pet any dogs while on earth and are they in heaven but wild, old, and homeless? So many questions.

Personally I think at the end of your life you just do what happens when you dream. You ever had the wild dream where you're getting chased or running for something and it seems to take hours but you wake up and it's only been like 4 minutes? I think that's what happens when you die. You just have some sort of wild happy dream as your body realizes this is the final scene, bar's closing. And you probably see people you love and old pets and maybe you're at the best concert you've ever been to (Beyoncé at the Superdome, 2013) and when it's time to go you just fade out like a turntable that's been unplugged or like a porn stream that ended and is now on the logo of the site and you're sitting there like "Wow, I didn't need to rub one out, what's wrong with me, Christ is watching."

And that is the last sentence of this book: Christ is watching.

Acknowledgments

Shouts to my parents. Thanks for leaving Jamaica and risking it all. I hope I've made you proud.

To Pilar, Tones, Jan, Leon, and Miles. I love y'all.

To Victor da gawd. Without you none of this happens.

To Christina Bazdekis and Victoria Cook. I was lucky enough to get connected to 2 of the best in the business.

To Victoria and Daiana and Sherri for keeping the brand strong.

To Donnie Kwak for starting this whole damn thing.

To anyone who worked with me at Complex, MTV2, Viceland, and Showtime.

To Dara Cook. Thank you for the good look.

To everyone at Red Bull Studios (220 West 18th Street, *airhorns*), thanks for taking in our humble little podcast and letting us become a threat to American youths.

To Greg Giraldo & Patrice O'Neal. You guys made this look like the thing to do. Never forgotten.

To the New York Public Library for giving me a job and place to expand my mind. Special shout-out to the Edenwald branch (my mother's library), Spuyten Duyvil, Mosholu, and the Science, Industry and Business Library branch (SIBL), all where I briefly worked. The fact that I went from restocking shelves to having a book on the shelf is pretty amazing.

To my cat, Charlie. You've been with me when we almost had to live in my car. Now you enjoy sunlight in a luxury apartment with high-quality cat food. Thank you for your support.

To the Bronx. You were rough to me and loving at the same time. The same place I met my first love and the first place I was illegally arrested. You made me realize it takes a special type of person to survive here and those qualities have led me to greatness. I would not be Desus if not for the Bronx. I love you so much.

And last but not least, The Bodega Hive.

You people listen to every podcast. Watch every episode. Buy the shirts. Come to the live shows. You are the most amazing fans in the world. The brand has come so far and you've been there through every step. We've gotten you through cancer, death of family members, families not accepting you. Some of you got through your bid while listening to us. Thank you. Thank you thank you thank you for even clicking our stuff.

The brand is strong.

PS shout-out to naughtyamerica. Ah ah ah *sucio* boys!

—Desus

I WANT TO THANK MAMI & PAPI PORQUE SOY EL HIJO DE TITO Y FIFA!! MY SUPERWIFE/PART-TIME THERAPIST/FULL-TIME LOVE HEATHER AND OUR FLAWLESS KIDS ADRIAN, AVERY, AMARI,

AND AZALEA—DADDY LOVES YOU! MY ORIGINAL COMEDY PARTNERS INGRID & TITO, TODOS MIS TIAS/TIOS & PRIMOS/PRIMAS QUE ME HACIAN CORO! I LOVE Y'ALL! BIG UP TO ALL MY FRIENDS WHO STOOD IN CYPHERS WITH ME AND HELPED ME SHARPEN MY CRAFT! TO THE TWO PLACES THAT SHAPED ME, THE DOMINICAN REPUBLIC AND THE BRONX, BOTH PLACES THAT PLAYED AN INTEGRAL ROLE IN WHO I AM TODAY. I LEARNED TO FIND HUMOR IN HOPELESSNESS. THIS ONE'S FOR THE BLOCK! KINGSBRIDGE! THROGS NECK! DUB CITY! CEET SPEK ASP ZEXOR YAMS LIVE FOREVER!! BEN AT RANDOM HOUSE AND DAN AT ICM FOR MAKIN IT HAPPEN! AND THE ONLY TEAMS THAT MATTER: VICTOR LOPEZ, CHRISTINA BAZDEKIS, VICTORIA COOK, & MARCIE CLEARY!! PLUS THE ID-PR SQUAD: SHERI 305, VANESSA AVOCADO, AND ALEX GOOTEY MANE.

MLB x INC x TRC x SAD x PPP x 2DX x WTO!! SHOUT-OUT TO VICTORIA DIEZ TOO CUZ I ALMOST FORGOT TO SEND THESE!! HOLLA!!

LAST BUT NOT LEAST, BIG UP TO THE HIVE! YOU BRING A REAL TANGIBLE SATISFACTION TO THIS WHOLE PURSUIT THAT MAKES ME GO HARDER! YOUR BOYS ARE WITH YOU NO MATTER WHAT YOU GOIN THROUGH! PEACE & LOVE. THANK YOU!!!

—MERO

ABOUT THE AUTHORS

DESUS NICE and THE KID MERO are multitalented comedians, writers, podcasters, and now authors who currently co-host Showtime's first-ever late-night talk show, as well as the long-running *Bodega Boys* podcast.

Their bond was forged in the early days of Twitter, where the Bronx natives and former schoolmates reconnected and shared an affinity for complaining about their day jobs, coupled with funny pop-culture commentary. This led to stints on Complex and MTV, the start of their hit podcast, and a critically acclaimed daily late-night show on Viceland.

In early 2019, the duo brought their skills to Showtime, premiering their new late-night show, *Desus & Mero*. Twice weekly, they offer their hilarious takes on the latest news and sit down with an all-star lineup of guests that span the cultural landscape, infusing the format with their signature brand of kinetic comedy.

ABOUT THE TYPE

This book was set in Minion, a 1990 Adobe Originals typeface by Robert Slimbach (b. 1956). Minion is inspired by classical, old-style typefaces of the late Renaissance, a period of elegant, beautiful, and highly readable type designs. Created primarily for text setting, Minion combines the aesthetic and functional qualities that make text type highly readable with the versatility of digital technology.

DESUS NICE · AKA · YOUNG CHIPOTLE · AKA · POCKETS STAY
BOUTROS BOUTROS GULLY · AKA · SLOBODAN MIGHT · K
AKA · YOUNG HOT TAKE · AKA · DESUS H. FUEGO · AKA · MR. NANDOS
NOVENTA Y CUATRO · AKA · MIKHAIL GOIN OFF · AKA · THE JOUVE
AKA · PULLIN UP FROM 40 WITH YOUR SHORTY · AKA · DONT T
KNOW YOU! · AKA · THE ORIGINAL MY +1 GOT A +1 SO DONT M
THE JAMAICAN JEW · AKA YOUR PROBLEMATIC BAE · A
AKA · ELI LITBY · AKA · DESUS NICE · AKA · YOUNG CH
· YOUNG DAY PARTY! BOUTROS BOUTROS GULLY · AKA
· MR. MIL NOVECIENTOS · AKA · YOUNG HOT TAKE · AKA · DESUS H.
LIKKLE GUNGO PEA NOVENTA Y CUATRO · AKA · MIKHAIL GO
UBER POOL, I DONT · AKA · PULLIN UP FROM 40 WITH YOU
AKA · DESUS ROTHSTEIN KNOW YOU! · AKA · THE ORIGINAL MY +1
E · AKA · POCKETS STAY FAT THE JAMAICAN JEW · AKA YOUR
DESUS NICE · AKA · YOUNG CHIPOTLE · AKA · POCKETS STAY
BOUTROS BOUTROS GULLY · AKA · SLOBODAN MIGHT · K
AKA · YOUNG HOT TAKE · AKA · DESUS H. FUEGO · AKA · MR. NANDOS
NOVENTA Y CUATRO · AKA · MIKHAIL GOIN OFF · AKA · THE JOUVE
AKA · PULLIN UP FROM 40 WITH YOUR SHORTY · AKA · DONT T
KNOW YOU! · AKA · THE ORIGINAL MY +1 GOT A +1 SO DONT M
THE JAMAICAN JEW · AKA YOUR PROBLEMATIC BAE · A
AKA · ELI LITBY · AKA · DESUS NICE · AKA · YOUNG CH
· YOUNG DAY PARTY! BOUTROS BOUTROS GULLY · AK
· MR. MIL NOVECIENTOS · AKA · YOUNG HOT TAKE · AKA · DESUS H
LIKKLE GUNGO PEA NOVENTA Y CUATRO · AKA · MIKHAIL G
UBER POOL, I DONT · AKA · PULLIN UP FROM 40 WITH Y
AKA · DESUS ROTHSTEIN KNOW YOU! · AKA · THE ORIGINAL MY